Remembering
Judson
House

To Donna
and all
from Robert

Eighteen

Remembering Judson House

EDITED BY

ELLY DICKASON

and

JERRY G. DICKASON

JUDSON MEMORIAL CHURCH
NEW YORK

Judson Memorial Church
55 Washington Square South
New York, NY 10012

Printed in the United States of America
printing number
1 2 3 4 5 6 7 8 9 10

Library of Congress Cataloging-in-Publication Data
Remembering Judson House / edited by Elly Dickason and Jerry G. Dickason.
p.   cm.
Includes bibliographical references and index.
ISBN 0-9702935-0-X
1. Judson House (New York, N.Y.)—History.   2. Church charities—New York (State)—
New York—History.   3. Church work—New York (State)—New York—History.
II. Dickason, Elly, 1940–   II. Dickason, Jerry G. (Jerry Grove)
HV530.R27   2000
361.7'5'097471—dc21
00-058965

Various permissions to reprint either words or photographs appear in the text.
All uncredited images are reprinted here with the generous permission
of the Judson Health Center, 34 Spring Street, New York City.
A special thanks to Alice Garrard for the use of her photographs, as marked in the text.

Designer: Shirley Chetter

To
Dean Wright

Visionary, selfless leader, man of God

"Something closed must retain our memories,
while leaving them their original value as images.
Memories of the outside world will never
have the same tonality as those of home and,
by recalling these memories, we add to our store of dreams;
we are never real historians, but always near poets,
and our emotion is perhaps nothing but an expression
of a poetry that was lost."

—Gaston Bachelard, *The Poetics of Space* (1958)

Contents

FOREWORD by Howard Moody   xi

PREFACE by Peter Laarman   xiii

INTRODUCTION by Elly and Jerry Dickason   xv

ACKNOWLEDGMENTS   xvii

THE BUILDING   1

The History of the Judson House Plot Up to 1899 by Irene Tichenor   3
The Property from 1899 to 1999 by Grace Goodman   7
A Custodian's Description by John Tungate   25
The Garden by Alice Garrard   51

THE JUDSON HEALTH CENTER   57

The Judson Health Center, 1921–1950 by Jerry G. Dickason   59
Eleanor A. Campbell by Elly Dickason   93
"Problem Parents" by Dr. Eleanor A. Campbell   100

THE JUDSON STAFF   107

Robert Boyd   111
Dean Wright   114
Alice Spike   119
Paul Spike   122
Norman O. Keim   127
Bernard D. Mayes   130
Beverly Waite   137
Joseph and Judy Pickle   139
Al Carmines   147
Ed Brewer   156
Larry Kornfeld   162
Ro Lee   166
Arthur A. Levin   168
Joan Muyskens   172
Arlene Carmen   177
Roland Wiggins   181
Lorry Moody   185
Lee Hancock   187
Mark Rubinsky   191
Bill Malcomson   195
Paul Chapman   197
Andrew Frantz   200

THE CHURCH IN URBAN LIFE PROJECT   205

Bernice Lemley   207
Juell Krauter   212
Robert A. Yangas   214
Donald H. Birt   216
Beverly Bach Cassell   219
Donald R. Ferrell   222
Marcia Freer   224
Larry G. Keeter   225
Jim Thacker   232
Reathel Bean   236
Michael Johnson   240

THE JUDSON STUDENT HOUSE   245

Seymour Hacker   247
Patricia White   250
McKinley Brown   252
Robert Newman   253
Tom Roderick   258
Christopher Holt   262
Sandy Padilla   264
Lurline Purvis   272

THE JUDSON GALLERY   275

Bud Scott   277
Allan Kaprow   286
Phyllis Yampolsky   288
Marc Ratliff   290
Claes Oldenburg   292
Tom Wesselmann   303
Jon Hendricks   307
Geoffrey Hendricks   314
Kate Millett   319
Nye Ffarrabas   321
Raphael Ortiz   335
Over His Dead Body by Jill Johnston   339
Jean Ovitt   343

THE RUNAWAY HOUSE   347

Aaron Crespi   349
The Judson House Gang by Steve Lerner   352

PEOPLE WHO DON'T FIT INTO ANY
OF THE PREVIOUS CATEGORIES   359

Mei-Mei Hull   361
Julie Kurnitz   366
Ed Lazansky   369
Carman Moore   371
Paul Richter   377

INDEX   379

Foreword

There could be no more fitting eulogy for a building than *Remembering Judson House,* a collection of testimonies from living witnesses as to what this place meant to them. When I was asked to write this foreword, the first thing I thought of was the song "This Old House," written by Stuart Hamblen. Its poignant lyrics are about the humanization of a physical structure, making it analogous to the infirmities and mortality of an aging human being. The refrain of the song goes:

> Ain't gonna need this house no longer
> Ain't gonna need this house no more
> Ain't got time to fix the shingles
> Ain't got time to fix the floor
> Ain't got time to oil the hinges
> Or to mend the window panes
> Ain't gonna need this house no longer
> He's getting ready to meet the saints.

It is true that buildings are always more than bricks and steel. They are living entities that harbor history and memories, and they are susceptible to deterioration and death just as we are.

Judson House has been a home to myriad ministries that would not have been possible without its structure: a health clinic where Italian-American women learned how to keep their babies healthy, an international dormitory where young students from Africa prepared to return to serve their decolonized countries after World War II, a gallery for avant-garde artists and a residence for would-be artists, a runaway house for wandering and displaced kids searching for their identity. Judson House was a living space, metamorphosing in every generation to serve a new need that appeared on its door-step.

Its attached garden was a shady refuge. Its towering trees looked down on noisy parties full of wine and song, antiwar protests and human rights rallies, the quietness of worship services, and acts of parting when the cremated remains of church members were mixed with the soil of the flower beds.

There were times when Judson House was neglected and some-times abused, but "this old house," with cracking walls and paint-peeling shabbiness, was always ready to shelter the lives of young and old and the work and ministry of its mother, Judson Memorial Church. In its checkered history, Judson House has been called many names, but it has primarily been a home, a landmark place for the lives of transients, wayfaring strangers, lost souls and pilgrims who stopped and stayed. In the following pages we will read ringing tributes and heartfelt confessions of what Judson House meant to some of its devotees.

Oh Judson House, love of our lives, this book is your warm and affectionate epitaph.

HOWARD MOODY
Senior minister emeritus
Judson Memorial Church

Preface

J okingly, but with a hint of seriousness, Elly and Jerry Dickason told me that when the Judson community fully understood and appreciated the rich history of Judson House that this volume lays open, the congregation's action to sell the property would be rescinded and enough money would be raised in the twinkling of an eye to restore the old place for another century of service.

I only wish this kind of magic were possible and that the money needed to restore Judson House would have fallen out of the sky. No one has enjoyed the plunge into the unknown that the decision to sell the Judson House land has entailed. The greatest fear, I think, is that we will trade in a history that has been vibrant and yeasty and full of daring for a bland future in which Judson behaves more and more like any other institution in our increasingly homogenized culture. I believe there is also a sense out there that the old crumbly building metaphorically signaled Judson's absolute independence in a way that six thousand square feet of Judson space within a spanking-new New York University Law School building won't ever be able to communicate.

Those of us working on the sale of the building have done everything possible to combat the sterility threat. We have found ways to link our new space directly to the landmarked main church building, so that the Judson spirit can freely infiltrate the space that NYU Law will build for us. More important, we staunchly resisted efforts by the Law School's lawyers to put boilerplate use restrictions in the condo agreement governing our space. It was clear they did not understand how much our freedom matters to us; they do now.

Deep down, however, we all know that the question of how much the spirit of the old Judson House can be sustained in a new era has little to do with legal documents or space layouts. It has everything to do with us: with how youthful and how feisty our own spirits feel, and with whether we still see the church as the vehicle for all forms of spiritual and artistic and social renewal and for all expressions of liberatory praxis. We could keep the old building, keep the garden, and still lose the passion, still let our light flicker out.

My hope and my prayer are that along with renewed and revived physical spaces, Judson members and friends will come to realize that along with having had some fabulous good old days, this church as an outpost of freedom has some great new days lying right ahead of it.

PETER LAARMAN
Senior minister
Judson Memorial Church

Introduction

During the summer of 1998, while on vacation and with time to think, we conceived of the idea to put together a book that would consist of reminiscences by people who had lived and/or worked at Judson House. During the first half of 1998, the members of Judson Memorial Church had been debating, with great emotion, what to do with the building on Thompson Street. It was falling apart, and the church did not have the money to fix it up. The church certainly did not have the funds to bring the building up to code in order to house new programs. It looked as if the building might be sold to a developer, who would tear it down to put up something new.

At the time of our vacation, we were both reading *The Poetics of Space* by Gaston Bachelard (1884–1962), a French philosopher. Bachelard talks at length about the meaning of spaces we grow up in and how these spaces have a lasting influence on the rest of our lives. The book convinced us that the memories of a space are just as important as the space itself. If we could not keep Judson House, then at least we could preserve the collective memories of what went on inside.

At the end of that summer we took the idea of a book to the Judson Board, which endorsed the project enthusiastically. We mailed about twenty invitations to people we knew had lived there—staff and former staff, some former students from New York University, a few program associates. It was going to be a fairly thin book.

Slowly the contributions came in. And then people began telling us about others who had lived at the house. We followed up with more invitations, and invariably more names surfaced. This whole process took far longer than we had anticipated, but with each new piece, the book became that much more complete.

Still, we were unable to locate some former residents we would have liked to include. Foremost among these are Betty and Richard Murphy. Betty served as housemother of the Student House while Richard completed his medical studies. The many references to Betty in the following pages attest to her great warmth and charm.

A visit to the Judson Health Center on Spring Street, which had been the main occupant of Judson House from 1921 to 1950, produced a treasure trove of old documents and photographs, which enabled us to cobble together the history of that long-term tenant.

We have grouped the chapters into several sections. Each starts with an introduction of the program, followed by individual reminiscences. We have made a strong effort to double-check the spelling of names and the dates offered in various contributions. What we have not done is to tinker with people's memories of what happened. Certain events are described by two or three people and never quite sound the same. After all, one person may have experienced them as very different from someone else who was there. One story that is told with three or four different endings is that of the chickens that were or were not killed in a "happening" that did or did not take place in the Judson garden in 1967.

Since we first made plans for this book, the Judson congregation voted to sell Judson House and the garden to the New York University School of Law. Judson House is no more. It is our hope that the stories in these pages will keep the memories of the building alive.

ELLY DICKASON
JERRY G. DICKASON

Acknowledgments

We have been overwhelmed by the generosity of the many people who offered us assistance in compiling both the text and the illustrations for *Remembering Judson House*. The biggest thanks are due to the former Judson House residents who took time to write down their memories and share them with us. There would not have been a book without them.

In addition, we want to acknowledge the following by name, listed in alphabetical order:

- Shirley Chetter, who scanned the photos and designed the book;
- Nye Ffarrabas, who entrusted us with original photos from her collection;
- Alice Garrard, Grace Goodman, Abigail Hastings, and Irene Tichenor, who researched and wrote about various aspects of Judson House history;
- Robert E. Harvey, great-grandson of Eleanor Campbell, the founder of the Judson Health Center, who provided us with invaluable information on Dr. Campbell's life;
- Jon Hendricks, who lent us original materials relating to the Judson Gallery in the 1960s;
- Peter Laarman and the Board of Judson Memorial Church, who provided financial assistance to bring the book to publication;
- Dana Martin, Director of the Library, American Baptist Historical Society, Rochester, New York, who went far beyond professional courtesy to give us access to old Baptist City Society archives and ended up doing some of the research himself;

- Barbara Moore, who gave us permission to use photographs by the late Peter Moore;
- Claes Oldenburg, for loaning us copies of the magazine *Exodus;*
- Michael Rivera, current director of the Judson Health Center, who let us borrow files and photos from the Center's early archives;
- Bud Scott, for allowing us to reprint illustrations from *Exodus.*

ELLY DICKASON
JERRY G. DICKASON

Remembering
Judson House

THE BUILDING

This section consists of four chapters: (1) an overview, by Irene Tichenor, of the history of the lot up to the time that Edward Judson bought the set of buildings on Thompson Street in 1899; (2) a review of the building as property, by Grace Goodman; (3) the personal reminiscences of John Tungate, who was Judson's sexton and maintenance man from 1968 to 1978 and who, by his own admission, had a very physical relationship with Judson House; and (4) memories of the Judson Garden, by Alice Garrard.

The History of the Judson House Plot Up to 1899

IRENE TICHENOR

Before Europeans arrived on what is now Thompson Street, Lenape Indians lived in this area and called it Sapokanican, which meant "the tobacco plantation." The focal point of this fishing and planting community was a landing on the Hudson River at the present Gansevoort Street. It was a good spot for landing canoes and became a post for trading with Hoboken and the southern tip of Manhattan. Sand hills and swamp also covered much of the area, with an overgrowth of brambles and rushes. A small stream, Minetta Brook, ran through the area. It began with two tributaries that joined near what is now 18th Street and flowed south to the northwest corner of the present park, then turned southwest and continued along today's Minetta and Downing streets, emptying into a salt marsh near the foot of Canal Street.

During the Dutch period (1624–1664) there continued to be a tobacco plantation on land that had been cleared by the Lenapes. The name changed from Sapokanican to Nortwyck. The rich land around Minetta Brook attracted the attention of Wouter Van Twiller, second director general of New Amsterdam, succeeding Peter Minuit in 1633. Van Twiller took the entire Minetta basin, including Judson's current property, as his personal country farm or *bouwerie*. His homestead was on a hill at present Eighth Street and MacDougal. Van Twiller pocketed the tobacco profits rather than turning them over to the colony. For this and other reasons he was recalled in 1638.

The West India Company, which ran New Amsterdam, had a handful of African slaves. Van Twiller's successor granted some of them a quasi-freedom in 1644 and allowed them to take up land on the outskirts of town. Some of these so-called Negroes' Farms were clustered in what is now Greenwich Village. At least one plot occupied the southwest corner of today's Washington Square Park; others ran along the banks of Minetta Brook.

During the British era (1664–1783) the name of the Nortwyck settlement became Greenwich and was the location of country seats of numerous well-to-do colonists. Many of these large estates survived the American Revolution but were soon subdivided into smaller farms.

After the Revolution, Greenwich gained enough people to become known as a village. In 1789, New York City decided that for the health of its inhabitants it would bury victims of contagious diseases out of town. At that time, Greenwich Village was several miles north of town. The City bought the present Washington Square, drained and filled in the swamp, and used it for burying not only the contagious but also the indigent. The park was a potter's field for the next twenty-five years or so. In addition, its trees would serve as gallows for convicts of Newgate Prison when it was opened in 1797 at the Hudson River and current Tenth Street.

In 1811 the City commissioned a street grid plan for Manhattan Island. Greenwich locals protested the redrawing of their streets which, naturally, followed property lines on which their houses sat, so the area west of Sixth Avenue was granted an exemption from reorienting its streets to the axis set for the less developed part of the island. But Judson's plot, later subsumed by the Village, was subject to having existing roads rerouted to conform to the plan. For example, Amity Lane, which bordered the farm of which the Judson site was a part, was rotated about 30 degrees counterclockwise to become Amity Street, later renamed West Third.

A yellow fever epidemic in the port city of New York on the southern end of the island during the early nineteenth century caused an influx of people into Greenwich Village. When the crisis subsided, some of those people stayed, and this in part accounted for a rapid quadrupling of the local population and the conversion of the Village from small farms to streets of row houses by the mid-1820s.

Washington Square acquired its current name on the fiftieth anniversary of the signing of the Declaration of Independence in 1826, and for a few years it was used as a military parade ground. That didn't work very well, however. Since some 22,000 bodies were buried there, heavy horse-drawn artillery sometimes fell through the graves. By 1850 Washington Square would have the configuration of paths that it has now, and in 1852 the first fountain was built.

The eastern and western parts of what is now called Greenwich Village had entirely different identities. The Village itself was originally the part nearer the Hudson and was a bustling area of small tradesmen and artisans. East of Sixth Avenue above the Square lived grander merchants and bankers, and they called their neighborhood "Washington Square," not "Greenwich Village." Fifth Avenue was not yet an address to boast about. Only in 1824 was it opened from the square to Thirteenth Street, covering over the Minetta Brook that continued, as it does today, to run beneath. Until 1825 much of the area immediately south of the square was still farmland, not yet divided into blocks in accordance with the 1811 grid plan.[1]

As for the Judson House lot in particular, official land records at the New York City Register's Office show the Herring family as the first post-Revolution owners of the land that now includes Thompson Street. They had it surveyed in 1784. Four years later Elbert Herring sold it to William Ward Burrowes, who in turn sold it to John Ireland (called "gentleman" in the records). Ireland owned it for forty years before it was surveyed for parceling into lots in February 1825 (which suggests that this was when the 1811 street grid plan actually reached Thompson Street). Ireland began selling lots shortly after his survey. In fact, there was quite a flurry of real estate transactions in the next few years. From 1825 to 1832 the Judson House lot changed hands six times. Small businessmen such as grocers and bakers were among the early owners. During the next decade, ownership of the Judson House lot was divided into ninths, presumably by a will. In 1842 the shares were bought up and reunited under the ownership of Edward N. Tailer.

---

1. Useful secondary sources for the history of Greenwich Village include the following: Gold, Joyce, *From Trout Stream to Bohemia* (New York: Old Warren Press, 1988); Gross, Steve, *Old Greenwich Village: An Architectural Portrait* (Washington, DC: National Trust for Historic Preservation, 1993); Miller, Terry, *Greenwich Village and How It Got That Way* (New York: Crown Books, 1990); and New York Landmarks Preservation Commission, *Greenwich Village Historic District Designation Report* (New York: The Commission, 1969).

The selling price of the Judson House lot had gone from $1,125 in 1825 to $4,050 in 1842—not a surprising increase in a blossoming area. No buildings are mentioned in the land conveyances until the next sale of the lot seventy-four years later—the sale to Edward Judson on July 27, 1899. He bought it from Edward Tailer's executor for $30,000, and that conveyance does mention "land with buildings thereon" and that the sale is "subject to lettings to present monthly tenants." For all these reasons, it seems likely that Edward Tailer erected three buildings sometime between 1842 and 1852 when they first appear on an atlas by Matthew Dripps.

Putting three small buildings on a standard 25- by 100-foot lot was unusual; virtually every other lot for blocks around had one house, typically at least half the depth of the lot. So this seems to have been rental property from the outset. Each of the three three-story brick buildings had approximately a 25-foot square footprint plus a small yard. The two northerly ones shared a party wall.

Lest the reader think this block remained a sleepy former *bouwerie,* in the 1860s there was a two-way horse-drawn trolley line going along Thompson Street. In the 1870s an elevated steam railroad was added along Amity Street. Incidentally, West Third Street formed one long block from Thompson to MacDougal streets; Sullivan Street was not extended from West Third to the park until about 1903.[2]

In 1888 Edward Judson had purchased the four corner lots on Thompson and the park for the purpose of erecting a church that would be a memorial to his father and into which his Berean congregation would move from Downing Street. The next year he bought the two lots to the west and five years later one more lot to the west and eventually would lease yet one more lot. The result was not only the church itself with its tower, but an apartment hotel for income as well.

Edward bought the Judson House lot in July 1899 with a mortgage from the American Baptist Missionary Union, the organization that had been created to support his father in the mission field in Burma.

---

2. This information comes from various insurance atlases, e.g., by Matthew Dripps, William Perris, G. W. Bromley, and the Sanborn Map Company.

The History of Judson House as Property, 1899–1999

GRACE GOODMAN

The twentieth-century history of the property behind Judson Memorial Church divides itself into four somewhat over-lapping periods, according to uses. These periods may be referred to by the names most commonly used during each era to refer to the property: "The Annex," 1900–1921; the "Health Center" and "81 West Third," 1922–1950; The "Student House" and backyard, 1950–1967; and "Judson House" and the Garden, 1968–1999. This chapter will deal with the property as property—its physical changes and its legal and financial shifts.

THE ANNEX PERIOD, 1900–1922

Acquisition of the Property, 1899

Edward Judson purchased the corner lot and the buildings known as 235, 237, and 239 Thompson Street in July 1899, in his own name, for $30,000 ($5,000 down and a mortgage for $25,000 from Robert W. Tailer, the seller).[1] However, by November 1899 (if not from the start), he was thinking of conveying this property to the church:

> I am inclined to think that it would not be unwise for us to take in the property at the corner of Thompson and Third Streets, in this way securing at least three advantages: (1) protection for our church edifice from that quarter;

---

1. NYC Register, land conveyances, Liber 74, p. 323.

(2) the safe and fruitful investment of money which cannot be now paid on our mortgage indebtedness; (3) the acquisition of a building admirably fitted for a parish house—both as regards site and interior equipment.[2]

Apparently the church's trustees approved; on January 12, 1900, the property was legally conveyed to the Corporation of the Memorial Baptist Church of Christ (the legal name) by Edward and Antoinette B. Judson, his wife, for $30,000, with the church assuming the mortgage.[3]

In the meantime, Edward Judson had engaged the architectural firm of McKim, Mead & White (the same architects who designed the church building) to renovate and expand the three small houses on this lot into one building, for $14,000. This they did by filling in the façades into one continuous brick wall with a brownstone footing and a cornice at the roofline for the entire length of the building, closing up the three original front doors and constructing a new door in the center of the building, and repositioning windows to be evenly spaced. In the back of the building, the former three houses could still be detected, since the added connecting portions did not extend out to the lot line, as did the walls of the original houses.

According to the alteration application filed with the New York City Buildings Department in November 1899, the plan was to create a tenement or lodging house of thirty-eight rooms, described as "bachelor apartments," with twelve rooms on the first floor (street level) and thirteen rooms on each of the second and third floors. Each floor would have two toilet-rooms with windows opening onto ventilation shafts. A central staircase would connect the three residence floors and the below-street level basement, which the application said would be used for "stores" (unclear if that meant storage or business, probably the former). In addition, a subbasement would

---

2. Letter Nov. 23, 1899, from Edward Judson to the secretary of the congregation's Board of Trustees, George Welwood Murray (senior partner in a Wall Street law firm and long-time financial adviser to John D. Rockefeller, the church's principal benefactor at that time); American Baptist Historical Society (ABHS) Archives, Rochester, NY; Group 1048, Box 2, Correspondence re: Judson Memorial Church, 1887–1914.

3. NYC Register, land conveyances, Liber 220, p. 47.

Thompson Street, looking north. Judson House is on the other side of the elevated subway, which ran along West Third Street. Date of photograph unknown (before 1924).

contain heating equipment (coal-furnaces and storage for the coal); the basement would be reached by exterior stairs down from the street level into a narrow trench extending along the entire front of the building. The work was completed as of May 26, 1900, and approved for occupancy at least by November 1900.[4] This basic layout existed for the rest of the century, although some rooms were combined into larger apartments from time to time.[5]

Early in the twentieth century, the Judson Hotel, next door to the church on Washington Square South, arranged to lease the new Thompson Street building to house its staff.[6] By 1912, documents show that some fifteen "servants" and two "clerks" lived there (possibly each using two small rooms?).[7] The building became officially known as the Annex, meaning an annex to the Judson Hotel.

Transfer of the Property to the Baptist City Society, 1913

The Judson Hotel property itself was owned by the church corporation, with the intention that income from the hotel lease (which now included the Annex lease) would cover a large portion of the church's capital expenses. Through a nationwide fundraising campaign, the church had previously raised a "Memorial Fund" to help pay off the costs of purchase and construction of the church build-

---

4. Municipal Archives, Folder on Block 541, Lot 26; Alteration 2568/1899 (undated).

5. The enlargement of rooms may have begun even before the proposed renovation was built: a Nov. 23, 1899, memo from the Department of Buildings disapproves the alteration application on a number of points, including the fact that some of the proposed rooms contained less than 600 cubic feet—a Building Code violation. However, by amendment to the application dated Dec. 6, 1899, the architects indicate that the objections will be taken care of (just how, not specified), and on Dec. 11, 1899, the Superintendent of Buildings approved the application. Municipal Archives, Folder on Block 541, Lot 26.

6. The Hotel lease was with Margaret Knott of the Knott hotel family; a new lease, signed on Feb. 1, 1911, included the Hotel and the Annex. City Register, Liber 226, pp. 216–220. It appears that these leases may have had ten-year terms; another lease of the same properties was made Aug. 30, 1921, for a term to expire Oct. 31, 1931, according to recitals in contract of sale of the Hotel property to NYU in 1925. Judson Archives.

7. March 25, 1913, booklet published by New York Baptist City Society, describing the Judson properties. In Judson Archives.

ings. Another part of these costs was covered by selling annuities paying 6 percent for life, in the expectation that the church would benefit from what was left of the principal when the annuitants died. Besides covering construction costs, the Memorial Fund took care of 2 percent of the annual 6 percent annuity payments, with the hotel lease covering the other 4 percent.

But by 1909, that fund was used up; the annuitants were living far longer than expected, and the church had to assume the 2 percent (some $4,000 a year).[8] Also, by the end of the first decade of the new century, many of Judson's wealthy church members had moved uptown and joined other churches, leaving a congregation of relatively poor people from the neighborhood south of Washington Square, an Italian immigrant ghetto for the most part. Probably the most significant financial change, however, was the loss of several thousand dollars a year from John D. Rockefeller, a Baptist who had been Edward Judson's patron since they met in 1882. Mr. Rockefeller, then one of the wealthiest men in the United States, had concluded that "scientific philanthropy" required him to give "wholesale" instead of "retail," which meant that he stopped giving to individual churches—including, in 1910, Judson Church—in favor of giving to institutions such as mission societies that covered numerous church projects.[9] The New York Baptist City Society was the local recipient that Rockefeller's fund manager recommended for his New York-area Baptist contributions.

In 1910, Edward Judson got himself elected to a four-year term as President of the City Society (of which his former seminary student and one-time assistant pastor, Charles H. Sears, was by then the executive director). When none of Edward Judson's funding appeals

---

8. Letter April 5, 1909, from Edward Judson to Dr. T. J. Harris, former church trustee, describing the church's financial plight and attaching a proposal to borrow money on the Annex. In Judson Archives. In the proposal, Judson referred to the Annex properties as "never an integral part of the church property" but instead just a place to invest some of the Memorial Fund at a better return than was available in bonds or mortgages. "The fact is that through our policy of regarding the Annex ... as sacred funds which we wish to hand down intact to our descendants we are in danger of letting the vitality of the church sink so low that no amount of money used in the future, however wisely, will bring about its recovery." Despite this plea, the borrowing plan was not approved.

9. Brumberg, Joan Jacobs, *Mission for Life* (New York: Free Press, 1980).

Judson House, 1926.

to individual wealthy donors proved sufficient, talks began with the City Society about making some kind of fiscal connection to the Memorial Church. Edward would have preferred to give an "ecclesiastical mortgage" that would have the City Society pay for everything except the "spiritual side," which the congregation would cover, in hopes that this would induce Rockefeller to give to the City Society for Judson, but his advisers told him that such a plan would not be "irrevocable" enough for Rockefeller.[10]

After much anguish, Edward Judson and the Memorial Church's trustees and congregation finally agreed to turn over all their properties (with both their revenues and their liabilities and obligations) to the City Society "for the purpose of its administration for mission-

10. Letter Nov. 13, 1912, from Edward Judson to "My dear kind friend" (not otherwise identified); ABHS Archives, Group 1048, Box 2, Correspondence re: Judson Memorial Church, 1887–1914.

ary work in the lower part of this city." The City Society in turn agreed to administer them as a program of the Society, without interfering with the "spiritual autonomy" or existence of the Memorial Church.[11] In the spring of 1913, formal deeds were given and registered soon thereafter.[12] With the endorsement of the national Northern Baptist Convention at its 1913 annual meeting, the City Society embarked on another nationwide fundraising campaign to underwrite what it called the "Judson Memorial." This became the overall term for a number of projects, not all located at the church site. About the same time, the church itself began to be called Judson Memorial instead of Memorial Baptist Church of Christ, its formal name up to that point.

The property transfer made no operational difference to the use of the Annex; the City Society simply took over the existing leases with the Knott family, who ran the hotel.

Edward Judson died shortly thereafter, on October 23, 1914. About a year later, the church called Alonzo Ray Petty, a well-reputed preacher from Los Angeles, as its new senior pastor. He served from 1915 to 1926, cooperating closely with the City Society on all fiscal and property matters and serving as chief staff for all the City Society's Judson Memorial programs, which expanded over the next several years.

City Society Acquires 81 West Third Street, 1917

The other lot behind the church building, next to the Annex property, was occupied by a single three-story house, some 40 feet deep, covering about one-third of the lot, whose address was 81 West Third Street. (Some insurance maps from the mid-1800s show a small structure in the middle of the yard behind this house, possibly a cooking shack, but apparently it did not survive long into the new century.) In October 1917, under terms of a bequest, a family named

---

11. City Society booklet March 25, 1913, pp. 19–21.

12. City Register of Conveyances, Liber 226, pp. 216–218 (recorded Nov. 28, 1913); includes conveyance of the church's interest in its lease with Margaret Knott on the Hotel and the Annex, and its interest in the underlying property of the church, the Hotel, and the Annex.

Judson House façade, 1999. Photo by Alice Garrard.

Malony conveyed the lot and house to the City Society, for a token amount of $5,601, mostly to buy out a minor's interest.[13]

The City Society treated this new acquisition as part of its Judson Memorial properties and used it principally as rental housing from then on, although it appears that many of the rentals were more for the purpose of providing housing for City Society staff than purely for income. This included some staff assigned to the

---

13. Register of Conveyances, Liber 3035, pp. 14–16, Liber 3039, p. 387.

Judson Neighborhood House that the City Society began to operate around this time at 179 Sullivan Street. There are also some
references in the Judson Archives to rentals to various New York
University-connected persons, and a bill, dated May 7, 1919, from
the church to NYU for $7.50 for NYU's share in removing dirt in
the yard, so there must have been some shared use with the University at that time.[14]

There is also a reference to 81 West Third Street as being the
"home" for a few years prior to 1921 of the Nokomis and the
Cherokees, a couple of boys' athletic clubs that the Judson Memorial sponsored, which used the church gymnasium for part of their
activities.[15]

What use, if any, was made at that period of the yard in back of
the lot is not clear. Correspondence from January 1922 states that
the church had agreed with the hotel to construct a covered passageway between the hotel and the 81 West Third Street building, and
further to connect the top floor of that building with the Annex—all
this presumably to allow indoor travel from the hotel to the Annex
for its staff. The City Society's attorney, Edward Clinch (later a
judge and also later a president of the Northern Baptist Convention), recommended that this obligation be fulfilled, especially since
the hotel had effectively surrendered the use of the yard at 81 West
Third without any abatement of rent. This suggests that the hotel
lease actually covered the back of that lot at that time. There is,
however, no record that such a passageway was ever built.

THE HEALTH CENTER PERIOD, 1922–1950

The Health Center Is Established, 1921

In 1920, Dr. Petty had met a young physician, Dr. Eleanor Campbell, who had a dream of providing clinic services to children and
families in lower Manhattan, but she did not have a good location
for this dream. Ray Petty convinced the City Society that a health
center would be a far better use for the Annex, and in 1922, the
property changed tenants and names.

---

14. Judson Archives; Folder "A Ray Petty Correspondence 1918–20 (1 of …)"
15. The 1922 Judson Annual Report, p. 29. In Judson Archives.

The "Health Roof" of the Judson Health Center in the 1920s.

As of January 21, 1922, the City Society entered a new lease with Dr. Campbell, covering the basement; first, second, and third floors; and roof at 235–237–239 Thompson Street for a period of almost ten years (February 1, 1922, to October 31, 1931), at a rent of $250 per month, for the purpose of operating a health center "for preventive and therapeutic health work to include a hospital, dispensary, and nursery." [16] The tenant was to arrange and pay for all alterations necessary to bring the facility up to code for such uses; the landlord would continue to do exterior maintenance and repairs as needed. Dr. Campbell entered a separate lease for the same time period with the Judson Hotel Company to buy steam heat and electric light from the plants belonging to the hotel (but actually located, for the most part, in the subbasement of the church) for $2,000 a year. [17]

Dr. Campbell engaged architects Raymond M. Hood and J. André Fouilhous to do interior renovations on the Thompson Street property, which involved extensive plumbing additions and some moving of walls, as well as fitting out the roof for use. Rooms were remodeled to serve as offices and also as examining and waiting

16. Indenture dated Jan. 21, 1922. In Judson Archives, Box C.14.
17. Draft indenture (unsigned) in Judson Archives.

rooms, a dentist's office, an X-ray room, a kitchen, and an apartment for the superintendent (location not specified, but possibly the basement apartment at the corner of Thompson and West Third streets).[18]

At some point, possibly in 1925, a connecting door was broken through the party wall between the top floor of 81 West Third Street and the third floor of the Health Center building. After that change, the top floor of the Thompson Street building was blocked off from that building's central stairs and could be entered only from 81 WestThird. Despite the lease to the Health Center of the entire building, the Health Center had apparently agreed from the beginning that the top floor, with thirteen rooms, would continue to be used for housing, either of hotel staff or of City Society tenants.[19] The Health Center used the rest of the building, including the roof.

There is also a report dated July 28, 1921, from the City Society's committee on Judson, which states that after negotiations, the hotel had agreed to give up its lease on the Annex so that the new Health Center could use that building but that the hotel wanted to have the use of an equal number of rooms at 81 West Third Street, at the same rental. Since it appears that the Health Center did not use the top floor of the Thompson Street building after all, it seems likely that at least some of the hotel staff stayed there; perhaps others received rooms at 81 West Third Street. To cover necessary alterations to make 81 West Third suitable for rental housing, and also

---

18. Letter dated April 11, 1950, from F. J. Coppinger of Triangle Painting Co. to Albert B. Ashforth, Inc., proposing prices to paint 26 named rooms and hallways. Judson Archives, Box on Judson Health Center. The letter contains a room-by-room description of the clinics not found in earlier documents.

19. The Oct. 1, 1925, Indenture of Sale from the City Society to NYU of the Judson Hotel property recites that a lease was entered Aug. 30, 1921, between the City Society and the Hotel to rent the Hotel and the top floor of the Annex for $18,012.68 per year. A memo dated Oct. 17, 1950 (unsigned, unaddressed) concerning "Interview of Oct. 11, 1950 with Joel Cohen" states that City building records then showed "a certificate of occupancy as of 1925 for the use of a hotel on the Third floor and the rest of the building as the Health Center." Judson Archives. A memo May 9, 1949, from Deputy Comm. of Housing Division to Superintendent, Department of Buildings, in Municipal Archives Folder on Block 541, Lot 27, mentions the long-standing use of the top floor for housing (by 1949, reported as for students of religion).

to cover some unrelated heating upgrades, insurance, and new carpeting for the church, the City Society voted to take a three-year $20,000 mortgage on the Thompson Street property at 6 percent interest, with the right to pay off $1,500 of principal each year. The plan was to amortize the loan over ten years out of the hotel income, plus church income. Apparently, the City Society ultimately took only a $15,000 loan against the Thompson Street property, and in 1930 extended the remaining $8,000 another three years at $5\frac{1}{2}$ percent; in 1934, some $3,500 was still outstanding.[20]

The Rest of the Judson Memorial Properties During the 1920s–1940s

In October 1925, the City Society sold the hotel (including the church tower) to New York University for use as a dormitory. The agreement included provisions for NYU to assume the City Society's lease with the Judson Hotel, which included the use of the top floor of the Health Center building and 81 West Third Street. NYU agreed to pay $3,500 a year for use of the latter properties, which were still owned by the City Society.[21] The sale brought $225 to the City Society's Judson Memorial Fund; this sum is reputed to have been set aside at least in part to start an endowment to maintain the Church in perpetuity.

Dr. Petty resigned as pastor at Judson in March 1926 to accept the pastorate of Grace Temple Baptist Church in Philadelphia, one of the most prestigious pulpits in the nation. The City Society thereupon named the Rev. Laurence T. Hosie (who had previously been assigned to the struggling Second Avenue Baptist Church and had also worked at the Presbyterian Labor Temple) as Judson's pastor.

---

20. Letters dated May 16, 1930, and Feb. 17, 1934, from the Mutual Life Insurance Company to the City Society; ABHS Archives, Box "Includes Judson Church Ca 1916–1944" folder "No. 79 West Third Street Judson."

21. Judson Archives, Box C.14, Lease; Indenture of Sale dated Oct. 1, 1925. The sale also included a provision that if NYU acquired the Hotel lease, it could cancel the lease, but if that occurred, the top floor of the old Annex would become available to the Health Center for its use, and new arrangements would be made to rent 81 West Third Street. It appears that this term was not carried out, and the top floor continued to be used by the City Society during the entire time that the Health Center occupied the building.

He served from April 1926 to September 1937, focusing much of his work on social programs responsive to the economic depression.

In July 1926, the City Society also acquired the lot immediately to the west of these properties, 83 West Third Street, which also contained a three-story house of about the same size as that at 81 West-Third, but with a one-story addition in the rear. That building deteriorated sharply, and by 1933 it had to be demolished, leaving a lot that stayed vacant for the rest of the century.[22] The Judson Memorial staff used this house, while it lasted, for more rental housing. Subsequently, the church let a Public Works "play project" use the vacant lot to let the boys in the project try making a garden; they planted a glorious flower garden on the entire lot, outlining plots with used brick from the demolished structure. Apparently, they also pulled a lot of loose bricks out of the remains of the party wall with 81, to the distress of the City Society's property administrator, who pointed out that when 83 was demolished, they had deliberately left about 18 inches of wall "to give some support to the poor west wall of 81."[23] In light of the fact that 81 West Third itself collapsed some seventeen years later, this demolition and weakening of the remaining supporting wall appears, in hindsight, to have been doubly unfortunate.

In September 1939, the City Society sold the lot at 83 West Third Street to the Bertolotti family, who lived next door, for $10,500 in cash.[24]

---

22. Register of Conveyances, Liber 3559, p. 292; Municipal Archives Folder on Block 541, Lot 28,and ABHS Archives, Box "Includes Judson Church Correspondence 1933–42," folder "Judson Apartment House." The property had been owned by a Joseph West since 1853; his heirs conveyed it to the City Society by deed July 29, 1926; letter dated Sept. 15, 1939, from Charles Sears to Elmer Sanborn; ABHS Archives, Box "Includes Judson Church Ca 1916–1944" in folder without tab or identification.

23. Letter Aug. 15, 1935, from Edward C. Sanborn to Stanley B. Hazzard (executive of the City Society); letter Sept. 12, 1935, from Laurence T. Hosie (minister at Judson) to Hazzard; in ABHS Archives, Rochester, NY, Box "Includes Judson Church Correspondence 1928–39," folder "Judson Memorial 1933–1937."

24. Letter dated Sept. 26, 1939, from T. Raymond St. John of the firm of Hays, St. John, Abramson & Schulman, to Rev. Charles H. Sears of the City Society. ABHS Archives, Box "Includes Judson Church Ca 1916–1944," folder with broken tab, no identification.

According to an article in *The Villager* of Oct. 9, 1939, the Bertolottis had operated a well-known restaurant since around 1900 in the ground floor of their resi-

As the depression deepened, the Judson Church congregation continued to shrink. Its income declined to the point where the church could no longer pay for housing for their minister, Rev. Hosie, and his family. Therefore, when one of the tenants at 81 West Third Street vacated an apartment there, the Judson Board offered the apartment to the Hosies, who lived there the rest of their time at Judson.[25]

By 1937, the English-speaking congregation at Judson Church had dwindled to almost nothing. However, the Italian-speaking congregation (which had been started during Edward Judson's era and had operated continuously with an Italian-speaking pastor, with services on Sunday evenings) was holding its own. The City Society decided to merge the two congregations under the leadership of the Italian pastor, Rev. Renato Alden, and so asked Rev. Hosie to resign, which he did, effective September 30, 1937.[26]

For the next ten years, the City Society hired a series of clergy and lay executive directors for the Judson Memorial work, which included leading services at the church after Rev. Alden moved on to other work. The last of these executive directors was Rev. Elbert R. Tingley, who came in 1946 and resigned, apparently in frustration over his inability to make any headway on any major program, as of April 24, 1948.[27]

THE STUDENT HOUSE, 1949–1968

The Health Center Becomes the Student House, 1949–1951

In 1948, the City Society appointed the Rev. Dean Wright as director of the Judson Memorial's Student Program, and a year later, the Rev. Robert W. Spike became the senior minister at Judson Church. These staff members and their families lived at 81 West Third Street.

---

dence at 85 West Third Street—a house where, in the nineteenth century, Edgar Allen Poe lived for two years while writing "The Fall of the House of Usher" and other works. "Papa" Bertolotti had been trying to buy the lot at 83 West Third from the City Society since 1931, to build a matching house for all his children and their families.

25. Unpublished manuscript by Laurence T. Hosie, in Judson Archives, Box C.09.

26. Judson Archives, Box C.09.1936.Hosie; folder "Hosie 'Dismissal' Correspondence.

27. Judson Archives, Box C.08.1946–48 Tingley.

After a period of persuasion and negotiations, the Thompson Street building took on a new incarnation and became known for the next two decades as the Student House. In 1950 Dr. Campbell agreed to move the Health Center to a new location, and the City Society agreed to underwrite renovations and alterations to the building to make it suitable to house students and some staff.

These renovations were done in 1951 by the J. B. Snook architectural firm. They restored the central stairs to the third floor, cleared out the Health Center equipment, and built an apartment on the north end of the second floor for use of various church staff. The bulk of the building remained very small residence rooms, with one toilet and a shower room on each of the second and third floors, a kitchen and dining area in the south end of the basement, and an all-purpose meeting/recreation/lounge room at the north end. The north end of the first floor was turned into a second staff apartment for use by the house parents for the students.

From 1950 to 1965, Judson organized the Church in Urban Life program, which involved about twenty students who lived at Judson house from June through August. In addition, Judson House always rented rooms to year-round students from NYU and other colleges in New York City. The last of these lived at Judson House in the mid-1960s.

Building Problems

In the spring of 1950, the City Society had a thorough inspection made of both the Health Center and the 81 West Third Street building. This revealed several structural problems that required immediate attention. The Health Center had some sagging floors and a bulge in its western exterior wall, which were not an imminent danger. At 81 West Third Street, the north and west walls showed new cracks, and the inspectors suggested that the normal settling of the foundation might be aggravated by the pile driving at the site of NYU's new law center a half-block away. The inspectors advised keeping close watch on this condition.[28]

---

28. Letter dated April 26, 1950, from Daniel E. Merrill, Architect, to Rev. Robert V. Russell, City Society. Judson Archives, Box C.10.1950s Health Center.

Later that year, 81 West Third Street suddenly developed a noticeable bulge in its front wall, causing it to be immediately evacuated. The building was razed soon after.

The Judson Gallery

Initially engaged by Robert Spike as a seminary student doing his internship work and later hired by Howard Moody as an associate minister, Bernard "Bud" Scott lived at the Student House from 1957 to 1960. Under his leadership, the church in 1958 opened an art gallery in a pair of basement rooms at the north end of the House. The gallery rooms were walled off from the rest of the House and were entered by an exterior iron stairway, under the fire escape. This area remained a separate space until about 1975, when it was returned to residence use by connecting it to the first-floor staff apartment via a spiral staircase.

Changes in the Student House Program

After 1965, the Church and Urban Life program at the Student House faded, and the space was used to take in a variety of persons who needed housing; for a period there was an effort to provide housing for students at the City's art schools that had no dormitories of their own.

In 1961, to house Al Carmines, the new assistant minister, another apartment was created on the south end of the first floor. Later Al moved into the larger apartment on the north end of the first floor that had been occupied by the Student House house parents.

"JUDSON HOUSE" AND THE GARDEN, 1968–1999

The Runaway House

The last residence program to occupy the Thompson Street building was a short-lived program for runaway teens during the height of the hippie culture in the Village in the late 1960s. The hard wear given to the premises by these youngsters, on top of the hard use given by all the other occupants over the years, effectively destroyed the building's suitability for lodging, other than the few apartments that continued to be occupied by Judson staff.

The Center for Medical Consumers

The apartment on the south corner of the first floor, used by Howard and Lorry Moody in 1975–1976 while Grace House, the parsonage on 18th Street, was being renovated, in 1978 became the home of the Center for Medical Consumers. The center continued to occupy this site until 2000.

The Garden

Sometime in the late 1960s, Art Levin, together with Lee Guilliatt and others, organized a work party to lay a brick floor over the old backyard portion of the 81 West Third Street lot. Thereafter, this "garden" was used by the church for its summer worship services when the church building was stiflingly hot and for many other activities. The site of the old house on this lot remained unpaved and served as a staff parking lot, accommodating up to four cars.

Judson Church Regains Title to Its Real Estate, 1979

Curiously, the process of transferring all Judson properties—the church, Judson House, and Grace House—from the New York Baptist City Society back to Judson Memorial Church took several years. In a letter dated June 14, 1977, Allen Hinand of the City Society informed Judson Memorial Church of "last night's vote" to return the properties to Judson. The actual transfer of the deed did not take place until November 28, 1979, and the congregation observed a Celebration of the Return of the Property in a festive service on Sunday, December 2, 1979. This marked the end of a dependent relationship with the NYBCS that began in 1913.

Uses of Judson House, 1970s–1990s

The top floor remained unused except for some archival storage and a two-room office, constructed there in the late 1990s for use by the minister emeritus when he was in town.

The south half of the second floor was similarly unusable and essentially unused until 1995, when an office suite was created out of several rooms at the West Third Street end for use of the Employment Project begun by Paul Chapman.

The roof of Judson House in 1999. Photo by Alice Garrard.

The rest of the second floor (aside from a staff apartment at the north end) was occupied variously by overflow offices from the first-floor Center for Medical Consumers and by a workroom for assembling the church's archives.

In 1992, the church voted to allocate the first-floor apartment at the north end of the building to Howard Moody, who retired after thirty-five years as senior minister. In the interim between Moody's departure to his home in California and the church's calling the Rev. Peter Laarman in January 1994, this apartment was used by the interim minister, Rev. Bill Malcomson, and his wife, Laurie. Thereafter, the Moodys returned to take up residence for six to eight months every year.

The south-end basement apartment was allocated to the church sexton, Roland Wiggins, in 1982. The bare-bones meeting room (formerly the dining room) was used for Sunday School classes and overflow meetings as needed; the north-end lounge (periodically redecorated with used furniture and some new accessories) served as the church's preferred location for small meetings throughout the week.

On December 16, 1999, Edward A. Powers, moderator of Judson Memorial Church, signed the document that turned the deed to Judson House over to the New York University School of Law.

A Custodian's Description

JOHN TUNGATE

John Tungate arrived at Judson in 1968 and for the next ten years took care of the physical needs of the church building and of Judson House.

There was nothing platonic about my relationship with Judson House. As the maintenance man and janitor I knew Judson House in the most physical of ways. I knew its sound, its smells, its problems, and its dirty secrets. I even knew what it looked like inside its walls and floors and ceilings. Judson was my home and work for many years. Its physical problems became my problems, day and night! It was the kind of familiarity that Al described in his oratorio "A Look at the Fifties," when he talked about how you come to know and love "the smell of your own gym floor."

Before I tell you anything about my experiences at Judson House, I have to make a few things perfectly clear. They are nicely summarized in one of Al Carmines's oratorios performed at Judson Church during the early 1970s. Like most of what Al wrote, they are clearly words to live by.

I know everything, (at least I think I do),
The rest I make up, the rest I make up
Some things I'm sure of, other things I'm not so sure
The rest I make up, the rest I make up.

Taking this as the guiding light for recounting my memories and experiences at Judson House, I warn you that the responsibility for any lapses in memory, exaggerations, incorrect information, or out-right lies rests solely on the shoulders of the editors, who should have known better than to ask me what I remember about Judson House from so long ago.

Coming to work at Judson Church in 1968 was a perfectly natural decision for me since I had just finished two years of active duty as a medic in the U.S. Army. I made the decision to work at Judson in the same way the army made all their personnel decisions: Almost all the cooks had been either auto mechanics or carpenters in civilian life, and 95 percent of the auto mechanics had never used a screwdriver before. So, it seemed perfectly reasonable to me to work at a church since (1) I had given up on all forms of organized religion years ago to become a solitary Zen Buddhist; (2) I had no previous experience whatsoever as a janitor or maintenance man; and (3) I felt I was the perfect candidate for this job at Judson Church.

I had not yet heard back from my first choice of a new civilian career (as a letter-carrier for the U.S. Post Office), so I took the job as the church janitor at Judson and began my new duties under the careful tutelage of a conscientious objector doing alternative service named Reathel Bean. I trailed around Judson Church and Judson House in my combat boots and crewcut and newly bought blue denim uniform of overalls with the over-the-shoulder straps while learning from Reathel which of the fifty-odd keys I carried on a big ring went to what door.

Like many newcomers to Judson I was still naïve about certain aspects of life in New York's Greenwich Village and at Judson. I couldn't at first understand why I seemed to attract the attention of some of the male dancers that rehearsed in the church gym and the meeting room upstairs: What was so interesting to them about a young, muscular, crew-cut army veteran still wearing his combat boots, with a huge ring of keys, and all sorts of tools hanging off his leather belt? As I changed the side I wore my keys on, I found it seemed to attract different people. What could all this mean? I thought, "How friendly they are to an Army veteran; and even while the Vietnam War is still going on!"

Thank goodness Reathel was there to help me. Although Reathel was from a small town in the Midwest, he had been around Greenwich Village for a while and was quick to help explain the secret language of the heavy ring of keys. Reathel told me that many of these male dancers were sons of chiropractors and they were very concerned about me hurting my back when I was carrying these heavy keys on one side. That cleared up any confusion I might have had about what it all meant. (Thanks, Reathel!)

I have not been in Judson House for over twenty years. I have driven by it once or twice, but I can still see it clearly in my mind's eye. For at least ten years afterward, I could have closed my eyes and told you where every light switch and outlet were (and I could have done the same for all of Judson Church, too). I knew every sound of every door, every gate and set of stairs. Even today, you could test me with recordings of the slamming of any of the doors and I could tell you instantly which one was the side door to the church, which one the security door or back door to the offices, which one was the double glass doors to the sanctuary or the steel door from the cage room to the gym. I could tell the sound of the Garden Room sliding door and its screen door in my sleep from my room in Judson House.

THE GRAND TOUR

Let me try to describe to you what the physical building was like, take you on a tour of its rooms, and tell you what I can still see and hear when I close my eyes and remember Judson House.

Judson House is a three-story brick building at the corner of Thompson and Third Street in Greenwich Village. It is a narrow building, with its façade running from Third Street uptown along the west side of Thompson Street until it meets the corner of the Judson Church building. Its footprint is roughly rectangular but it has insets or wells along the backside of the building. This technique was used often in New York City tenement buildings to meet the New York City Building Code requirements for light and ventilation. By cutting out a portion of the rectangular footprint and making an open shaft way or well, inner rooms could still meet the city codes for natural light and ventilation even when another building was built right against it, as it was done with the rowhouses in New York and other cities.

Judson House has one such cutout in back that is big enough to be called a small courtyard. It is just a little lower than the basement floor of Judson House, with an outside area drain. I close my eyes and imagine that I am standing there again: I can see two doors that open onto this courtyard, one from what was the old kitchen when Judson House was a student's residence, the other door opening onto the narrow back hall to a separate apartment, where Joan Muyskens, the church secretary, lived part of the time when I was at Judson.

The main front entrance to Judson House is on Thompson Street, roughly in the middle of the building. There are two low stone steps up to the front door, then a wood landing inside, then several more wood steps up to the first floor level. The wood landing and steps are covered with linoleum, and there are bright metal "nosing" strips on each stair trap.

There are three more doors in the front of the building, each one partly below street level, going into the building at the basement level.

Façade

The façade on Thompson is set back from the sidewalk by two open wells that extend down to the subbasement below, thus allowing for windows and doors below the sidewalk, on the basement level. At the Third Street end is a gate in the steel railing that surrounds one well. There are steep steps down to a steel landing outside the door to the basement apartment. After another gate, a longer set of wooden steps goes down to the subbasement. Similar gates and steel landings give access to the front door to the kitchen, to the left of the main entry, and to the Judson Gallery at the north end.

At the north end, a fire escape stairs comes right down to the street level suspended over the other well. It is enclosed in a steel security mesh so it can be opened only from the inside and (theoretically) keep anyone from climbing up from the street. The fire escape runs up between the church building and Judson House to the second-floor hall window. The fire escape continues to the third-floor window of Judson House and then up a flight of steel steps to a door cut into the thick back wall of the church building. This door connects to the "fluff room" over the rose window and to the spiral staircases down to the dressing rooms on two levels and up to the secret walkways and spaces hidden above the sanctuary ceiling.

The exterior walls of Judson House are brick, painted red, with cut stone as sills and lintels for doors and windows. The windows are double hung, with old-fashioned weight boxes and chains. The counterweights inside are cast-iron and torpedo shaped with the numbers indicating their weight cast into them on the side and a loop at the top to attach the chain.

The roof is flat, and made of built-up bituminous layers laid down hot, the old-fashioned way.

The Judson House Parking Area

If you look out the back windows of Judson House you see the Judson Garden courtyard below, and beyond it—up a few steps—is the Judson Garden itself and the parking area. You can also see the wood fence separating the garden from the parking area and beyond it the brick wall on Third Street with a sliding garage door built into it. The heavy garage door slides toward the Thompson Street side (to your left from here) toward the old storage rack against the wall that is not visible around the corner of the building. The bottom of the door rubs on the concrete and you have to stand with your back braced against the side jamb to push it open. The sound of the garage door opening is distinct and recognizable through the open windows of the second floor. Here there is an old wood rack with mostly scraps and junk. Here, too, Howard Moody sometimes parks his car, and I keep my Volkswagen bus and canoe.

This parking area behind Judson House is a good place to overhaul a Volkswagen bus engine. Here, you can jack up the back end of your bus as high as the jack will go, then build a platform of wood scraps under each rear wheel. You keep jacking and building the platform until you have room to slide a wheelbarrow under the engine from underneath between the rear wheels of the bus with its rear end now tilted up at almost a 30-degree angle.

By cutting a hole in the back sheetmetal floor over the engine, and building a 2×4 tripod, you can use a block and tackle and lower your engine down into the wheelbarrow. Then you can wheel it through the garden to the back door, and there discover that the engine is so light that you can pick it up and carry it into the janitor's work room in the basement and set it on the workbench. After overhauling it you can carry it back out and install it in reverse order.

Inside the Walls and Floors, Technically Speaking

The inside walls (except where new sheetrock has been installed) are of plaster over wood lath. The "brown coat" plaster has fibers in it, probably horsehair. The wood lath is on furring strips on the outside walls. The furring strips are nailed into the masonry of the outside wall except that a "trick" was used in some places in Judson House on the inner course of the brick walls: The 3/8-inch wood lath was sometimes laid into half of a horizontal mortar joint instead of mortar—one course near the ceiling and one near the floor, and sometimes a third in the middle. This would allow the nailing of the furring strips directly into the wooden strip buried in the wall. (This wasn't always such a good trick because when I took down the plaster, the wood lath had dried out and become loose inside the wall.) The interior separation walls are of rough cut 2×4s (the old full-sized ones) with some partitions of thinner 2×3s.

The floor joists are wood, often full-sized and rough-cut. Bridle irons have been used in some places where headers cut across a run of joists, and the joists fit into pockets, or "seats," in the brick masonry walls. The top corners of these joists have been "firecut" to allow them to fall free of the wall in case of collapse during a fire. In this way the entire masonry wall will not fall down. The old wood flooring is wide tongue-and-groove strip flooring (probably pine) fastened to the joists with cut nails. It is partially blind-nailed, partially face-nailed.

The Sounds of the Front Hall

I can still hear, as plain as day, all the noises as someone—let's say Al Carmines—enters 237 Thompson Street. There is the muffled sound of a key being inserted on the outside of a two-inch thick wood door. It makes the door resonate in a certain way as the key enlarges the pins inside and pushes up against the spring-loaded brass pins above, then suddenly there is a rush of street sounds—the noise of cars and voices bouncing off the wall of the Catholic church on the other side of Thompson. There is the soft creak of the hydraulic door-closer arm at the top of the door. The hinges are on the side closest to the park and they, too, make a soft rubbing sound as Al's shoe hits the metal edging on the first step inside the door.

He will reach the second step—his shoes rattling the metal nosing again—before the door slams hard against the electric door-release strike and shakes the whole wall and rattles the loose pane of glass on the second floor window right above the door, in my room. It is all over in a few seconds: Al's deep voice humming a few notes as he turns right and crosses to the heavy steel door to his apartment; the click of the brass knob retracting the latch on the mortise lock; and his voice, still humming, cut off in mid-sound by a soft clunk, as the self-closing hinges seal his door from the first-floor hallway. Through the closed door you can still hear him thump up the steps just inside his apartment, the sound of those steps unlike any other anywhere else in Judson House. Then it's quiet again, only a lingering smell of cigarette smoke in the hallway and the muffled sounds of the street outside.

First Floor South Memories

If you turn left instead of right, there is another heavy steel fire door with self-closing "Bommer" type hinges that have adjustable steel tensioning pins. The lock is a brass mortise lock set, with a brass cylinder, a deadbolt, and brass knobset. The doorframe is also steel, and on the hinge side is the fire rating label for the door. You enter the hallway with windows on your right and continuing down the first floor hall, there are dormitory type rooms on the left. Past the windows on the right is the door to the bathroom. It is large with one toilet, one sink, and one white-painted steel shower stall. The single bulb of the ceiling light does not give enough light to see the scum and soap built up inside the stall. There is no door on the stall—only a built-in rod and a dirty plastic shower curtain. The base is precast concrete, and the steel is rusting where it meets the base.

This is the same space that I later renovated with the help of volunteers. Linda Simmons, an architect, helped us keep it simple and straightforward. We gutted the corner space (at Thompson and Third) into one large room, and instead of concealing all the pipes and electrical conduits, we simply painted them bright colors and let them be open and visible (in keeping with the times, we "let it all hang out"). It was in the old bathroom on this floor, years before this renovation, that I first learned how to cut sheetrock.

Although Arlene Carmen, the church office manager, used to say that "John Tungate can fix anything," it was really not true. But I got that reputation and had to work very hard to keep my public image untarnished and to live up to Arlene's expectations. Therefore, I was constantly having to learn new skills to cope with the things I got called on to fix. Sooner or later I had to fix everything from the old Gestetner offset printer and typewriters, to door locks, light fixtures, and any part of the church, building, or theater set that could possibly have a problem. Eventually I got pretty good at it, but thank goodness Arlene didn't see some of my "rich learning experiences" that preceded my eventual competence, or I might have had to reapply for that letter carrier job after all.

CUTTING SHEETROCK THE EASY WAY

On this particular day I had to patch the ceiling in the bathroom that was right at the inside corner of the building with one window facing the little "courtyard" that was formed by the first-floor hall on our side and the parking area and garden on the other.

A carpenter from Canada affectionately referred to as "John Canada" was visiting, and he quietly watched as I got ready to cut sheetrock the way I had always done it, that is, I'd put on a dust mask and goggles and coveralls, mark my cut on the sheetrock, and then one, two, three, I'd cut out the pieces I needed with an electric "skill saw." After the dust had cleared enough to see again, I'd climb the ladder, and nail up the sheetrock pieces I had cut. If the piece was quite large, I would use a "T bar" to help hold the piece up. Then I would begin the slow task of cleaning up the room, top to bottom, to remove all the sheetrock dust. That electric saw sure threw a lot of dust all over the place.

Well, "John Canada" watched me do this once without saying anything and then politely suggested that there was an easier way than using a 120-volt, $7\frac{1}{2}$ inch, 2,800 rpm standard #487 all-purpose hand circular saw (made by the Skill Corporation) that had enough power to coat a normal-sized 8.5×11-foot room with .024 inches of white plaster dust with only one cut in a taper-edged, 4×8-foot sheet of $\frac{5}{8}''$ U.S. Gypsum type "x" sheetrock. John Canada then showed me how the rest of the world cuts sheetrock (with a knife and no dust), and I was truly amazed! I never told Arlene about this, not wanting to bother her with such minor technical details.

ON WITH THE TOUR

Upstairs on the second floor is another apartment above Al's. This was Beverly Waite's apartment when I first came to Judson, and later this was the apartment for the "house parents" for the runaway project; finally Arlene Carmen moved into it.

On the third floor there is no apartment at this north end. The whole third floor is divided into dormitory-type single rooms with a central hallway running the full length and with a bathroom on each side of the floor.

From the first floor to the basement, the main stairs are narrower. At the bottom of the stairs is another hallway. Like upstairs, each side door from the hallway has a heavy steel-clad fire door with self-closing hinges separating the stair hall from the rest of the building. And like upstairs in the hall, there is a flush metal door built into the wall, hiding the electrical fuse panel. Inside are round plug fuses in two vertical rows. When electricity fails, this is where you must hunt to replace the blown fuse.

Changing a Blown Fuse

Willy, the electrician, once showed me the easy way to check for a blown fuse at the panel in the first-floor hallway where there must be almost thirty fuses. Sometimes you can't tell if a plug fuse has gone bad simply by looking at it. At times the fusible line won't "blow" and darken the little window. Then you have to unscrew each fuse and test it and replace it when necessary.

Willy said doing it that way took too long. He would just lick the tips of his thumb and first finger and shove his hand behind the panel and touch each of the fuse holders in turn, working his way down each row until he would say "here it is." He would quickly unscrew the bad fuse and pop in a new one. Sure enough, that was it! Willy saw how impressed I was and explained to me how it worked. If the fuse was good, the electricity would flow through it and you wouldn't feel any current in your fingers, but if the fuse was blown, it didn't have a path to travel and all the electricity would instead go through your fingers. But you had to wet your fingertips so you could feel it better.

"Feel right here," he said, reaching into the panel and touching two big terminals on the panel with his wetted fingertips, "this is 220." Touching two smaller ones, he said, "This is 110; you'll be able to tell the difference right away." I licked my two fingers and stuck them on the two big terminals at the bottom of the panel and learned to recognize the feeling of 220 volts of electricity running through my fingers and my hand and my arm and my leg and my toes. I told Willy I had gotten a pretty good idea already; I didn't need to try any other fuses.

A Janitor by Any Other Name...

As we resume our tour, in the basement ahead of you is the janitor's workroom. Here there are a workbench and storage shelves and cabinets. This is where I keep my tools and cleaning supplies. I have another room like this in the church basement. The one in Judson House does not have the same sign on the door that the one in the church does. In Judson Church, the sign on the door says "Sanitational Engineering Consultant" (that meant me, the janitor, and it made me feel a lot more important).

I did not put up my title on my janitor's room door in Judson House because of an amazing transformation that took place, almost like Paul's miraculous conversion on the road to Damascus. In my case, I was on the way to put toilet paper in the ladies' bathroom at the foot of the front stairs. Up until then I had been only a janitor and handyman, but on that day it all changed when Howard Moody, the senior minister, came out of his private office just as I was passing through the main office area with my arms full of toilet paper. There I am and Howard comes out with a paper in his hand and tells me that he has discovered that my position at the church is really that of church "sexton." I was even "sacerdotal" and had never even known it.

As Howard told me this and explained that I was even eligible for a Baptist pension because of my intimate relations with the holy sacraments, I suddenly felt a warm rush in my cheeks and an unearthly lightness to my body (despite all the toilet paper I was holding). I was dizzy with joy. "I'm sacerdotal!" was all I could keep saying to myself as I floated down the stairs and unwrapped a roll of toilet paper and placed it gently and serenely in its little holder next to the toilet. My life was never the same again.

Basement Layout

The basement has no dormitory rooms. From the south end to north, starting at Third Street, there is first a small apartment (inhabited for some time by Joan Muyskens, the church secretary, and her guard dog Lisa), then the kitchen, then the main hall stairs and janitor's room, then the Judson Lounge, and then, at the far north end, the Judson Gallery. A rear window from the main hall opposite the janitor's room has been converted to a short door, with steps going out to the garden. A similar door was made out of the rear window to the Judson Gallery.

The Old Kitchen

I can picture the old kitchen as it was when the building was still an artist's residence. The metal wall cabinets have a mural painted continuously across them, and there is a lot of dark green in the mural. It is a scene or landscape, and I think people are in it. The old commercial stove is on the back wall by the courtyard. The base cabinets are of wood and also painted with scenes and people. Later I will turn these cabinets into a base for my workbench when the kitchen becomes a workshop for me.

Judson Lounge

The Judson lounge has a low (tin?) ceiling, and there is dark, highly varnished exposed red brick in this room, with a structural column somewhere near the middle of the room. There is a couch and furniture here. This room is the "living room" of Judson House, one of the few rooms, other than the kitchen, gallery, or apartments, big enough to have a group of four or more people together at once. Lots of things have happened in this room.

The Judson Lounge is where I taught my home repair classes at night. The basic entrance requirements for the class were (1) to read

Plato's "Meno" dialogue, and (2) to bring in something broken, such as a portable appliance, so we could see how to "remember" to fix it. Although Arlene Carmen was always saying, "John Tungate can fix anything," it was really Plato who taught us that we already know how to fix things but have temporarily "forgotten." Zen taught us to humbly meditate on the possibility that it might be easier to buy a new appliance rather than go through the hassle to fix it. This was all before *Zen and the Art of Motorcycle Maintenance* was published, so it is clear that the Judson Lounge was in the forefront of pioneering the Zen approach to maintenance. We had a lot of broken toasters and hair dryers left over after the class that never got fixed, but at least I got a date with Stu Silver's ex-girlfriend as a result of the class, so it wasn't a complete loss.

It was also in this room that our "communal living" group met. It included Alice Eichholtz, Tom Craft, Carol and Phil Eichling, Jane Schram, and many others. We were all eager to explore the new openness and sexual freedom of the time. It turned out to be much more difficult than we expected, not only emotionally but also in the simple mechanics of it. So, in this room I wrote my not-too-well-known ode to the sexual freedom of the sixties and seventies, "Multiple Relationships":

> Multiple relationships,
> Two Janes, a Jean, and Joan,
> Can cause one lots of trouble
> When speaking on the phone.
> Your lips begin to form her name,
> Your thoughts begin to stray,
> And what comes out in syllables
> May cause you pain that day.
> So here's to sexual freedom
> And here's to telephones,
> (You'd better speak distinctly)
> Two Janes, a Jean, and Joan.

It was in the Lounge also that I had my typical conversations with Stu Silver in those days. Whoever of us entered the room would start out with a question like, "What time are they going to the airport?" The other person might respond, "They had to cancel their flight because the limo got a flat tire on the BQE, so they're thinking of going to Rio instead." The response to this might be, "I thought Charlie's ex-wife threatened to kill him if he ever went to Rio again?" We would sometimes go on for fifteen minutes like this, never knowing where it would take us. We always played it completely straight-faced, so that someone in the room not "in the know" would not have a clue that it was all completely made up on the spot. (It has been rumored that Stu went to Hollywood and became a well-known writer for TV shows. I hope it's clear that he owes much of his success to his early formative experiences at Judson House.)

Runaway House and Staff Apartments

Judson House became a runaway house in 1968. Art Levin started and sponsored this project. (He was always so quiet and unassuming about all the projects he started that it was hard to tell what Art was up to at any given time.) Some of the kids who came to stay had been living out on the street for many months. The number of runaways living on the streets of New York in those years was at epidemic proportions. Prostitution, drugs, and cold and hunger were familiar to most of them. Judson House gave them a safe place to sleep and to talk and think about their lives and to look at the realistic possibilities and decisions for their futures.

At first, I was not much involved with the runaway program. I do remember that I had to help fix up the kitchen, where a long-haired, bearded guy named Bob Lamberton cooked something that the counselors and runaways called a "macrobiotic diet." But soon I had more involvement with the runaway project than I needed. At first the kids and counselors thought I was just a nasty janitor, a straight authority-figure type. Later they all got to know me better, and then they recognized me for what I really was deep down inside—a nasty janitor, a straight authority-figure type.

The Runaways Fix Up Their Rooms

With the runaways, everything started out innocently enough: "Can we borrow some paint to paint our rooms?" "Can I borrow a hammer and screwdriver for a little while?" Then it was: "Can I use your saw for just ten minutes?" I began to think that these street kids were learning from my example and wanted to better their skills, learn a trade, make a positive move by helping to fix up Judson House. Slowly, I began to feel truly "sacerdotal."

Then I made the mistake of going up into the dormitory floors where these runaways had their rooms, to see all the "projects" they had made with the tools, paints, and materials they had borrowed from me. "Acid trip" is a sixties term, and I'm not really sure what it means, being sacerdotal and all, but I'll bet you twenty bucks it describes what I found on the upper floors of Judson House that day.

The first room I went to inspect stands out clearly in my memory. When I went to open the door to this room I noticed that it seemed to be hung on the outside of where it used to be and had the hinges on the wrong side. I opened this door, and inside I found a second door hung with the hinges on the opposite side. When I opened this door, I was looking into a pitch-black hole. I tried to step into the room and promptly fell over the bottom of the inner door because it had been sawed off from the upper part. The lower section of this "Dutch door" was only 18 inches high. I opened it, too, and once again stepped into the darkness. I felt the wall for the light switch I knew was there, and flicked it on. A dim light came on, but I still could barely see.

The whole room—walls, ceiling, floor, baseboards, window, window glass, light fixture, even the light bulb itself—had all been painted flat black (with my can of flat black paint). The closet door was gone; the bed was gone. Nothing in the room was the same as before the runaways came to Judson House. I retreated to my janitor's room in the basement and tried to remember my Zen training. I locked the door with shaking hands and kept telling myself that my thoughts of strangling runaway children were inappropriate for a church janitor, especially a sacerdotal one claiming to practice Zen Buddhism.

After I had calmed down, I went back up and inspected the rest of the rooms. Some of the art work in the rooms was really very creative, consisting of psychedelic patterns, "God's eyes," and murals similar to some of those executed as street art on the sides of buildings on the Lower East Side. I eventually became good friends with the staff and many of the runaways, and I began to be invited to share in this macrobiotic diet thing.

Brown Rice and Spoon Rings

To this day, it is hard for me to picture Judson House without also seeing brown rice, fried eggplant, God's eyes, peace symbols, and spoon rings. One very successful (supervised) project was to make rugs out of carpet remnants and carpet tape and glue. The designs often included a peace symbol or the Chinese yin/yang symbol. (If you don't know what these things are you probably aren't old enough to be reading this.) Some of the arts and crafts were made and displayed, and even sold, in the empty apartment that later became Joan Muyskens's place. Like the rest of New York's hippie generation, the runaways made bead necklaces and spoon rings. A trip to the Salvation Army thrift shop would net a whole load of old silverware to be made into spoon rings. Even I got caught up in it. My janitorial instincts did not want to waste the cutoff fork or spoon ends, so I began making cute little jewelry animals too. The tines of the forks made keen legs and the spoons could become turtles without too much effort.

I Teach the Runaways How to Cut Plywood

One time, when the Runaway Project was in full swing, five or six of the kids had gathered around to watch me do some kind of repair that involved plywood. They were really impressed by all the things I could do, all the stuff I knew, and how thorough and knowledgeable I was about all my projects. They were asking me questions and getting my head all swelled up with praise and attention. By the time I was ready to cut in half this big 4x8 sheet of 3/4″ plywood, I was on a roll.

I hoisted that heavy sheet up, and in one deft motion laid it flat on the folding table. As all eyes were on me, I made a quick check to see that the cord on my skill saw was clear and I carefully lined up the blade with the pencil mark on the plywood. As the group stood back in quiet admiration, I ran the saw accurately along the left side of the pencil mark and in one smooth motion cut the plywood cleanly in half. As I slid half the plywood off the table and back to the floor, it became immediately apparent that, in my great pride in my own prowess, I had somehow also managed to cut the folding table that was under the plywood, metal edge and all, cleanly in half.

A silence fell over the room as we all just looked at the cut-in-half table and tried to pretend nothing had happened out of the ordinary. Then, without another word said by anyone, one by one the kids got up and politely walked out of the room.

DRIFTWOOD, SOHO, AN OLD TOWN CANOE, AND THE JUDSON HOUSE KITCHEN

From trips upstate in my canoe I used to bring back driftwood tied to the top of my bus. The canoe would go on the wood storage rack against the wall of Judson House, and the driftwood would take its place with all the other pieces of driftwood that were deposited in various hiding places around Judson House or Judson Church. There was always an extra empty room somewhere in Judson House crying out for me to fill it up with driftwood or those other special things I used to collect at night from in front of all the warehouses and small manufacturing companies south of Houston Street. In those days, there was no "SoHo" with its glitzy restaurants and art galleries. It was a strictly industrial area except for the scattering of artists' lofts. At night, if you walked the dark, empty streets south of Houston and east of West Broadway, you only found an occasional "wino" or "bag lady" barricaded for the night in some alley or doorway. Here and there the big "A.I.R." signs were painted on the shaftway of the buildings to tell the fire department, in case of a fire, that an "Artist in Residence" was living there. I used to find old packing crates and pieces of machinery or a bolt of discarded material still perfectly usable. The packing crates were of rough-cut wood from all over the world. When I planed and sanded some of those rough boards, they became strange smelling exotic hardwoods from Africa, Asia, or South America. When the Judson House basement kitchen was empty, I used it as a workshop because of its size and good lighting. Here I built an "antique" cabinet for Joan, planed my exotic woods found in SoHo, and worked on my woodcarvings and driftwood craft projects.

Also in those days, Jean Ovitt had opened a little gallery on the Lower East Side. I was a major contributor in my own right in those days, keeping Jean's gallery full of things made by me late at night in the old kitchen at Judson House. If you weren't around New York

City in the early 1970s, you would find it hard to believe how many little stores were opened up by my generation of hippies who wanted to drop out of the "capitalist society" dominated by the "military-industrial complex" (remember the sound of those words?). St. Mark's Place was only the most dense section of such stores, but you could go all over the Lower East Side and find little restaurants, leather stores, sandalmakers, candlemakers, tie-dye clothing, and of course, Jean Ovitt's store, where my driftwood tables and wood sculptures and scrap metal objets d'art and sheet metal wind chimes attracted crowds of art connoisseurs from as far away as Fourteenth Street. Today, I still have three of my "masterpieces" created in Judson House. One is carved out of a triangular end of a structural rough-cut wood beam, and another is an unfinished three-foot tall wood sculpture called "Maddono" that is currently occupying a place of honor next to the sump pump in my basement. It is a hooded figure looking at a child's face and head as a projection of his own lower anatomy, and might be considered "dirty or religiously offensive" by those not as open-minded as you and I. (This is why I put a little cover over it when the gas man comes to read the meter.)

The Maddono sculpture is from a large piece of a London Plane tree. The tree used to stand in Washington Square Park about thirty feet into the park from the northeast corner. It was cut down during the first great "renovation" of Washington Square Park in the1970s, when the City of New York, in its great wisdom (learning from the Chicago school of sociology and wishing to give jobs to otherwise unemployable sociologists called "city planners") decided to close down Washington Square Park, put up temporary fences around it, cut down some of its large trees, and redesign it completely.

Why did they close a perfectly good park, cut down the trees, and put a construction fence around it for one year? Because it was so poorly designed to begin with? Because it was not functional as a park? Was it possibly because the police had a hard time driving vehicles through it to clear out the hippies smoking marijuana and playing bongo drums, or maybe because New York University did not like the way Washington Square Park had become a center and a symbol of the new free-spirited street life of the hippies right on the doorsteps of their expensive real estate empire?

I would not be surprised if you took a tour of all the secret rooms around Judson House and the church and found some of my driftwood art still there. Look out along the fence separating our garden from the messy store yard next door. Look in the church, up in some of the tiny rooms at the top of the spiral staircase ("stage right"), near the door that goes out to the fire escape stairs down to Judson House, and down a few steps from the "fluff room" over the sanctuary and rose window. (The lights never worked up there since the fire that buckled the lead in the rose window years ago, so take a flashlight with you.)

A GIFT FROM THE FIREMEN

Today, in my dining room, on the top of a china closet, there is a rusted metal sculpture on a nice chestnut base with a felt bottom. It was a gift to me from eight New York City firemen who came to inspect the subbasement at Judson House one day.

The fire department in New York used to go around and inspect buildings in their precinct—especially public buildings—for fire safety and also to familiarize themselves with the interior of buildings they might one day have to enter to fight a fire.

Because Judson was such an "unorthodox" church, with theater performances in the sanctuary and dancers rehearsing in the gym, and runaways modifying the normal means of egress from bedrooms, we were always nervous and on our best behavior when the New York Fire Department wanted to inspect. I did my best to give them a good tour and made sure they liked us and weren't going to be overly critical of the minor lapses in housekeeping that sometimes occurred as I struggled to control the "messiness" from the hundreds of "artists" (of all kinds) that practiced their trade at Judson.

On this particular inspection day I had recently cleaned up the trash that people threw down the outside wells in front of Judson House on Thompson street, so I was not too worried when they asked to see the Judson House subbasement. The subbasement door is almost one and a half stories below the sidewalk. To get to it, you first go to the corner of Thompson and Third streets, open the metal gate, and go down a few steel steps to the steel platform outside the basement apartment. Then you open another gate and go down the long flight of wooden stairs to the bottom of the stairwell.

I went down all the stairs to the door to the subbasement where they were going to inspect. I unlocked the padlock, opened the door, turned on the single light, and came back up. I was now holding open the lower steel gate just outside the apartment door so they could go down and see how nice and clean the subbasement was.

I stood there chatting with the firemen for a while as they parked their fire truck and left the driver in it to receive calls on the two-way radio. As they were preparing to go down I was talking about all those things firemen like to talk about, things like advances in rubber boot technology, the proper techniques to axe down a door, and different brands of your standard number 484 brass nozzles for 3″ fire hoses. This is always a sure way to develop a good rapport with firemen.

Now, these firemen were all big men, dressed up in their big, heavy fireman's coats and hats, and carrying big flashlights, big axes, and all sorts of other big heavy tools and equipment. The first big fireman started down the wooden stairs, then the second, then the third. By the time the seventh fireman got to the top step, the first fireman had not quite reached the bottom of the very long flight of wooden stairs. There were now seven big firemen on the wooden stairs to the subbasement. Suddenly there was a groaning sound followed by a loud crack, and seven fire hats disappeared into a jumble of arms and legs, boots, and pieces of broken, rotten stair treads at the bottom of the Judson House stairwell! There were several brief loud swearwords, and then it became quiet. I was right next to the last fireman at the top of the steps, still smiling and holding the gate open for him to step off into what was now only open space. I was afraid to breathe, or stop smiling, and I didn't dare look him in the eye.

Visions of fire-prison (or wherever they send janitors who break the New York City fire regulations) began to swim in front of my eyes. But then, down below, a fireman began to snicker, then another one began to laugh. Pretty soon all eight firemen were roaring with laughter as they tried to dig out the poor guy on the very bottom. Only then did I dare breathe again and I started laughing myself.

The disheveled firemen agreed goodheartedly to not write up a violation. To show my gratitude, I gave them my special VIP tour of Judson Church. This included such popular attractions as the trap door in the stage left dressing room, the massive complex of piping under the giant walk-in baptismal font in the sanctuary, and even the spiral staircase that starts just above the bathroom fan in the ceiling of the Garden room and goes all the way up to the "fluff room" over the rose window. I did not show them the catwalk above the sanctuary ceiling that leads to empty spaces under the roof where you could fit a good-sized apartment, or where you can look down into the sanctuary through the ceiling grilles and see whatever is going on without being seen or heard yourself. I was saving that special treat in case I had to appease them for some bigger crisis later.

After the firemen left, I set about cleaning up the broken stairs and figuring out what to do to replace them. At the top of the stairs, the main support had been a small steel I beam that was anchored into the bricks on each side. It had rusted badly over time and had pulled out of the wall completely. As I removed it from the opposite wall, still stuck to part of the bricks, it looked strangely like two long-necked swans, one with head outstretched, and one with its neck slightly bent. I took the rusted beam into the Judson House kitchen and attached it to a nice piece of chestnut that I later carefully sanded and finished. I then glued a piece of felt on the bottom of the chestnut base, and, "Voilà," as we say in the art world, there was an instant piece of art!

AL'S APARTMENT IN JUDSON HOUSE

No matter what other people might tell you, I had nothing to do with the construction of Al's apartment in Judson House. When I first saw it, it had already been "renovated" by Bruce Mailman, one of Al's theater people.

The first time I saw it was not long after I first started work at Judson. Al told me there was "something wrong with his toilet," and could I take a look at it. This was the first time I saw Al's "wide innocent eyes" look, and his "I'm so helpless" body language, both of which I came to know only too well over the years.

Once I found my way to the sunken bathroom and toilet ("second door, stage left") and flushed it, I realized that somewhere under that false floor of built-up plywood and indoor-outdoor carpeting someone had hooked up the hot instead of the cold water to the toilet, so that every time Al flushed his toilet a little cloud of steam would rise out of the bowl and slowly make its way up toward the ceiling. I don't know why Al was upset about it—who likes a cold toilet seat anyway?

Going inside Al's apartment from the hall, you had to go up some steps to a long, narrow, raised walkway that ran to the far end of the big living room, which was sunken down on your right.

Off on your left were, first, the bedroom, then the bathroom, and then the kitchen, but only the kitchen floor was at the same level as the walkway. The bedroom and part of the bathroom were at the original floor level, so there was a "sunken bedroom" and a "sunken bathtub."

Except for Al's grand piano at one end and the built-in bookcases along one wall, you saw nothing but wall-to-wall gray indoor-outdoor carpet and a couple of gray carpet-covered cubes for furniture. It was the perfect space for loud music, serious drinking, and wild dancing. The opening and closing nights of Al's plays at Judson always included a party at Al's apartment. These cast parties usually included at least one "set" of songs with Al at the piano, and always some Bessie Smith records. Al's parties always came with excitement and fear. There was always the exciting possibility of getting carried away, of losing control, and there was always the fear that you might give in to feelings and desires you tried to keep hidden deep inside. An opening-night party in Al's apartment, with its flat gray indoor-outdoor carpet, was the bare stage for all those raw and tender and hopeful things that might come true, and then again might not. Disappointment, sadness, and loneliness could be found there, too. I won't tell you how it felt to leave alone after all the night's possibilities and hopes were gone. Those stories and memories belong to those of us who were there.

JUDSON GALLERY

The Judson Gallery next to the Lounge was empty a lot of the time I was there. It had been used more regularly when Judson House was the Judson Student House and full of mostly art students. In the 1960s, many artists had become caught up in experimental art forms that usually involved action or participation by the audience. It was called "Performance Art" or "Happenings," and some of this took place in the Judson Gallery. Art was also becoming highly politicized in those days. One of the artists, Jean Toche, with long hair and bushy beard and twinkling eyes, called himself "The President in Exile of the Walloon States of Belgium." He and Jon Hendricks and other artists at the gallery played an important role in my own transformation from a crew-cut ex-G.I. janitor in combat boots to a long-haired, bearded advocate of Zen, who wore beads and a sari (any other generation would probably call it a dress) and who attended at least one antiwar rally. Actually, I was a Zen Buddhist before I went in the army, but the rest of my transformation took place at Judson, aided and abetted by these shy-looking, soft-spoken artists.

EX-G.I. JANITOR BECOMES HIPPIE ANTIWAR PROTESTER

Before an upcoming antiwar rally in Washington, D.C., Jon Hendricks asked if I would help him and other participants get ready by driving my Volkswagen bus to pick up some "supplies" they needed. Since most people around Judson did not have a car, and almost no one had an off-street parking lot like I did, behind Judson House, I of course agreed to help.

We drove to the West Village over by the Hudson River between 14th Street and Little West 12th Street, where the wholesale meat district is. The meat district was more active then, in 1969 and 1970, and there were huge beef carcasses hanging off hooks outside in the street on overhead steel tracks, waiting to be wheeled inside where rows of thick-armed butchers in blood-spattered white clothes were laughing and talking and chopping up big pieces of dead animals into smaller ones to be sold as "cuts of meat" in the food stores all over the city. Jon Hendricks bought no less than twenty plastic one-gallon bottles of cow's blood, and pounds of raw intestines, pig's hearts, and other ugly-looking internal organs.

I don't know where we hid it all in Judson House overnight (nobody told Arlene, thank goodness). The next morning when the charter buses arrived to take everyone down to Washington for the rally, Jon had everything all neatly wrapped up and looking innocuous enough, as he loaded it into the luggage compartment under the bus. Jon gave everyone their final instructions on the bus, and that's when I heard of his plan. He had even held "rehearsals" in the preceding days to tell the others what to expect from the police, from the media, and from other people at the rally.

Once we got down to Washington and joined the other marchers, the "Performance" planned by Jon Hendricks began. We opened the packages on the street and then stuffed the various entrails and organs inside our clothing, with parts of them hanging out of our shirts or pants so they looked like they were part of our own bodies. We looked as if we had been cut open or blown apart, but were still alive. Then we took the gallon jugs and poured the blood all over each other and over our clothing. We were careful to throw away the empty containers in the public garbage cans, as Jon had told us, so the police could not arrest us for "littering."

We tied ourselves together in a long line and limped and hobbled, chanting "Stop the war, stop the killing." Some of the women in the group were screaming. It was probably on the news—if not I'll bet the FBI has tapes of it all. We did not last the whole march. We walked for maybe ten blocks, screaming, shouting, and wailing. We not only horrified many of the people around us but we ourselves began to forget we were only acting and started to lose our sense of control. Someone in our group started sobbing, and then someone else threw up. It became hard to tell the difference between the horror I was pretending to feel and the horror I was beginning to experience. Some of us started crying uncontrollably and others were shaking and unable to shout anymore. We sat down on the ground and we held each other and stopped trying to speak as the crowd of marchers surged around us and the flies buzzed at the sticky blood drying on our faces and hands.

We were completely drained. We had not been prepared for what we, ourselves, were going to feel. We untied ourselves from the line joining us and removed all the guts from inside our clothing, and put it all in the trash receptacles nearby, as the police watched our every move. We were still barely able to talk as we rejoined the marchers. The police lost sight of us as we were surrounded by the thousands of other bodies and carried along. When we got to where the huge outdoor fountains were, we jumped into the cool pool water to wash off the sticky blood. The water around us turned slowly red. I looked up and the water pouring out from the fountain above us was red with blood ... gallons and gallons, red with blood.

JUDSON HOUSE AND WINOS

Even though I was a sacerdote, I still had to perform certain unsacerdotal functions that nobody else seemed willing to do. One of the unfortunate functions that went along with being the janitor was that of bouncer and policeman.

Our front door was the boundary between the "no drinking" zone enforced in Washington Square Park and the last place you could finish off your cheap wine after walking from the nearest liquor store at Bleecker and Thompson streets (in the same building as the Village Gate). The winos would all stop at our front steps to argue and shout, and to finish off their Ripples and Thunderbirds. They would then leave the empty bottles or break them right there, or else would throw them over the railing into the well down to the subbasement for me to clean up with all the other trash and litter that people threw down as they passed by Judson House. I was constantly battling the winos and street people who used the front steps as their own private bar and lounge.

THE JUDSON GARDEN COMMITTEE

Since I was a sacerdote and also the total maintenance staff at Judson, I was also an un-official member of both the Judson Building Committee and the Judson Garden Committee. One day the Garden Committee had a big cleanout party. I don't recall where everything came from, and the Building Committee might have been involved, too. I don't know if Ken McNutt was already the chairperson for the Building Committee, but he did chair that committee for many years while I was at Judson.

You have to understand that the Judson Community was forced by necessity to have people play multiple roles. Just as "multipurpose space" was a building committee buzzword in those days, people around Judson were multipurpose and often were on more than one committee. So it might have been both committees that held a cleanout of Judson Garden and Judson House. The effort netted so much stuff to get rid of that we had to get one of those big rental vans and call the New York City Sanitation Department to see where we could dump it.

"STOPPING BY THE FOUNTAIN AVENUE LANDFILL ON A (NON) SNOWY MORNING..."

In those days New York City had several landfills or garbage dumps open at any one time. There was no such thing as recycling. "Saving the environment" was a phrase not yet in use. So instead of recycling we got to take all the stuff we found around Judson to a "landfill."

The New York Sanitation Department gave us a special permit to dump at the Fountain Avenue Landfill, in Brooklyn. None of us had ever been to the landfill before, but some of us had seen it and smelled it as we drove by on the Belt Parkway on the way to Long Island or Jones Beach. We piled the huge rental truck full of old furniture and junk and then drove to Brooklyn with our special permit. As we drove toward Fountain Avenue, off in the distance hung what looked like a cloud over a low mountain, except the cloud kept changing shape. As we got close, we could see that the cloud was really thousands of seagulls hovering over the mountain of garbage.

From the security gate, where a guard checked our permit, we could now see that this "mountain" had a road going up to the top and that the road had a long line of white garbage trucks on it. We now entered another world. The sun was blocked out as if by an eclipse. We entered a dark landscape where there was no earth and no sky. The smell was everywhere, and our ears were filled with the high-pitched screams from the thousands of seagulls that hovered just above us, darting down past the truck windows to land for a moment and then take off again.

The road up was the only flat surface, shiny and smoothed by all the truck tires. Everywhere else the ground was made up of pieces of something unrecognizable, a flattened surface of garbage here and there punctuated by a piece of jagged metal or pipe sticking up into the air. We inched our way up the slope in the endless line of garbage trucks. When the line stopped, we realized that the shaking was not just the engine of our truck. The whole mountain was moving and rumbling, and ahead a roaring sound could be heard or maybe felt above the crying of the gulls. As we approached the top, the garbage suddenly leveled out. One by one the trucks in front of us turned and disappeared to someplace we could not see, on the other side. Nearby a flagman signaled to us to move forward. As we came over the crest of the hill, we saw a small valley filled with all the white garbage trucks with their backs raised into the air, each backing or moving away from a different spot on the cliff.

A bulldozer was coming right toward us, pushing ahead of it the flopping and flailing corpses of bedroom sets and TVs, couches and ironing boards. As we watched, another man signaled to us impatiently to turn around and back the truck toward the edge of the cliff. The bulldozer was right next to us now, missing us by only two feet, close enough to feel the heat from its engine and feel the rental truck swaying from the weight of the bulldozer as it compressed the garbage under our wheels. The noise was deafening, and we could not hear each other's shouts from a few feet away. All around us was noise and movement as if a Hieronymus Bosch painting had come alive. White trucks with their back compartments being hydraulically lifted up on an angle into the air looked like huge insects with their abdomens arched and distended, depositing their eggs on the fetid soil. Around our heads were swarms of seagulls diving headlong and fighting over the garbage, trying to get the freshest rotted food and meat before it was consumed by the waiting maggots and clouds of flies around us. With the earth shaking and accompanied by the screaming of the gulls and the smell of rotted flesh, we struggled to unload our rental truck in the strange light. We drove away from there as fast as we could.

The Fountain Avenue landfill is closed now, but that day, the Judson Garden Committee, like Odysseus before them, were among those few who actually visited Hell and returned to tell about it.

JOHN TUNGATE
runs a construction business in Bedford Hills, New York.

The Garden

ALICE GARRARD

After church volunteers covered the garden ground with bricks at the end of the 1960s, Judson Church began to use the space intensively during summers. ─────────────────

I am told a building once stood, and eventually fell, on the rectangular plot that has been the Judson Garden for as long as I can remember. It has been a summer sanctuary and the backdrop for many informal gatherings, garden parties, cookouts, celebrations, and farewells. I recall jubilant parties after the hard work of planning and orchestrating the annual Judson Bazaar. We miraculously pulled off the first one in September 1972 and continued to organize eight or ten more, until we had completely run out of white elephants and old clothes to sell. At least once, the day-long event included a beer garden.

Over the years, informal cookouts took place in the garden, along with more organized shared meals and sing-alongs. After work on a few prearranged Friday nights in July 1981, we gravitated to the garden with whatever we had brought to throw on the grill and just hung out. During the summer of 1990, several week nights found us there, brown-bag suppers in lap, talking with Howard Moody about "Life after the Centennial" (the big homecoming weekend celebrating that event would occur in October). In the late 1990s, these garden get-togethers were enriched by the voices of Andy Frantz and Emmy Bean (and doubly so when they sang together), Cheri Kroon, and Vicki Manning. We listened to the lively picking and playing of Andy, Lenny Fox, Reathel Bean, Jerry Dickason, Paul Holzer, and others.

With the arrival on staff of Aziza as special program associate in 1994, garden events took on new energy and intensity. "Licks 'n'

Licks," a unique jazz series coordinated by Aziza and members of the Single Mothers Workshop, exposed children living with their families in temporary housing to the history and power of jazz. Accomplished musicians and artists volunteered their time to lead workshops for the families and perform for them, and anyone else who dropped by, in free Sunday afternoon concerts in the garden. Unlimited ice cream, an equally big hit with the kids, was provided courtesy of Ben & Jerry's.

Through the Open Mic, overseen by Aziza but run by junior high and high school students, young poets, dancers, singers, writers, visual artists, and performance artists from all over the city came together every month to perform for and support one another. Most of the year, they gathered in the gymnasium, the Garden Room, or the Meeting Room, but each summer they, too, spilled into the garden. At dusk one Sunday in August 1996, Judson's little bit of Village green became the backdrop for "Sacred Ground," a dance performance created by Aziza to honor natural environments—and natural hair—with text and choreography inspired by the Judson garden and conversations with members of the congregation.

For many years we entered the garden for services and other events via a fairly treacherous route—down steps from the sidewalk, through Judson House, past Roland Wiggins's patio, then up more steps. On Sunday mornings, congregants sat facing the back of the church and the rose window, our folding chairs wobbly on the garden's undulating brick carpet. For services, the church's old upright piano was wheeled out onto the small balcony off the Long Room to accompany the singing. The pianist could neither see nor hear what was happening in front, resulting in many comical moments.

By the 1990s, the congregation—older and less sure-footed—had begun to enter the garden directly through the Long Room. The only drawback was that latecomers or parents, after dropping off their children in Sunday School, had to walk past the pianist, worship leaders, and assembled congregation to take their seats. Eventually, this setup was changed, and the chairs were turned around to face the back of the garden and rowhouses along West Third Street. For many years, the Prostitution Project bus peeped back at us over the fence separating the garden from the minuscule Judson parking lot. The sound system, indoors and out, was too loud for those close to the stage and too soft for those in the back. Whatever the seating

The Judson Garden, 1999. Photo by Alice Garrard.

configuration, it was always a challenge to pass trays of bread, wine, and juice for communion and finish by the time the communion hymn ended. Wise pianists just kept playing.

Judson Church is unique in giving its ministers most of the summer off for study, reflection, travel, and recuperation, and for turning summer services over to members of the congregation and visiting speakers.

"Sermons" by lay people are often introspective and self-revelatory. In the 1980s, Reathel Bean shared "Reflections on the

What is a garden without pink flamingos?

Rainbow Soup Kitchen" and performed songs by Loudon Wainwright III and Woody Guthrie; Grace Goodman revealed "Scenes from Judson History"; Jim Pentecost spoke of "Life After Addiction"; and Randy Jones and Emily Jean Gilbert offered "Thoughts About Money." Allen Hinand mused on "Celebrating Presence and Absence," and seventeen summers later, in 1998, his daughter Marcy stood in the same garden pulpit to reflect on "A Whole New World in Philanthropy."

In the 1990s, Holly Bean pondered "Arrogance and the Limits of Truth"; Carol Cellman, "Aspiring to Less"; and Dave Murdoch, what it was like to grow up Catholic. Janel Cariño spoke of Freud; Susan Godfrey, of "Spiritual Roots"; and Mary Russell, of "Truth-Telling in Women's Lives."

Steve Arrendell walked into Judson—via the garden—for the first time in the summer of 1990. Five years later, he led a service there, telling us about his involvement with a needle exchange program in East Harlem. Elly Dickason, a native of the Netherlands and an editor, shared "A Reflection on Calvinism" in 1991 and her passion for "The Power of the Word" in 1996.

Over the years I had the pleasure of speaking at summer services, but I was happiest on the other side of the podium—still a little groggy, clutching a cup of coffee from the corner deli, and listening as others spoke of their experiences and passions above the sounds of tinkling wind chimes, chattering birds, wailing sirens, and the shouts of angry frat boys next door awakened by robust congregational singing. The occasional leaf drifting into my lap was an unexpected benediction.

In my mind, we are all in the garden and will remain there: Miriam Corbett, smiling from under her straw hat; Irwin Mann, tennis racket in hand; Jo Dean, bringing in plants from her garden; Bob Hoffman, with an invitation to share. Michael Kelly and Judith Thomas huddle conspiratorially on a weathered bench pushed against the wall of Judson House. On another sit three generations of Thomasons, paper plates balanced on their laps. Reathel Bean, Lee Guilliatt, and I hobble about on crutches, slowed by unexpected tumbles. At summer's end, the children return to the garden, more grown up than before—blossoming, sprouting closer to the sun until eventually they will clear the garden wall: Sam Bean (with a mustache now), Blaine and Myles Dickason (so tall!), Megan Wolff (suddenly with short hair)—growing, growing, gone.

For many years, Margaret Wright readied the soil and filled the flowerbeds and boxes. In the mid-1990s the shovel passed to Jerry Dickason, who faithfully rallied the volunteers each spring.

In 1998 and 1999, knowing that our time in the garden was limited, we ventured out earlier in the year and stayed later. The seasonal migration used to occur on the first Sunday of July, right after Gay Pride Sunday, and we would retrace our steps after Labor Day. In 1998 we lingered in the garden until mid-October, and only partially because the Meeting Room was being painted.

John Burroughs once said of a garden he loved: "I come here to find myself. It is so easy to get lost in the world." The Judson Garden cradled us and served us long and well, providing a patch of blue or a glimpse of moon in an inky sky—a respite from the sights, if not the sounds, of the world outside. It gave us a place to be alone, together.

Adam and Eve once had a garden; eventually they lost it. Many years later, Adam said of Eve (according to Mark Twain, not the writer of Genesis), "Wherever she was, was Eden." So it goes. Wherever the Judson community gathers—to celebrate, to mourn, to bear witness—is the garden.

ALICE GARRARD
walked into Judson Church for the first time in June 1971. Both ministers were away. The service was led by members of the congregation.

THE JUDSON HEALTH CENTER

The Judson Health Center began its life in January 1921 in the basement of Judson Memorial Church. In July 1922 it moved next door into Judson House, where it occupied most of the building until the summer of 1950. The Center continues to operate its clinics on Spring Street in New York City, still providing services to newly arrived immigrants.

This section consists of three chapters: a history of the Judson Health Center, by Jerry G. Dickason; a profile of its founder and long-time director, Dr. Eleanor A. Campbell, by Elly Dickason; and the text of a 1936 radio address by Dr. Campbell.

Judson Health Center, 1920–1950

JERRY G. DICKASON

In 1951, Mayor Vincent R. Impellitteri of New York presented Dr. Eleanor A. Campbell with a testimonial scroll honoring her thirty years of service as the general director and co-founder of the Judson Health Center. In these thirty years, the center had logged in one million visits, both at the clinic and in people's homes, a phenomenal accomplishment considering the Center's humble beginnings.

In 1920 Judson's minister, the Rev. Dr. A. Ray Petty, had invited Dr. Eleanor A. Campbell to start a clinic at Judson Memorial Church to serve the Italian immigrant population just south of the church. Dr. Campbell was a recent graduate of the Boston University School of Medicine. He had heard that she was planning to get involved in a public health program, and he wanted her in his district. Dr. Campbell later recalled that the Rev. Petty had said: "I just cannot stand the crooked legs of the children down here." [1]

The Rev. Petty was keenly aware of the health conditions and the lack of health care services in his neighborhood. He had already been working with the New York Association for Improving the Condition of the Poor (AICP) to establish a Baby Health Station at 114 Thompson Street. [2] The Department of Hygiene was sponsoring

---

1. Campbell, Eleanor A. "Judson Health Center," n.d. (c. 1934). Four typewritten pages ending with "Eleanor A. Campbell, M.D., General Director, Judson Health Center, New York." Judson Health Center Archives, 34 Spring Street, New York City. Dr. Campbell was a member of Madison Avenue Baptist Church at the time. Rev. Petty probably knew her through Baptist association activities and in all likelihood was aware of the prominence of her mother, Elizabeth Milbank Anderson, in social and welfare circles.

2. Department of Health of the City of New York. *Annual Report,* 1920, p. 178. Municipal Reference and Research Library of New York City.

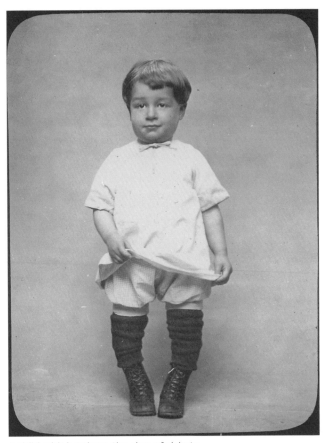

A child with bowlegs, the sign of rickets.

baby health stations throughout the city to reduce and control the morbidity and mortality of infants and young children.[3]

The 1920 U.S. Census reported 44,250 people living in the Greenwich Village district, largely of Italian origin. The Zoning Law of 1916 outlined the Village as starting on the corner of West Street and Bank, from there northeast on Bank to Hudson Street; south one block on Hudson to West Eleventh, northeast on West Eleventh to Seventh Avenue, left (north) on Seventh Avenue to Fourteenth Street, right on Fourteenth to Sixth Avenue, right (south) on Sixth

---

3. Ibid., p. 165.

Avenue to Waverly Place, left on Waverly Place to Fifth Avenue, diagonally across Washington Square Park to West Broadway, down West Broadway to West Houston, right on West Houston to West Street, and right on West Street back to the corner of Bank Street.[4]

The death rate per 1,000 in the district was 14.35 compared to 12.93 citywide, and the infant mortality rate, under the age of one year, was 95 per 1,000 compared to 85 citywide. There were 9,000 preschool children, ages two to six years, who did not have access to the kind of medical services offered by baby stations and public schools in other areas of the city.

New York City's Department of Health had recently experienced innovative leadership in health matters that went against the political leadership of the time. In 1914 Mayor John P. Mitchel had appointed Dr. Sigismund S. Goldwater and Dr. Haven Emerson as commissioner and assistant commissioner, respectively, of public health. During the next four years, Goldwater and Emerson inaugurated a system of district public health services that embarked upon a host of new programs, giving evidence of the efficiency of neighborhood health services.[5]

On January 1, 1918, John F. Hylan, a Tammany mayor, took office and appointed Dr. J. Lewis Amster as health commissioner. Dr. Amster served for four months before resigning with a blast against the mayor.[6] Dr. Royal S. Copeland was next appointed commissioner. Copeland terminated the health districts and abolished the health service bureaus. However, the district health concept continued to function largely because the local voluntary agencies saw the value of working together to improve their community's quality of health. Their collective dedicated professional staff presented an excellent public image for the city's Department of Health, even though the latter hardly supported their efforts.[7]

---

4. Ware, Caroline F. *Greenwich Village, 1920–1930.* Boston: Houghton Mifflin, 1935. Reprinted by Farrar, Straus & Giroux, Octagon Books, 1977. Taken from a foldout map between pages 8 and 9.

5. Duffy, John. *A History of Public Health in New York City, 1866–1966.* New York: Russell Sage Foundation, 1974, p. 266.

6. Ibid., p. 284.

7. Ibid., p. 276.

THE WORK BEGINS

Dr. Campbell accepted Rev. Petty's offer in the early summer of 1920. She began her work by conducting a survey of the district to determine the new health center's needs and direction. She found two health agencies in the Judson Church area: a tuberculosis clinic and the baby health station on Thompson Street. The tuberculosis clinic was probably at the Bowling Green Neighborhood Association, established in 1916 as a health and social center on the Lower West Side in which the AICP and a number of other volunteer organizations worked together. Two years later, the AICP coordinated the founding of the Mulberry Health Center, an Italian section of more than 40,000 between Canal and Houston streets and between the Bowery and Broadway. The primary aim of the Mulberry Health Center was to provide neighborhood health and social services. The focus was mainly on health education and preventive medicine for prenatal and child care up through the fifth grade.

Seeing the health needs so great, Dr. Campbell and Rev. Petty converted two rooms in the Judson Church basement into medical, diagnostic, and nutrition clinics. These rooms were adjacent to the gymnasium. The director and staff offices were in the corner of the church, and the dental clinic and the diet kitchen were in the Judson Neighborhood House, two blocks away at 179 Sullivan Street.[8] And, like the Bowling Green and Mulberry Health Centers, Dr. Campbell and Rev. Petty solicited the help of volunteer agencies, including the AICP, and the Department of Public Health for services and personnel to establish the Judson Health Center.[9]

---

8. Judson Health Center. *Measuring the Work of a Health Center: A Report of Four Years' Work of the Judson Health Center.* New York: The Center, 1925, p. 13. Judson Health Center Archives. The New York Baptist City Society managed Judson Church's affairs and property. In 1918 the City Society had acquired the Judson Neighborhood House, at 179 Sullivan Street, under the joint auspices of the Woman's Auxiliary of the Mission Society (WA-NYCBMS) and the Woman's American Baptist Home Mission Society (WABHMS). The house had been a Christian center for several years before that, and it opened in September 1919 as a community social service agency similar to the Greenwich House on Jones Street. The Neighborhood House had strong ties to all of the church programs. The Society sold it on September 28, 1951.

9. Duffy, pp. 321–322.

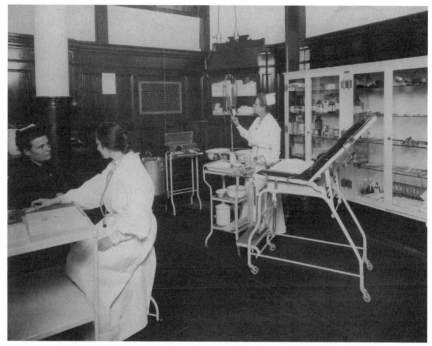

The Women's Medical Clinic in the basement of Judson Memorial Church, 1921.

THE CENTER OPENS ITS DOORS

The Judson Health Center opened its doors in January 1921 with four full-time, paid staff members—two nurses, a secretary, and an Italian interpreter. The part-time staff included a dentist, a dental assistant, an oral hygienist, and a dietitian. There was also a volunteer medical staff consisting of the full-time general director (Dr. Campbell) and four physicians who gave part-time service. Through an arrangement with the Maternity Center Association, a salaried physician came once a week to conduct the prenatal clinic.[10] Every week that first year, the Center conducted thirteen diagnostic and medical clinics, four dental clinics, five oral hygiene clinics, and two nutrition classes. During the first year there were no field workers to make home visits except for the occasional house calls made by members of the staff. The Center was completely unbudgeted that first year, and the expenses were covered by the funds Dr. Campbell was able

10. Judson Health Center, p. 13.

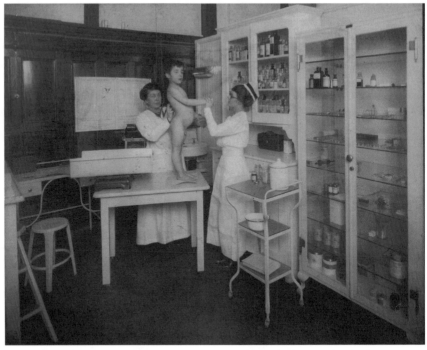

Dr. Eleanor Campbell and Ruth Morgan, R.N., examine a child at the Health Clinic in the basement of Judson Memorial Church, 1921.

to secure from month to month. Much of the money came from her own inheritance.

By the end of 1921, the Center was well known in the neighborhood, and it became overwhelmed with the demands for medical services. Such meager and simple space as the church provided was no longer adequate to meet the medical needs in the community. Dr. Campbell later wrote: "I shall never forget those early years—a crowded group of mothers and babies on one side of the screens, many crying, and on the other side a basketball game, the ball occasionally coming over onto a baby's head. Which interfered with the other most is a question." [11] The Rev. Petty responded to the space need by making the basement and next two floors of Judson House (known at the time as the Annex) available to the Center at a rent of $3,000 per year. The Center incorporated in February 1922. Dr.

11. Campbell, p. 1.

Campbell wrote: "We kept the name Judson out of honor to the Church which helped us start, but [we] are an entirely independent, non-sectarian corporation, carrying a rounded educational and preventive public health program, and are alone responsible for financing it."[12]

Dr. Campbell raised the funds for renovating the new space and for expanding the programs. The Milbank Memorial Fund, founded by Dr. Campbell's mother, Elizabeth Milbank Anderson, pledged $25,000 toward the operating budget in the new facility.[13] The Fund also pledged $20,000 to remodel and equip the new space provided that Dr. Campbell raise the additional $28,000 needed from other resources. The Rev. Petty was instrumental in persuading the American Baptist Home Mission Society to donate $20,000, which secured the Fund's additional matching pledge.

In July 1922, the Center moved into its new quarters, which housed "seven clinic rooms; two large and two small waiting rooms; four dental rooms equipped with four chairs; offices for executive, registration, field, nutrition and social services staffs; a well equipped diet kitchen; a milk station; two nurseries and a roof playground." Dr. Campbell also secured pledges for future operating expenses. The Laura Spelman Rockefeller Memorial (LSRM) made a grant of $12,500 to remodel and equip the roof with a playground and infant nursery. The LSRM also guaranteed grants of $3,333.33 for 1922, $9,000 for 1923, $6,000 for 1924 and $3,000 for 1925. The Milbank Memorial Fund granted $15,000 to remodel, equip, and operate the preschool nursery for 1923.[14] Within one year, Dr. Campbell raised approximately $100,000 to develop an impressive health care service for immigrants and the poor. (One hundred thousand dollars in 1922 would be the equivalent of approximately one million dollars today.[15])

---

12. Ibid., p. 2.

13. For information on the Milbank Memorial Fund, see "The Quiet Milbank Millions," *Fortune*, May 1959, pp. 137, 166, 168, and 176.

14. Judson Health Center, p. 14.

15. Derks, Scott, ed. *The Value of a Dollar: Prices and Incomes in the United States*, 2nd ed. Lakeville, CT: Grey House Publishing, 1999, p. 2. A one-to-ten ratio is a general estimate of today's value of the money mentioned in this chapter—1920 to 1950.

THE CENTER EXPANDS ITS SERVICES

Over the next two years the Center extended its health care activities. It assisted the baby health station down the street with the care of baby-feeding and prenatal cases. It opened nurseries for malnourished, rachitic, and convalescent children. It introduced Alpine light treatment, and thanks to the New York Rotary Club it added a physiotherapist to its orthopedic staff. A dental clinic was enlarged from one to five chairs. The Center also opened an eye clinic and a cardiac clinic.[16]

The 1924 records show a total clinic attendance of 22,000 plus approximately 14,000 field visits.[17] The *World* newspaper reported that the Judson Health Center had become the largest in the nation.[18] It employed a staff of fifty-one workers, which included physicians, dentists, dental assistants, nurses, dietitians, social service visitors, interpreters, clerks, and stenographers.

The Center's mission was to:

1. encourage people of the district to undergo thorough physical examinations at stated periods;
2. correct such physical defects as the examinations disclose, and to make such curative measures the medium through which preventive health lessons may be taught;
3. educate people of the district in proper habits of diet, exercise, rest, cleanliness, and general hygiene.

The methods adopted by the Center to accomplish these goals were grouped as follows:

1. service that is largely preventive in character, since the aim in view is to induce the people of the community to patronize the clinics before they become ill in order that they may learn of the measures to be adopted in helping themselves to keep physically fit.

---

16. Judson Health Center, p. 14.
17. Ibid.
18. "Health Centre Files Report for 5 Years," *World,* October 8, 1925, p. 21.

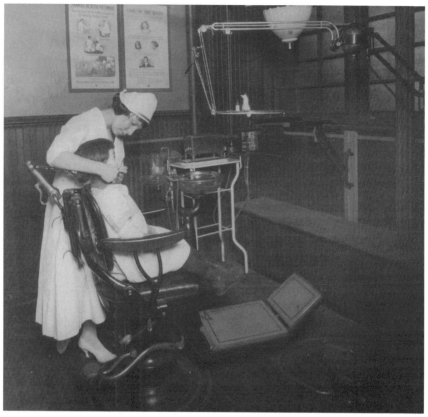

The Oral Hygiene Clinic in the basement of the Judson Neighborhood House on Sullivan Street, 1921. The hygienist is Elfrieda Lawrence.

2. clinic services, where curative measures are applied in the treatment of minor physical ailments and where the correction of physical defects is followed up and supervised.
3. education service, which includes health talks and health demonstrations by the physicians, the nurses, the dietitians, the social service workers and the interpreters; demonstrations in the Health Problems Nurseries for the mothers and older girls in the care of babies; clubs and classes for parents and children; group work in the public schools of the neighborhood; health exhibits and health contests.[19]

---

19. Judson Health Center, p. 17.

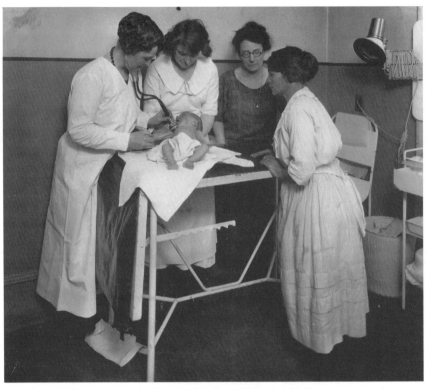

A mother, right, looks on as Dr. Campbell, left, and Mrs. Cargill, the nurse, examine a baby while Mrs. Franconi, the interpreter (in dark dress), explains the findings to the mother.

In 1925, Dr. Campbell embarked on a campaign to raise one million dollars. David H. Knott, former Sheriff of New York County, was chairman of the Campaign Committee and Robert Underwood Johnson, former ambassador to Italy, was honorary chairman.[20] Dr. Campbell often turned to her own family for additional funds, but by this time there were signs that she was wearing out her welcome. In a letter dated June 15, 1926, her cousin Dunlevy Milbank can hardly hide his irritation when he writes to his brother Jeremiah:

> To help Eleanor in her work during the coming five years provided she remains active in the management of it during

20. "Health Center Seeks $1,000,000 for Work," *New York Times,* October 13, 1925, p. 38.

that time as at present, I am willing to contribute $3750 on June 30th 1926 and $3750 on December 30th 1926, and thereafter in a like manner $7500 in each of the years 1927, 1928, 1929 and 1930, provided a Budget submitted by the Judson Health Center for the coming year approved by the Milbank Memorial Fund is satisfactory to me in my sole judgment, and on the failure of these two bodies to make such Budget satisfactory, any further payments by me shall cease.

I wish it further understood (and in this I understand you concur) that this payment of $7500 by each of us annually shall relieve us and the members of our families from any appeals for contributions or for benefits, fairs, etc., to raise funds for the Judson Health Center, and that at the end of the term of five years any obligation we may be thought to have toward the Judson Health Center for support of endowment will be considered to have been completely discharged.[21]

CHANGES IN PUBLIC HEALTH ADMINISTRATION

In 1926, the New York City Health Department was trying again to adopt the district health concept citywide. To show the effectiveness of the district concept, the Milbank Memorial Fund agreed to subsidize the Bellevue-Yorkville Health Demonstration Project. After eight years of centralized city health services, the demonstration project's aim was to document that district health care procedures were more efficient and effective.

In 1928 the child health stations in New York City became teaching centers for medical students. Many were assigned to the Judson Health Center, which was a boon to the staff. In 1929 "squad systems" of three physician inspectors, each trained in a different specialty, were used to examine preschoolers. These squad systems also inaugurated teacher observation systems in the schools. The teachers would refer cases to the school doctor. Dr. Campbell and the Center staff worked closely with several schools, including

---

21. Dunlevy Milbank, letter to Jeremiah Milbank, June 15, 1926. A copy of this letter was provided by Robert E. Harvey, great-grandson of Eleanor Campbell.

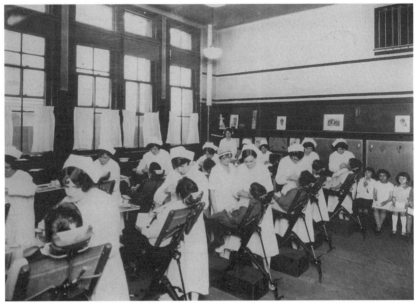

An oral hygiene clinic set up in a public school, 1920s.

Public School 38 and Saint Anthony's parochial school. (Public School 38 was in the building on the corner of the Avenue of the Americas and Broome Street that today houses the Chelsea Vocational School.)

Saint Anthony's sent all of its students to Judson for physical examinations. Dr. Campbell made note of the splendid cooperation and leadership of Mother Raphael and the Sisters of Saint Anthony who "not only bring the children to the clinics for examination, but likewise render invaluable aid in helping to have defects corrected and the physician's instructions heeded." [22]

In 1929 Health Commissioner Shirley W. Wynne appointed a Committee on Neighborhood Health Development. The Milbank Memorial Fund financed the work of this committee to formulate plans to establish individual health centers as part of the district concept. On March 21, 1931, the committee, in a report on "The Next Eight Health Center Districts," stated:

22. Judson Health Center, "'Selling' Public Health Down Greenwich Village Way." Five typewritten pages marked in pencil "Publicity," n.d. (c. 1930). p. 2. Judson Health Center Archives.

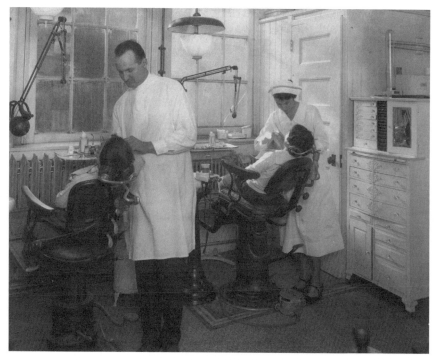

The Dental Clinic in Judson House, 1920s.

The city plan for district health centers calls for division of New York City into thirty health districts. Provisions already had been made in 1930 by the City for the following health centers: Central Harlem, Mott Haven, Tremont, Williamsburg-Greenpoint, Astoria-Long Island City, and Staten Island. It is now recommended, after careful consideration, that the next eight Health Centers should be located as follows: Manhattan: East Harlem and Lower West Side.[23]

The factors that supported a Lower West Side district were based on population, health, economic conditions, and facilities. In 1929,

---

23. Committee on Neighborhood Health Development. "The Next Eight Health Center Districts: Report of Committee on Recommendations of District Health Centers," March 21, 1931. This is an eight-page document with the ninth page being a Manhattan and Bronx map of Health Districts, 1930. Copy found in the New York City Municipal Reference and Research Library.

Parents bring their children to be registered at the Judson Health Center.

4,862 births were recorded; the 1930 census reported the population to be 302,118, of which 39,320 were children registered in the elementary grades. In 1929 the general mortality for this district was 17.8 per 1,000. This was the highest for any of the districts in the entire city. Infant mortality in 1929 was 82 per 1,000—the third highest in the city. The new-case rate for tuberculosis was 344 per 100,000 and the rate for other communicable diseases was 2,375; both were second highest in the city. These statistics reflected the deplorable economic conditions of the district. The health care agencies and facilities, although adequate, lacked coordination of services.[24]

Until 1932, the Judson Health Center's territory of operation within the district had extended from Washington Square on the north to Canal Street on the south and from Broadway to the North (Hudson) River. In May 1932, the Bowling Green Neighborhood Association, due to its retirement from health work, asked the Jud-

24. Ibid.

son Health Center to expand its geographic area, save for a certain section under the supervision of Greenwich House.

THE CENTER TEN YEARS LATER

Judson's health service statistics up through 1932 were as follows:[25]

WEEKLY CLINICS

6 Child Health	16 Dental
2 Eye	3 Heliotherapy
6 General Women's	3 Mental Hygiene

CLASSES

9 Nutrition	1 Prenatal
Parents Club Monthly	

STAFF

1 General Director	4 Nutritionists
1 Assistant General Director	1 Psychiatric Social Worker
4 Dentists	1 Psychologist
10 Physicians (part time)	16 Clerks & Interpreters
11 Nurses	1 Oral Hygienist
16 Student Volunteers	

STATISTICS

	1930	1931	1932
Clinic Visits	22,885	20,806	19,755
Office Conferences		6,257	6,346
Staff Visits to Home	16,688	22,414	17,469
Class Attendance	3,694	4,867	3,935
Total visits by or in the interest of Judson clients	43,267	54,344	47,505*

*For 11 months January–November only.

25. Judson Health Center. "Brief Statement Regarding Judson Health Center," December 1932 or early 1933. Judson Health Center Archives.

BUDGETS FOR 10 YEARS, 1923 TO 1932

Year	Amount
1923	$71,150
1924	$77,996
1925	$87,892
1926	$90,000
1927	$90,000
1928	$105,990
1929	$113,490
1930	$102,980
1931	$85,478
1932	$83,528

Personal Service Cost

Medical & Clinic Services	$6,275.00
Physician	$4. per hr.
Dental & Oral Hygiene	$5, 480.00
Dentist	$1.50 per hr.
Oral hygienist	$1500. per yr.
Nursing Service	21,240.00
#1 nurse	$1600–2000
Nutrition Service	8,500.00
#1 nutritionist	$1600–2000
Mental Hygiene Service	
#1 Psychologist	$2. per hr.
Clerical & Interpreting	10,970.00
Clerks	$750–1500
Supervisors	$2700–3000

By 1932, the Judson Health Center was cooperating more actively on emergency relief—this was the time of the Great Depression—and acted as an agent for the Federal Emergency Relief Administration (FERA) in the distribution of food and clothing. Dr. Campbell was in principle opposed to this kind of aid. She felt that a supply of free food and clothing was putting many small pushcart operations that sold these goods out of business, thus contributing to higher unemployment.[26]

26. Judson Health Center, *Annual Report of the General Directors*, 1933, p.14. Judson Health Center Archives. Because of the depression and the need to

The staff office at the Judson Health Center, 1926.

COOPERATION WITH OTHER AGENCIES

On January 17, 1935, twenty-nine organizations gathered at the Hotel McAlpin for a conference on the "Need for a Coordinated Health Program for the Lower West Side Health District." The conference was organized by the Department of Health. Bailey B. Burrett, director of the AICP, chaired the conference. He was also treasurer of the Board of Directors of the Judson Health Center. Twenty-nine voluntary organizations were in attendance, including the Salvation Army, the Judson Health Center, the Henry Street Settlement, and the YMCA.

The minutes of this conference indicate that Mrs. V. G. (Mary K.) Simkhovitch of Greenwich House felt that the coordinated district health program should succeed because there was real leadership in the person of the district health officer, Dr. Sophie Rabinoff.

---

economize, the Center did not publish annual reports for the years 1933 and 1934.

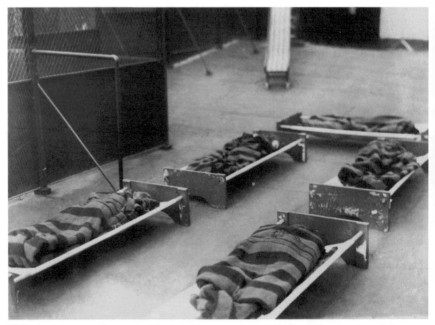

Children asleep on the roof of Judson House as part of their routine treatment for rickets, 1920s. The original caption to this photo read: "An American will emerge from each cocoon."

Dr. Eleanor A. Campbell of Judson Health Center commented on the infant mortality rate in the area, and mentioned that in the immediate neighborhood of Judson Health Center the rate had been reduced to a rate lower than for the city at large. She attributed this good record to the cooperation and coordination of the agencies in her vicinity, and believed that similar improvements would be evident in the future throughout the area.[27]

Dr. Sophie Rabinoff made a point of saying, in her presentation of the historical background and special health problems of the Lower West Side Health District, that there has been no attempt to unify and adapt health programs to meet the needs of the entire dis-

27. Department of Health New York City, Committee on Neighborhood Health Development. "Need for a Coordinated Health Program of Lower West Side Health District," January 17, 1935, pp. 6–7. New York City Municipal Reference and Research Library.

In the nursery of the Judson Health Center children are taught self-service. The midday meal is served by one of the little ladies, 1920s.

trict. Dr. Campbell may have taken Dr. Rabinoff's observations as a personal challenge. The Center's 1935 Annual Report, published sometime after the inclusion of the Audit's report for 1935 dated September 14, 1936, has an aerial photo showing the Lower West Side Health District in outline. The caption reads "Area Served by Judson Health Center on the Lower West Side of Manhattan." [28]

THE CENTER EXPANDS ITS JURISDICTION

Without question Judson Health Center's services were a major influence in the area, but Dr. Campbell may have overstated the Center's jurisdiction a bit. In the report Dr. Campbell wrote:

> We were requested by the Bowling Green Neighborhood Association, in May 1932, to expand our boundaries to include their old district west of Broadway from Canal Street to the

---

28. Judson Health Center, *An Oasis of Health: Annual Report 1935,* 1936, p. 9.

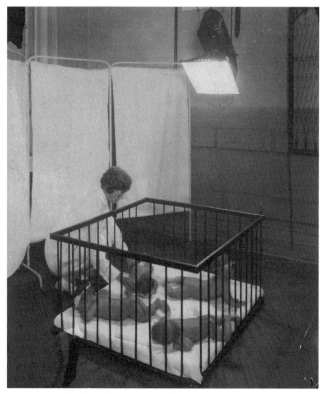

Infants receiving heliotherapy, 1920s.

Battery. This district was assigned to us after conference with the Department of Health, Child Welfare Federation, and Bowling Green. Since then we have operated a sub-station in this district.

At first we had use of clinic facilities for three days a week without rent, but when cold weather made heating necessary, we had to concentrate our clinic services to one-half day a week. When the old Bowling Green Neighborhood Association building was taken over by FERA we had to find new quarters. We are happy to have rented space at 84 Washington Street. There we have conducted our expanded services since May 1.[29]

29. Ibid., p. 25.

The following are the health service statistics for 1934 and for 1935, the first year Judson Health Center provided services for the entire Lower West Side.[30]

	1934	1935
Clinic visits	18,389	19,992
Field Visits	13,073	12,992
Conferences	8,561	9,811
Class Attendance	2,353	2,409
Total services rendered	42,376	45,204

FUNDRAISING

In the same 1935 report Dr. Campbell reported that the Center showed a deficit of $13,321.60. But with an influential and resourceful Board of Directors, this shortage was readily eradicated. For example, Mrs. August Zinsser, Judson Health Center board member, and Mr. and Mrs. Bartlett Arkell were among the distinguished patrons of an art exhibit of Dutch works organized by Dr. Campbell. This was a major society event to benefit of the Judson Health Center. The exhibit included seventeenth-century Dutch paintings of Rembrandt, Frans Hals, and Pieter de Hooch. Many were exhibited in America for the first time. Dr. Campbell organized annual fundraisers throughout the 1930s and 1940s. These were major occasions, and the attendees reflected New York City's Who's Who of the day.[31]

Never missing an opportunity to showcase the impressive efforts of her staff and the overall accomplishments of the Judson Health Center, Dr. Campbell organized an event for February 5, 1937, to acknowledge the Center's sixteen years of health care service. The reception was held at 80 West Fortieth Street, the studio of her father, Colonel A.A. Anderson. She invited Health Commissioner Dr. John L. Rice to be the keynote speaker. The event made the *New York Times* the next day: "Figures tending to show nearly a 20 per cent decline in the general mortality rate in the region served by the

---

30. Ibid., p.29. It is unclear why these statistics are lower than for 1930–1932.
31. "Dutch Art Exhibit—Judson Benefit," *The Villager,* December 3, 1936, p. 3.

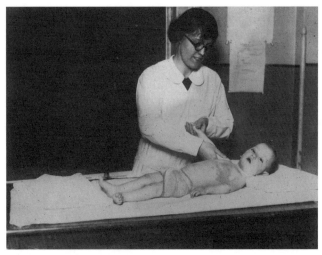

A physiotherapist loaned by the Rotary Club of New York to the Judson Health Center gives corrective exercises to a deformed child, 1920s.

Judson Health Center as compared with the rest of the lower West Side were cited by Health Commissioner John L. Rice yesterday as proof of the effectiveness of public health agencies in the fight to curb disease and death." [32]

DISTRICT HEALTH CENTERS

It was the private, voluntary health agencies, such as the Judson Health Center, that provided the backbone and muscle for the district health plan. In February 1937, the city's bureaus of Child Hygiene and School Hygiene were merged, along with the voluntary agencies participating in each district, into the Bureau of District Health Administration. To launch this new bureau, Dr. Rice initiated a three-year project to improve community participation in the district health centers. [33] The New York and Nathan Hofheimer foundations financed the project. The U.S. Public Health Service had placed a new emphasis on health education, and Dr. Rice had solic-

---

32. "Death Rate Cut 20% by Judson Center," *New York Times*, February 6, 1937, p. 19.
33. Duffy, p. 358.

ited funds, under the Social Security Act, for health education training programs for health personnel. Rice indicated that his goal was
to equalize the quality of service in all the health districts through
health education. Dr. Rice brought in Philip S. Broughton, director
of the U.S. Public Health Service, to direct the program. To coordinate community involvement, a number of advisory committees
worked together, and by 1939 no fewer than ten medical advisory
committees were in place.[34] Since Goldwater and Emerson's days,
the New York City Department of Health had always promoted
health education and disease prevention. But now health education
became the rallying cry for a program of integrated district health
care. It made good sense; coordinated efforts were efficient and eco-
nomically expedient.

THE CENTER REORGANIZES

Even though health education had been a goal of the Center from its
first days, the Judson Health Center, after a critical appraisal of its
program, made extensive changes in its operations. In 1939 Charles
H. Sears, executive director of the New York Baptist City Society
and also a member of the Center's Board of directors, invited the
Center staff to make a presentation on its new focus to the City Society. Therese Kerze, assistant director of the Center, told the City Society that the Center's 1939 programs were quite different from any
previous programs. The new focus was health education for prevention and early diagnostic procedures to eliminate unhealthy conditions before they got established.[35]

Miss Kerze identified a number of changes that had been put in
place throughout the district. The Center was actively involved in
uniting community health-oriented agencies for the purpose of coordinating efforts, and working in harmony, for better service to the
community. As part of the education component, the Center now
sold cod liver oil, skim milk, bandages, and thermometers. Along
with the sale, a staff member would discuss the use and value of
these items with family members and discuss health topics in gen-

---

34. Ibid., p. 359.
35. Kerze, Therese. "Report of a Modern Health Institution," November 2,
1939. Nine-page typewritten document. Judson Health Center Archives.

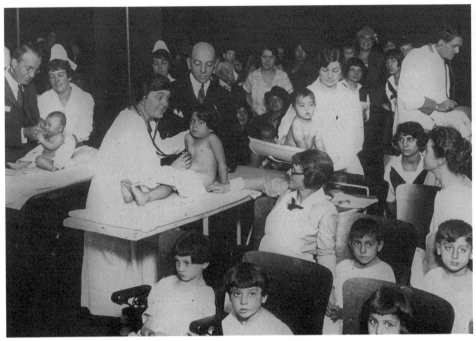

A "squad team" of physicians examining preschoolers, c. 1929.

eral. The Center had begun to advertise what it called "Well Clinics for Well Individuals" to reinforce good health habits and stress prevention and early diagnosis procedures.[36]

The Center had also made organizational changes in home visits. The staff now visited only those families who had not come to the Center in the past twelve months. "An infant who comes to the clinic regularly every month, we have found, does not need an additional monthly visit made by the worker into the home."[37]

Volunteers were a major source of personnel for the Center. At the same time, the Center felt it was making a contribution to the lives of the volunteers by "giving them an insight into the operation of a public health organization ... and by arousing ... a greater interest in health education."[38]

---

36. Ibid., p. 6.
37. Ibid.
38. Ibid., p. 7.

Staff education was a major innovation. The Center instituted in-service education and job training programs.

The Center also implemented several new group-work initiatives and classes in a broad range of health subjects. For the Society's benefit, Miss Kerze highlighted four specific programs:

1. Homemakers' club, consisting of mothers who are learning about the practical aspects of homemaking, low cost foods, budgeting and meal planning as well as cooking.
2. The Junior Club, composed of ten-year-old girls who learn about first aid and the care of children.
3. The Young Chefs Club, which teaches the rudiments of nutrition to eight-year-old boys.
4. The Girls Discussion Club for adolescent girls, the future mothers of the community. Some of the topics being discussed were home nursing, personal hygiene, sex education, etc.[39]

The Judson Health Center was leading the national trend of health agencies becoming advocates for health education. Health education and coordinated efforts were becoming the solution to a lack of public funds. The Center's new focus was a sign of the times. The Great Depression had taught people that the only way to improving one's life was through self-reliance. To learn that one could do something about one's health was a worthwhile education in itself. This can-do attitude would soon prove very valuable on a national level as the United States was drawn into World War II.

BUDGETS AND FUNDRAISING

The income for the Center, just before the war, for the first ten months of 1940, was $44,973.15. Expenses ran at $39,471.06, which left a balance of $5,502.09. This net income may have been the result of the sale of health care items that was begun in 1939. During this ten-month period the Center rendered 19,356 services.

---

39. Ibid., pp. 5–6.

Nonetheless, at the Annual Meeting of the Center's Board of Directors in January 1942, H. Adams Ashforth brought before the board a recommendation by Carlton M. Sherwood for raising money, and the idea was accepted. Dr. Campbell agreed to donate a salary for twenty-one weeks—February 2 to June 27—to pay Mrs. Charles P. Stone, a board member, to come on staff as promotion director. Her job would be to generate funds, enlarge the number of contributors, and advance the interest of the Center in all ways possible. In addition, the board granted Mrs. Stone a 10 percent commission on all monies raised over $10,000. [40]

Mrs. Stone was very efficient. She built one of the fundraisers around the arrival of the pandas at the Bronx Zoo. She organized volunteers to offer their cars to take the Center's children to see the pandas. She also put out the following publicity appeal:

> The only *live pandas* in captivity were sent here to us by the *Chinese* Government to give happiness to our *children.*
>
> The Judson Health Center has formed a volunteer group of "Pandas" who are taking numbers of children to the Zoo to see the Pandas—children who otherwise could not get to the Zoo.
>
> These children need milk.
>
> Will you help give *health* and *happiness* to these children, by filling the milk bottle with *dimes* or *dollars?*
>
> One of our volunteer group of "Pandas" *will call for the milk bottle* in a few days' time. Your contribution will be used to further the work of this charity, one of the oldest children's health centers in the City.[41]

On Wednesday, May 27, 1942, the Judson Health Center hosted a reception for Mrs. Eleanor Roosevelt, the First Lady at the time. Sit-

---

40. Judson Health Center. "Minutes of the Meeting of the Board of Directors," January 19, 1942, p. 4. The American Baptist Historical Society Archives, Rochester, NY (ABHS). Box "Includes Judson Church, 1933–1942," folder "Judson Health Center 1942." This folder includes the Judson Health Center Board Minutes from November 26, 1941, to April 27, 1943.

41. Judson Health Center. Letter dated May 8, 1942. Judson Health Center Archives.

Students from P.S. 38 participate in a health day celebration in Washington Square Park.

ting down informally in a basement room, she warmed the hearts of her small audience with high praise for the Center's work, which she had inspected thoroughly. She asserted that "education and health care should be equal obligations of the State.... The emphasis in the future should be placed on health work, beginning with prenatal care right on up as a prerequisite to education. If the State has an obligation to educate children, it should also have an obligation to see that they are in conditions to receive education." Mrs. Roosevelt went on to say that school health examinations were ridiculous. There was no uniformity or follow-up. Often it was too little too late. Had good health care been implemented at an early age, people could grow up "without suffering from things that take a lot of medical care." [42]

In October 1942 Mrs. Stone proposed to the board a "Stars on Ice" fundraiser to be held at the Center Theatre on December 23. At

---

42. "First Lady Sees Her Son Take Oath," *New York Times,* May 28, 1942, p. 14.

this gala, the board agreed to sell war bonds that the buyers would donate to the Center. This idea probably came from an event earlier that year. In May New Yorkers had paid $5,250,000 in war bonds to attend the premiere showing of the film "Yankee Doodle Dandy."[43] Mrs. Stone estimated that her event would gross $12,000 on admission and raffle tickets, exclusive of war bond sales.[44]

The Center's minutes do not report how much money was made, but the January 27, 1943, Annual Meeting directed the secretary to send a letter of appreciation to Mrs. Stone for the benefit. The board also voted to appoint Mrs. Stone as promotional director for another three months at a salary of $50.00 per week.[45]

WAR WORK

In line with the war effort, the Center added additional courses to train volunteers in nutrition and home nursing; both courses carried Red Cross certification. The nutrition classes also participated in the Mobile Kitchen that was located in the district. Miss Kerze was granted release from some of her duties so she could be a part-time consultant on home nursing and nurse's aides for the Red Cross in New York City. The war emergency caused several staff resignations, but the Health Center's reputation was such that it had no difficulty in filling the vacancies.[46]

The Judson Health Center archives contain little documentation about the Center's activities during the war.

In 1946 Dr. Campbell celebrated the Center's twenty-fifth anniversary by launching a campaign to raise $25,000. New York City Mayor William O'Dwyer opened the campaign at a ceremony in his office in City Hall. The funds were intended to establish a new psychiatric service and to reopen a Center branch in the Bowling Green Neighborhood section of the district.[47]

---

43. "$5,250,000 Is Paid to See One Movie," *New York Times,* May 27, 1942.

44. Judson Health Center. "Minutes of the Meeting of the Board of Directors," October 19, 1942, p. 1. ABHS Archives.

45. Judson Health Center. "Minutes of the Meeting of the Board of Directors," January 27, 1943, p. 2. ABHS.

46. Judson Health Center. "Minutes of the Meeting of the Board of Directors," November 16, 1942, p. 1. ABHS.

47. "She'll Be Guest of Honor at Judson Health Center," *New York Times,*

A mother's class, 1923. Mrs. Franconi is the teacher.

POSTWAR EXPANSION AND MOVE TO NEW QUARTERS

The Center continued its services and became more active than ever. Simultaneously, the New York Baptist City Society, who managed the affairs and property of Judson Memorial Church, became interested in providing Christian education to the great number of students who began attending colleges and universities after the war, many on the G.I. bill. Judson Memorial Church, next door to New York University, was a logical location for a Christian Education program aimed at students.

The Rev. Dean Wright began work as the Director of Student Work on September 15, 1948, and was given an apartment in 81 West Third Street, the building joining the west side of Judson House, as part of his salary. There was an odd assortment of people,

January 14, 1946, p. 14; "Aids Judson Center," *New York Times,* February 9, 1946, p. 8.

Girls participating in a Future Mothers Club, 1921.

unrelated to the operations of Judson Church, living at 81 West 3rd Street and the top floor of Judson House and the Society moved them out to make room for the students and staff of the new Christian education program. The facilities were not in good shape, and the Society authorized funds to make extensive repairs to make them habitable.[48]

In addition to the students moving into the top floor of Judson House, the City Society gave William Myers and his wife living quarters there. Myers was the director of a youth program sponsored by the Police Athletic League, and Judson Church provided free housing for him and his family.[49]

As Judson House now contained the Judson Health Center, a student dormitory, and staff housing, the building was in violation

48. Board of Managers. "New York Baptist Mission [City] Society Minutes," September 16, 1948, pp. 225–226. Bound Minutes of the New York Baptist Mission Society, 1945–1950, Vol. H. ABHS Archives.

49. Ibid., October 20, 1949, pp. 279–280.

of New York City's Multiple Dwelling Law. Dr. Campbell had a meeting with Robert V. Russell and Stanley B. Hazzard, officers of the New York Baptist City Society. Dr. Campbell brought a report with her, presumably from the Department of Housing, concerning the Multiple Dwelling Law violation. Immediately after the meeting, on April 13, 1950, Mr. Russell wrote to Dr. Campbell acknowledging receipt of the report. He informed her that the City Society would study the report in regard to any responsibilities to the Health Center the City Society might have under the existing lease. Mr. Russell took this letter-writing opportunity to bring up several issues with Dr. Campbell. He reiterated "that it is quite desirable that there should be closer liaison and cooperation between those in charge of the Health Center and those in charge of the program and activities now being carried on in the Judson Church.... We sincerely trust that closer relations can be developed between the two staffs." Since the church program was rapidly growing under the new leadership, there was a need for more space. Mr. Russell requested social facilities for the seventeen students in the dormitory, "and it would be of great assistance to our program if we could acquire the use of the rooms on the basement floor ... on evenings during the week (except Wednesday) and on Saturday and Sunday." [50]

The Center's rent of $3,000 per year had been reduced during the depression to $2,500, and Mr. Russell informed Dr. Campbell that the original rent would be reinstated, acknowledging that the market place would bring substantially more.

Dr. Russell's letter included an intriguing proposal: that the Health Center and Judson Church jointly raise the funds to build a new facility to house both programs. "This could be done on a cooperative basis, so that the rental of space by one organization to the other could be avoided; it would seem that such a new structure might be erected which would be tax free." If the project were developed, Mr. Russell offered Dr. Campbell the use of the basement and the first two floors of 179 Sullivan Street for the interim period.

Dr. Campbell agreed to the increased rent to $3,000 beginning April 1, 1950, and she informed Mr. Russell that Dean Dorothy Ar-

---

50. Russell, Robert V. Letter to Dr. Eleanor Campbell, April 13, 1950. pp. 2–3 of 6 pp. Judson Health Center Archives.

Members of the Young Chefs Club at work.

nold and Miss Ellen Black would be the representatives to discuss the proposed use of the Center's basement facilities by the students in the Judson program. She also indicated that Mr. H. Adams Ashforth and Mr. H. Stanley would work with the City Society on a possible project for a new facility.[51]

In between the lines of Dr. Russell's letters one can read a growing tension. Judson Church wanted Judson House for its own programs and somewhat resented Dr. Campbell's independence and near-complete control over the building next door.

Matters came to a head several months later, when the building at 81 West Third Street developed a dangerous bulge in one of the walls and had to be demolished. Judson Church had to find new quarters for the staff and the women students living there. Also, the male students living on the third floor of Judson House had used 81 West Third as access to that floor and now had to go through the Health Center to get to their rooms. Dr. Campbell probably felt that sharing her facilities with students would endanger the antiseptic environment and compromise the security of the clinics. In short order, she found new space and made plans to vacate Judson House by No-

---

51. Russell, Robert V. Letter to Dr. Eleanor Campbell, May 1, 1950. Judson Health Center Archives.

vember 1, 1950. In a press release dated July 20, 1950, the Judson Health Center announced: "Judson Health Center, Famous 'Health Desert' Service to Cold Water Tenement Population, purchases Former New York Dispensary Home on Spring Street. To Move From Thompson Street Quarters After 30 years. Change Dictated by Expanded Activities. West Side Work to Continue."

The press release went on to say:

> Twice in its career, the Center was requested by the Health Department to extend its territory. Today its district is bounded by the Hudson River, the Battery, Broadway/Fourth Avenue to 28th Street, Sixth Avenue to 14th Street, and along 14th Street to the Hudson. There now will be some slight alteration in boundaries to take in the East Side section in which the new quarters are located.... . The change is being made in talks with the District Health Administration of the Department of Health. Virtually all of the West Side Area is being retained in the Center's activities.[52]

On November 21, 1950, Ellen Black, R.N., administrative director of the Judson Health Center, wrote to Charles Merz, editor of the *New York Times,* announcing an open house for the Judson Health Center at 34 Spring Street. Along with the announcement was the request that Mr. Merz write an editorial highlighting the Center's accomplishments over the past thirty years. Mr. Merz obliged. On November 30, 1950, the *New York Times* published an editorial tribute that said, among other things:

> From very small beginnings, Judson expanded through the years, serving thousands of persons who might otherwise have been unable to provide vital health services for themselves, until now its staff estimates that it has provided altogether 995,000 such services—just short of the million mark. Though closely budgeted and with limited financial re-

---

52. Judson Health Center. "Judson Health Center, Famous 'Health Desert' Service to Cold Water Tenement Population, Purchases Former New York Dispensary Home on Spring Street." Judson Health Center Archives.

sources, the center has done a great work in building better homes and happier men, women and children in a congested, cosmopolitan section of the city.[53]

---

53. "Judson Health Center." *New York Times,* November 30, 1950, p. 32 (editorial page).

Eleanor Campbell

ELLY DICKASON

Written sources about Eleanor Campbell are scant. Much of the information in this chapter comes from Robert E. Harvey, great-grandson of Dr. Campbell's, who lent us many family documents. ⎯⎯⎯⎯⎯⎯

Eleanor Anderson Campbell was a woman larger than life. She came from a wealthy New York family. She went to medical school for the specific purpose of being able to help the poor. She founded the Judson Health Center and ran it for thirty-three years, setting standards in preventive medicine at a time when preventive care had not yet made it to the agenda of public health. She was beautiful.

Why is so little known about this amazing woman? The only public sources available for a glimpse into her personal life are her obituary in the *New York Times* of December 30, 1959; an entry in the 1975 edition of the *National Cyclopedia of American Biography* (and even that article spends more space on the clinic than on Eleanor); and *The Milbank Memorial Fund: Its Leaders and Its Work,* a 1975 work written by Clyde Vernon Kiser for the Milbank Memorial Fund.

Eleanor was born on March 2, 1878, to Abram Archibald Anderson, an artist, and Elizabeth Milbank Anderson. Her mother was a noted philanthropist with an early interest in public health and in women's education—she donated more than $1,000,000 to Barnard College, and that college's Milbank Hall was named after her. Large sums of money also went to the Children's Aid Society and the Association for the Improvement of the Condition of the Poor.

Eleanor's father, Colonel Anderson, was an artist of some note. His portrait of Thomas Alva Edison hangs in the National Gallery in Washington, DC. He was also an all-round bon vivant, spending

The staff of the Judson Health Center in 1921. Dr. Campbell is seated in the center.

about ten years in Paris pursuing his art while his family stayed in New York. When he was not in Paris, he oversaw Palette Ranch in Wyoming, a large development where he tried his hand at raising cattle and horses. All this was made possible by his wife's money. Anderson was instrumental in creating the Yellowstone Forest Reserve in 1902, and President Roosevelt named him superintendent. In 1933 Anderson published *Experiences and Impressions: An Autobiography of Colonel A. A. Anderson*. In this curious little book, Anderson talks about his life as an artist and as a rancher. He devotes three chapters to various bear hunts but none to his family life. Only at the end does he describe Mrs. Anderson, after she has died, as a

Dr. Campbell examines one of several boys while the mother looks on, 1925.

woman who "naturally encountered differences of opinion" but whose "every act was inspired by unselfish and noble motives." There is a chapter each for Eleanor, of whose accomplishments as the director of Judson Health Center he was very proud, and his granddaughter, who died at age twenty-five. He never mentions that he also had a son, Jeremiah Milbank Anderson, who died at age seven of diphtheria.

Elizabeth Milbank Anderson ascribed the death of her son to the unsanitary conditions of New York City. She began donating money to have bathhouses built in the area of New York City where she and Eleanor lived. The death of her brother and her mother's reaction to it must have made a deep impression on Eleanor, who was eight years old at the time.

As a girl of thirteen or fourteen, Eleanor accompanied an older cousin on a tour of tenements on the Lower East Side (this was called "slumming"). Even at this age Eleanor understood how demeaning and condescending the visit was to the women they saw.

The *New York Times* notes that she was "shocked by the sights and by the futility of her cousin's gifts and well-meant advice." The memory of that trip stayed with her.

Eleanor attended the Brearly School and Miss Spence's School for Girls in New York, graduating in 1896. She attended Bryn Mawr College from 1896 to 1898. Practically nothing is known about the next fourteen years, except that she enjoyed the social life and the pastimes afforded to the rich in New York. On April 7, 1904, Eleanor married John Stewart (Jack) Tanner, a medical doctor from Kentucky. As a wedding gift, Mrs. Anderson bought her son-in-law a seat on the New York Stock Exchange, and Jack Tanner became a stockbroker. In 1905 Eleanor and Jack had a daughter whom they christened Elizabeth Milbank Tanner, followed two years later by a boy, Milbank Tanner, who died at birth.

In 1910, Eleanor divorced her husband. He had made a trip to Paris alone, and word came back—through a private detective hired by her mother—that he had engaged in a relationship unbecoming a married man. Eleanor was willing to forgive him, but her mother, not wanting her daughter to have the same lonely marriage as she, insisted on a divorce. Eleanor's relationship with her mother became strained at this point.

In 1912, when she was thirty-four years old, Eleanor entered Boston University Medical School. Her daughter, who was seven at the time, lived with her maternal grandmother, who legally adopted the girl and renamed her Elizabeth Milbank Anderson, II. Eleanor received her M.D. in 1916 and spent two years as an interne in hospitals in New York City and Boston.

On January 1, 1918, Eleanor married Frederick Barber Campbell, a lawyer. What happened to that marriage cannot be found in public records, but by 1921 Eleanor was again divorced.

In 1920 Dr. Campbell began discussions with A. Ray Petty, senior minister of Judson Memorial Church, about a health center for the large Italian immigrant population just south of the church. The Judson Health Center opened its doors in January 1921. During the first eighteen months, the clinic used the basement of the church, but soon the program outgrew the space. In July 1922 the clinic moved next door into Judson House, where it occupied most of the building until 1950.

Mayor Vincent Impellitteri of New York City presents a
testimonial scroll to Dr. Campbell, March 15, 1951.

From 1921 to 1954 Dr Campbell ran the clinic and was its sen-
ior medical doctor. It was mostly her own money that kept it going,
especially at the beginning. In later years, the Health Department of
New York City paid for immunizations and for some of the salaries.
The clinic also received financial help from the Greater New York
Fund and was the beneficiary of various fundraising events.

One such event stands out. In 1936, friends of Dr. Campbell's
among the very rich of New York organized a show of paintings as a
fundraiser. The exhibit, held at the Schaeffer Galleries on 57th
Street, was called The Great Dutch Masters and included paintings
by Frans Hals, Meindert Hobbema, Pieter de Hooch, Jacob van
Ruisdael, and Rembrandt!

Alongside her work as the director of the Judson Health Center, Dr. Campbell also was heavily involved in the well-being of Deering, New Hampshire, a small town that she had begun to visit annually in the 1920s. In 1925 she bought an old farm there. Ray Petty, Judson's minister, also bought property, as did several other prominent Protestant families. This was the beginning of a growing colony of summer houses around Deering Lake. Not content with one property, Dr. Campbell kept adding farms and lots to her holdings; fifteen years later she owned 2,000 acres in and around Deering.

Spending summers in this rural community, Dr. Campbell realized that unfavorable health conditions and lack of proper medical care were not restricted to city slums. The Deering Health Center, financed by Dr. Campbell, opened its doors in 1927. In 1930 she created the Deering Community Center. Every summer the center held a camp for religious instruction, where entire families could come to enjoy the country and listen to good preaching. Ministers associated with this program were A. Ray Petty and Daniel A. Poling, a prominent clergyman who later, during World War II, preached at many active fronts at the invitation of General Eisenhower.

Through the Deering Foundation, Eleanor Campbell also paid for the college education of many young people who could not otherwise have attended.

Dr. Campbell's daughter, Elizabeth, was married to Henry Adams Ashforth. They had two children: Eleanor and Henry. Elizabeth died in 1930 of a streptococcal infection (this was before penicillin), and the Deering Center became a monument to her memory.

In 1951 Mayor Vincent R. Impellitteri of New York gave Dr. Campbell a testimonial scroll for "her fine efforts and accomplishments" on the occasion of the Center's thirtieth anniversary.

In 1954 Dr. Campbell retired. She was seventy-six years old. For another two years she was the clinic's president, and in 1956 she was made honorary general director. In 1957, the government of Italy awarded her its Star of Italian Solidarity for her help to Italian-Americans.

Eleanor Campbell died in Scarsdale, New York, on December 29, 1959, at age eighty-one.

We know that Eleanor Campbell was a lifelong Baptist and that she was a Republican. We know very little else about her as a person. She was a strong-willed woman, and especially toward the end of her career she became autocratic, used to having her way. Even friends described her as "difficult." There are no records of how her daughter's death affected her. If anything, it seemed to have propelled her to work even harder for better health conditions.

One thing is clear, though: Eleanor Campbell was an exceptional woman who made a difference in the lives of thousands of families.

Problem Parents

The following article is the text of a radio speech given by Dr.
Eleanor Campbell and broadcast on WMCA in New York on May 18,
1936. The content is amazingly modern.

T he biggest handicaps which some children have are their
parents. No parent would intentionally be such a handicap.
Yet many are without knowing it. We hear a good deal
about problem children. What about the problem parents?

I once heard a noted mental specialist say: "There are very few
problem children, there are a great many problem parents." In this I
thoroughly agree.

In my fifteen years at Judson Health Center as General Director
and one of the doctors, I have not been surprised at the effect of
slum life, with its unsanitary housing, terrible congestion and poverty, on our children. I expected that. What has surprised me has
been the frequency of the problem parent and what he or she was
doing to the child. These findings might be duplicated in the higher
economic areas of the city, though possibly overemphasized by the
close proximity of the crowded tenement, with the less chance of
clashing personalities to escape. In the same economic type of home,
where we have intelligent, cooperative and emotionally balanced
parents, with mutual understanding and love, we see radiant children developing physically and mentally into personalities who will
be a credit to America and who in the privileges of our democracy
may go far.

Far too many mothers bring their children to my clinic either
with such a complete indifference toward them, or with such overindulgence, that you know you cannot arouse cooperation. Sometimes they come with such mutual and emotional misunderstand-
ing—even advanced antagonism between parent and child—that it
has been a distinct shock to me. All too often the mother has come
saying, in front of the child: "He so fresh, he so bad, I can do nothing with him." The sullen little fellow of only five or six looks up at
the parent criticizing him to a stranger, with a look of resentment

and hate that is appalling. Right here we see the beginnings of a problem child, the developing of a mental and emotional attitude of antagonism which will be carried into the future relationships of life, the beginnings of a possible criminal. It is wise to have conferences to discuss the eradication of the crime problem. But it is not around a conference table that crime will be eradicated. It must be met first of all in the problem parent and the handling of the little child in its home. Henry Ward Beecher once was asked, "at what age should one begin to train a child." He answered, "a hundred years before he was born."

Therefore, the first essential is trying to prevent "problem parents." The real function of a Health Center is this. This is the reason that Judson has added to the usual medical and dental clinics, the nursing and nutrition departments of a Health Center, a mental hygiene or child guidance department. The success of this department depends not only on dealing with the so-called problem child, but the problem parent. One psychiatrist and social worker is teaching the public health nurse and nutritionist how to recognize mental health problems, the way to approach the parents, and how to convey health education to the problem parent.

When our Child Guidance Department was first added to the Judson Health Center, it was before the days of a mental hygiene service in the public schools. The attendance officer asked if he might bring to our clinic the truant and delinquent children of our district. Up to that time such children were brought to court, and thus started life with a court record. To prevent this he wanted to bring them to us. That winter we handled fifty-five children referred to us by him, and these were so adjusted by us that only two were taken to court. We made a study of the causes leading to delinquency in this group. First of all causes, in fifty-one out of fifty-five instances, were broken homes or disharmony between the parents—problem parents.

The problem parent is the result of various factors, often dating back to their own problem parents, "a hundred years before they were born," according to Mr. Beecher. Where it is due to marked mental inferiority little can be done. But these cases, fortunately, are a minority, and it is not these that chiefly interest us at Judson Health Center.

The first, and chief, cause is ignorance. Most of our parents, even where this noticeable antagonism seems to be developing, deep down in their hearts, love their children. With patience and tact, they can be shown, they can be taught to understand their children's needs, more easily in regard to their physical needs, than given an appreciation of child psychology. To many adults, the child is regarded as a "little grown-up," while he really lives in a complete world of his own, which an intelligent parent should attempt to learn about and appreciate. This can be done and when grasped gives an entirely different attitude on the part of the parent.

Ignorance of child care and need is appalling. Too many feel that the mother instinct is sufficient to make a person a good mother. Instinct may teach the lower animals care for their young, but it does not teach a human being to be a good parent. We must depend on education and scientific knowledge, too. Instinct does not teach us how to prevent rickets, to make our child immune to diphtheria, or to give him a chance to become a healthy, educated and emotionally balanced individual.

In the early years of Judson Health Center services, before we had won confidence and faith in our health leadership (which now make such experiences rare) a nurse made a follow-up visit of instruction in one of our homes. There were seven children, each more malnourished than the other. The two-year-old was almost crippled by rickets, and a little baby was in wretched condition. They were seven child failures. This baby had been brought to the clinic and the nurse had gone to teach the mother how to prepare the formula ordered by the doctor. As the nurse left she turned to see the mother pouring the formula down the sink. When she asked why, the mother answered: "My husband, he say I got seven children, you got none, I know more than you do."

But slowly and patiently we have been able to win faith in our teachings and to demonstrate what education in baby care can do. The health area where Judson Health Center has operated from the beginning and conducts its most intensive service, is one of the most crowded slum areas, with old-fashioned cold-water, walk-up tenements. When we opened fifteen years ago we had one of the highest infant death rates in the city, and at that time it was called by a health authority "The Health Desert of New York." Though the housing and economic conditions have not changed much, a study of average infant death rates made by the Neighborhood Health Development Committee covering the years 1929 to 1933 showed the

infant death rate in this health area to be the lowest in the whole
west side. It was lower than in a high income area, one of the lowest
in the city. Education can change the problem parent.

A second and more difficult cause for problem parents is the
emotional difficulties which they are suffering. Too often the parent
is unadjusted, upset and distressed. Study of our delinquent children
showed this. Often with parents afraid to let out their pent-up emotions on another "grown-up," the child becomes the recipient of
these emotions, of unjust fault findings, scoldings or whippings. A
mother comes saying: "My child, he hit me and slap at me." I ask:
"How often do you slap your child?" Or "my child, he so nervous,
he kick and scream," and I ask, "are you nervous, and do you let out
your emotions on him?" Often I get the answer: "I cannot help it, he
makes me nervous." I answer: "Which is the older, and which must
learn self-control first?"

A third, but less frequent and more hopeless cause is indifference.
Here, in the mother, lacking the normal affection for the child, we
have a personality problem to be handled by the psychiatrist. The
only hope for the child lies here, or in finding a new home for him.

The fourth, and worst, is the delinquent, the "criminal parent."
We cannot go back the hundred years of Dr. Beecher, but let us an-
ticipate the hundred years in the future. Here, where possible, children should be removed to foster homes with non-problem parents.

The depression of today has been a frequent cause of "problem
parents." Anxious parents lead to troubled children who are unable
to meet life today without fear and tension. Unemployment, lack of
regular income, the struggle to maintain one's family without going
on relief, is not only taking its toll in physical health but in mental
health. The parent who is habitually tense and fearful has had his
fears and anxiety increased in the last few years. Children who,
above all else, need security in the home day after day find parents
too preoccupied with worries over rent, discouragement over fruit-
less job hunting, to give them as much as a kind glance or a cheerful
word. Most children are so sensitive that these experiences leave
scars upon them. The Judson Health Center child guidance clinic
works to prevent these deprivations from leaving too deep a mark.
To illustrate:

A father of three children was able to support his family regularly until the factory where had always worked closed. Frequent

changes of job and periods in which he had none at all were more than he could bear. He became moody, withdrawn and suspicious, accusing his fellow employees of plotting against him. When he finally attempted to end his life he was sent to a mental hospital where he will probably have to remain always. Agencies quickly came forward to provide relief for his wife and children so that their worries about food and shelter were over. But the children have been exposed to his moods for the past five years. The oldest boy, a lad of ten, had been particularly disturbed by him. He became unable to sleep at night; he showed a fear of every knock at the door; he suffered pains around his heart so that he could not go to school, but would sit miserably about the house while his mother feared that he was becoming just like his father. Finally he came to our child health clinic for a heart examination. The doctor found no physical basis for his pains, but knowing that worries can cause pain too, he and his mother were sent to our child guidance clinic. Here the psychiatrist got to the root of his suffering and helped him to bring out fears that he had never dared to express to anyone before. The psychiatrist was able to give him the reassurance his sick father had never been able to give him. His mother also had a chance to find a friend in the clinic, who helped her understand her children, to meet the problem of raising her three children bereft of their father with a little more courage and understanding.

If crime is to be lessened, if America is to give a chance to its children for a normal, healthy, and adjusted life, it lies in seeing that parents cease to be problem parents, that when Mother's Day comes, it awakens in each individual the emotions and memories of the best and most helpful influence of life. Unfortunately, today that is not the case for everyone. Children in a Sunday School once were asked which was the hardest commandment to keep. The answer of one little boy was, "Honor thy father and thy mother." The home was investigated, and both parents were found to be drunkards.

There are major problem parents—but how many of us may be problem parents in "spots" or at off moments? We at Judson Health Center run into many blind spots on the part of the parent that interfere with their handling of their children. For instance, Barbara as the only child was the pride of her parents until a new baby brother arrived. The mother could not understand why Barbara suddenly became impudent, sulky, refusing to eat or go out to play. Disciplinary measures increased the difficulties and a tense situation of anxiety on the part of the mother and unhappiness on that of the child rapidly developed. When the mother learned that it was only natural for Barbara to be jealous of her brother and that she was struggling for the love she felt she had lost, her handling of Barbara altered — and, making the child feel the continuance of her family's love, Barbara learned to love her brother, too.

Another blind spot parents frequently show is in regard to their children's food fads. The mother comes complaining that the child will not eat without being fed, or that Mary has "no appetite," though she urges her to eat and does all she can to make her. The mother little realizes that Mary has learned to secure the attention so dear to all children—to obtain a greater share of mother's time and care than the brothers and sisters, through refusing to eat. Mary has already learned to control her mother, and malnutrition is a price Mary is willing to pay.

How often a mother, when tired or irritated, releases her feelings on the children. All of us who are mothers have to a certain degree been unjust in the handling of our children, and to that degree we have been a problem parent. One winter day when there was much ice in the streets, but a thaw had caused big puddles, a mother was taking her two little boys to school. Their suits were clean and neat, and their appearance showed care and consideration. One block from the school the mother sent them on alone. The little chap started to run, stepped on a piece of ice and sat down in a big puddle. The mother grabbed him, shook him violently, and slapped him, scolding in a shrill voice. It had been a pure accident and the little frightened, helpless child was not in any way guilty of willful wrongdoing. I have never found resentment on a child's part for punishment for wrongdoing for which he felt guilty. But nothing causes greater heart-breaks and antagonistic reactions on the part of a small child than treatment or punishment he considers unjust. The beginnings may be small, but the end results may be very big. "Blind spots" in parents which they have not faced may be the cause when Johnny grows up of social behavior which breaks mother's heart.

The answer to problem children, maladjustment and crime is in the home and the agencies trying to better the homes. Crime begins at home, and so does the remedy.

THE JUDSON STAFF

The history of Judson House took a sharp turn in 1948. Until that time, the building—group of buildings, really—had been rented out by the New York Baptist City Society (NYBCS) for others to use. In 1947, Melissa Russell, whose husband was the associate secretary of the City Society, became interested in Judson Church. She wanted to work out something with New York University so that Judson House would become a laboratory for Christian education at NYU. The students could live at the house for a minimal fee while being involved in this work.

About that time, Dean and Margaret Wright were planning to come to New York, where Dean was going to pursue a graduate degree at Columbia University. Dean was looking for a part-time job and approached the City Society. Mrs. Russell hired him to be the director of the new student program. Dean and Margaret moved into 81 West Third Street in September 1948 and began their work with the students.

A year after the Wrights came to Judson, Robert W. Spike, who was also in graduate school and also needed a part-time job, became the senior minister of Judson. He and his wife, Alice, and their son Paul moved into 81 West Third as well. This was in September 1949. At the time, the Judson congregation consisted of only a handful of people, and the real work of Judson took place in Judson House with the students. The Judson Council, which was the committee in the NYBCS that oversaw the affairs of Judson Memorial Church, proposed that Dean's job be made into a full-time position, and the NYBCS agreed.

The congregation slowly began to grow, and Bob Spike and Dean Wright felt that they needed more control over Judson House and Judson Church. The NYBCS had placed a woman in the church who oversaw the rental of various spaces to different groups, and

Dean and Bob had little to say over what she did. Her name was
Ruth Thompson, and she became the bane of everyone's existence.
There is a story about the Police Athletic League, which ran a program in the gymnasium below the church one night a week for the
Italian kids just south of Judson. One week Mrs. Thompson canceled the program so that she could rent the space to a group of ladies who wanted to give a Christmas party *for their dogs.* The
women were walking their dogs around the gym, and the kids had
their faces pressed against the mesh screen above the gym. They
were perfectly happy because they had never seen anything like it.

Things came to a head in the summer of 1950 when the building
at 81 West Third was condemned and razed to the ground. The
Wrights and the Spikes needed room in Judson House. At this time
also, the Judson Health Center was ready to move to larger quarters,
so most of the space in the building became available. That was also
the year of the first Church in Urban Life project, a three-month program for Baptist students from other parts of the country to study
the work of the church in an urban environment. Howard Moody
had been invited to run the project. Howard and Lorry arrived right
after the collapse of 81 West Third. There was no place for them to
stay other than the space that later became the Sunday School room,
just above the gymnasium in the church basement. To give themselves some privacy, they hung a blanket over the mesh wiring.

Dean Wright and Bob Spike requested a meeting with the NY-
BCS to see if Judson could not become more autonomous. Surprisingly, the Society acceded to their request, and from this moment
dates the modern Judson Church as we know it.

The earliest staff member represented in this book is Robert
Boyd, who moved into Judson House in 1947 to manage the students that lived there. Judson House offered an attractive alternative
to NYU housing, without any rules about curfew and such.

In the chapters that follow, a variety of staff, paid and unpaid—ministers (senior, associate, assistant, interim), some of the
spouses and one child, church secretaries, sextons, and program directors—provide a patchwork of more than fifty years of Judson
House history.

Two former staff members who contributed chapters are not
included here. Bernard (Bud) Scott, assistant minister from 1957 to

1960, was so totally involved in the arts that we have placed his chapter in the section on "The Judson Gallery"; and John Tungate's brick-by-brick and squeak-by-squeak description of Judson House, we felt, belonged more properly in the section called "The Building."

Robert Boyd

Robert Boyd is the earliest staff member represented here. ————————

In the summer of 1947 I arrived in New York City to begin teaching organic chemistry at New York University. I was staying at the Y on 23rd Street and had not yet found an apartment. One day, as I was walking down Washington Square South and passed Judson Church, down the steps came a young woman who had been one of my students at Antioch College in Ohio. After our initial surprise, she said, "Well, come in and meet my mother. She is secretary to the church minister, Rev. Elbert Tingley."

At that time, the New York Baptist City Society, and specifically Mrs. Melissa Russell who was running things there, was trying to set up a program to provide living arrangements for students at New York University that would also involve community service. The students would live at 81 West Third Street, which at the time was called Edward Judson Hall. The City Society was looking for a manager for the house who would also keep an eye on the students. I was interviewed by the Judson Council, and Mrs. Russell took a liking to me. Actually, they were desperately looking for somebody and hired the first sucker that came along! It was absolutely the most fantastic combination of events for me to have landed there.

My wife at that time, Carol, was working at a summer camp on Cape Cod, and unbeknownst to her I made the decision to take on the management of the building and move in. Then, of course, I had to persuade my wife, and apparently I did because soon we were living at 81 West Third. It was a great way to get started in New York. We were not paid a salary but had rent-free housing for taking care of the place.

There were two steps going up from the outside door, and we lived on that floor. In the back, looking out over the garden, was our bedroom. There was a kitchen in front. We did our own cooking and were not part of the students' meals. There was also a room that could be used as an office, which the City Society outfitted with a very nice desk from Wanamaker's. The City Society was very interested in getting things established.

My responsibility was to run the dormitory. The program was starting from scratch. I had promised we would try and see what we could do. In this building, a very strange combination of people had been occupying some of the rooms. One of them was a woman who soon retired from something or another related to the Baptists. Another was an elderly woman who was not in very good shape. One day she tumbled down the stairs. She was a great, big, husky woman. Her daughter came and fetched her one day and we never saw her again. That took care of two of them. That left the place open for what Judson wanted to do, namely, create a dormitory for students with an interest in community service.

NYU STUDENTS IN THE DORM

Now they had to get the students. By the end of the summer they collected a number from New York University. The students paid very little rent. Most of them were men. Some were army veterans but all in all they were an unusual bunch of people. Many were already employed. Some of these finally agreed that they did not fit in and moved out. One was a night clerk for the New Yorker Hotel. He would come in every morning with the New York Times and leave it on my doorstep. He was a great guy but he knew he wasn't cut out for this kind of communal thing.

My wife did a damn good job. She had to handle this college bunch of kids, war veterans mostly, get them to do stuff around the house, and I don't know how she did it. I don't know what the heck I was doing, to tell you the truth. There was no real job description, but it was pretty obvious that certain things had to be done. And the City Society was determined to make the program a success, so we received a lot of support.

The students were supposed to do certain things in the church and in the community, but Carol and I did not have to ride herd on them. If they did any community service at all, they did not tell us.

One of the young men who lived in the house was Charlie Croghan from Florida, another was Lou Reale. Another was Nocito. He worked for some furniture company in the swanky end of the furniture business, near Bloomingdale's. He managed to get a set of Eames chairs for the house.

Our heat and hot water came from New York University. All I would do is tell them we needed some heat. I made a point of becoming friends with the engineer at NYU. After that we had no more complaints about the heat.

DEAN AND MARGARET WRIGHT JOIN THE STAFF

In 1948 Dean and Margaret Wright moved in. Dean had been hired as associate minister to work with students. Dean and Margaret were a godsend. Danny Novotny was an interim pastor when we were there. I believe he was still a seminary student.

Carol and I were part of the Judson congregation. I remember being part of a pageantry honoring Adoniram Judson. We were a very small congregation. Some of the women were marvelous singers. Mrs. Cavalieri was the organist. We still had a baptismal font then up on the stage. The minister had rubber boots and a rubber gown: walk them in, walk them out. I have never seen anything like it since. I am a Presbyterian.

There were some memorable events and incidents during our stay. In 1947, during our first winter, there was a big blizzard. We had twenty-seven inches of snow. There was a young man who used to come around cleaning sidewalks and things like that. He shoveled snow for three hours and then quit without finishing the job.

Judson Church had an arrangement with the Election Board, which used the Long Room to set up the voting machines. I remember early one morning in November 1948 when someone was ringing our doorbell and banging on the door. It turned out to be two policemen: "We want to keep an eye on the voting machines." This was the Dewey-Truman election, and it was promising to be very close. So I let them in.

We lasted two years, and I had a great time. I hung around Judson for a while longer after we moved out of 81 West Third, singing in the choir. Then I stopped coming, and it was not until almost forty years later that I began attending Judson services again. In 1994 I became a member of Judson Memorial Church, finally.

ROBERT BOYD

continued to live in New York City, close to Judson, until his death on July 16, 2000.

Dean Wright

Dean Wright was minister of students at Judson from 1948 to 1952. _____

In 1947 Bob Spike was associate minister at the Granville Baptist Church in Ohio. He had graduated from Colgate Rochester. I had graduated from Yale Divinity School and got a job working with students, also in Granville. We were very good friends with the Spikes. I was doing student work for the state and Bob was related to the church, and we were the same age. Spike then decided that he wanted to get his doctorate degree at Columbia. He and his family moved to New York, and he took a little church in Queens, a small Baptist church, that was just part-time while he was doing his graduate work.

Margaret and I decided we might come back, too. I would follow the same course and study at Columbia. I would need a part-time job as well, so I approached the New York Baptist City Society (NYBCS). As luck would have it, my request came at a good moment.

Judson House was occupied by the Judson Health Center, which was begun in 1921 by Dr. Eleanor Campbell to bring free medical care to the Italian immigrants in the neighborhood. The clinic occupied the ground and second floors. On the third floor were rooms that were rented out to various people, including two men who were part of the quartet that sang at Judson services each Sunday.

We still had an organ then. A woman who had been a home missionary who played the organ had married an Italian from the neighborhood. Her name was Mrs. Cavalieri. She played the organ, the quartet was on the balcony, and the congregation was below in pews, which we still had then. We also had carpeting, which made for very good sound. We had a seminary student, Danny Novotny, who came only on Sundays to preach. This was his field work. None of the Judson Council people, of course, came to church.

A LABORATORY FOR CHRISTIAN EDUCATION

The wife of the secretary of the NYBCS was Melissa Russell, and she was a very strong, bright woman. She had been at the YWCA for years as a volunteer. Mrs. Russell became very interested in Judson. She was also interested in the NYBCS's Department of Christian Education. Her idea was this: She would work out something with New York University so that the Judson House would become a laboratory for Christian education at New York University. Students would be involved and some of them could even live in the house. The Judson congregation had nothing to do with it. When I say congregation, there were fifteen people there, and that would be counting the Spikes and us.

So when I asked the NYBCS if they could offer me a part-time position, Mrs. Russell had this grand idea and took it to the Judson Council. They said this is great, go ahead. Margaret was on her way to New York at the time. Mrs. Russell interviewed her and I got the job. In her letter of August 25, 1948, in which Mrs. Russell officially offered me the position of Director of Student Work, she enclosed the following job description:

1. to develop and carry out a plan of work with the students attending New York University
2. to be a staff representative to work with the New York University Christian Association
3. to be a representative of the New York Baptist City Society on the Board for Protestant Student Work in New York City
4. to carry responsibility for the Roger Williams Club and to strive to interest the residents of the Judson dormitory in the Club
5. to work out a relationship with the Department of Christian Education of the New York Baptist City Society as applied to students
6. to develop a subcommittee for student work, working with the committee on Program and Personnel of the Judson Memorial Church.

Mrs. Russell did add in her letter that I might want to have a new job description after being at work for a while.

That's how we got to Judson House. We moved in in September in time for the school year at NYU. We decided we wanted to make what space we had available to students. We lived on top of 81 West Third in a nice apartment with two bedrooms. We could walk right across the passage to get to the third floor of the building on Thompson Street (81 West Third and the building on Thompson Street were collectively referred to as Judson House). In the summer our apartment was unbearably hot. There was no insulation, just a metal-pressed ceiling with a skylight. But our living room was big, and later we had student meetings at least once a week. When we moved in, Robert Boyd and his first wife were living on the first floor of 81 West Third. They were in charge of the building at the time.

THE STUDENTS MOVE IN

We advertised on bulletin boards at NYU. When students started moving in, we put the men on the third floor of Judson House (this was not yet the day of mixed dormitories). The rooms on the first and second floors of 81 West Third were for women. One woman was black. Her name was Camay Procter. She was the daughter of Cab Calloway. We did not know this at the time. Her dad had said that he would pay her way through college if she would break with her mother, and she refused to do that. Instead she gave up her name and she chose Camay for the soap and Procter for Procter and Gamble. She had a great sense of humor. She moved in with a friend, also black. Camay had all the personality in the world but she never talked about her dad. We did not know who he was until she got married and we were invited to the wedding at her father's estate in Long Island.

Patricia White, another student, was from Wooster College in Ohio, very WASPish. It was about as big a mix as you can imagine, including a student from India, people who would otherwise never have met. The man from India, for example, had never made a bed in his life (everybody had to do their own cleaning). He was used to servants, and house work was beneath him.

We had a little room up on the third floor of the Thompson Street building where they could do some cooking, but it was not really meal-type cooking. Anyone who lived there had to give four hours a week of community service, and that could be all kinds of things: helping in the church (although that was not pushed at all), working with a political party in the Village, lots of things.

When Danny Novotny finished his internship as a seminary student, Bob Spike came from Queens part-time, except he ended up doing a lot more. Bob and Alice Spike and their son Paul first moved in where the Boyds had lived, in the building at 81 West Third.

During the summer of 1950 we were out west visiting my family, and when we came back the building was gone. It had developed a big bulge overnight and basically collapsed, so it had to be torn down right away. We had to find housing for some of the students and for us, and we found it on the second and third floors of a very nice brownstone on Jane Street. I don't know why these people rented to us. We lived on the third floor and the students lived on the second floor in bunk beds. Bob Newman was in that group.

THE FIRST CHURCH IN URBAN LIFE PROJECT

We had planned to have a summer service project that year. The idea was to bring students from other places in the country to New York to work in the city and to study the work of the church in the city. Howard and Lorry Moody came to run the project.

Howard and I had known each other in Ohio and had worked together on various projects and committees. Howard had chosen to be ordained at Judson earlier that year. When we wanted someone for the summer project, Howard and Lorry were our natural choice, and they loved the city.

This summer program was strictly for Baptists and had nothing to do with the year-round program with NYU students. The Baptist students did their own cooking and had a wonderful time. It was a terribly hot summer. Some of the students ended up sleeping on the fire escape in back of the building.

On several occasions the students went up to Harlem to help serve at one of Father Divine's dinners. People who had nothing would come for a meal, but they would dress up. This was at a time when a lot was happening in Harlem. Father Divine had his angels, white women, who would hand out the food, and they would say "no salt." This was long before people knew that salt was bad for people with heart problems.

That was just one activity the students were involved in. During the day they went to their various jobs to earn money and at night we had discussions and speakers. The students also went to plays and movies.

The Judson Health Center moved out of the building in 1950. Margaret and I moved back into the Student House and Judson took over the whole building. The Spikes moved to the floor above us. We now had a full kitchen and we hired a cook and became more of a co-op.

As time went on with Spike, a few more people were coming to church, but still the largest group that met was the students. Young people who lived in the Village, who had no connection to the house, would also come to the evening meetings.

JUDSON BECOMES INDEPENDENT

About that time, the Judson Council voted to give us a tremendous amount of authority. That was the beginning of Judson's autonomy. When Howard was called in 1956, it was not the Judson Council but the congregation that called him. Checks were still signed at the City Society, but in terms of program, Judson was now on its own.

Margaret and I left in 1952 a month before our daughter Cynthia was born. Around this time the congregation began to withdraw from being a church for the university. This happened gradually as the church reset its priorities. At the end of the 1940s, many veterans had returned to school on the G.I. Bill, and there was a great need for student housing. In later years, students were better off financially and were not necessarily looking for cheap housing and a commitment to do community work. There never was a time when a church committee said: "Now the work with students is over." It was a natural transition. Students still lived in the house, but it was no longer a program of the church. Still later, in the 1960s, the students moved out altogether and artists moved in.

DEAN AND MARGARET WRIGHT
live in Montclair, New Jersey.

Alice Spike

Alice Spike is the widow of Robert Spike, who was senior minister at
Judson Memorial Church from 1949 to 1955. _____

When exactly did you live at Judson House?

From mid-1949 to some time in 1955. Then we moved to 235
East 18th Street (Grace House).

Did you live on Thompson Street or 81 West Third?

We lived at 81 West Third until it was condemned in 1950. Then
we moved to 237 Thompson Street.

Who else lived in the building while you were there?

Betty and Dick Murphy lived below us at 81. We were on the
first floor. Dean and Margaret Wright were on the top floor.

At Thompson Street we were on the second floor, the Wrights
were on the first floor, the Murphys on the ground floor. Students
lived on the top floor. Verne Henderson, an associate minister at Judson, was there toward the end of our stay.

*Do you remember people from the congregation? Would you re-
member some of their names?*

Evelyn and Bob Poole. Evelyn was Bob's secretary. Bob Poole
played Santa for the children every Christmas. Doris Todd was a
great member, and Miriam Corbett was very active, too.

Do you remember any of the students by name?

Johnny Mui (he liked raw meat). Omar. Camay Procter. She was
the daughter of Cab Calloway, a very funny and talented girl. Pat
White, a very nice girl and active in the church. Dick Murphy was
studying medicine; he and Betty were raising the first few of their
five little girls.

Was your son John born while you lived there?

Yes. He was born at New York Women's Infirmary on November 8, 1951. The great distances we had to walk to the supermarket and Paul's school were memorable. Paul started school in September 1951 at Saint Luke's School. It was about a mile away and a long push with a baby carriage after John came. Paul was four and could not go alone nor come home alone.

The people who lived around us worked or went to school and worked. So we did not have a stream of visitors but had a life much like other city residents.

Dean Wright was co-pastor and minister to students. He was excellent in that work, and Dean and Bob were a great team.

Do you remember any irritating peculiarities of the building, such as leaky faucets, poor plumbing, or inadequate heating system?

When we put Paul to bed, at Third Street, we overdressed him as the heat went off at 11 p.m. This too hot/too cold system resulted in pneumonia at age two and again at age four, when we were on Thompson Street.

Do you remember any incidents you can laugh about now but were not so funny when they took place?

NO. We laughed at everything that would ever seem funny. Morale was very high.

Please add anything else you think may be interesting.

We occasionally saw famous people in ordinary places. One day during the Washington Square Outdoor Art Show I looked out the second-story window and saw Steve Allen and Jayne Meadows looking at the paintings below. A theater group at Judson put on a play in the church sanctuary. One of the actors was Sidney Poitier. The press corps was less numerous and less obnoxious then. At that time New Yorkers respected the privacy of celebrities.

One of Bob's greatest interests was a program of recreation for young people from the neighborhood. They were mostly Italian and Catholic. Many had strayed from ideal behavior at the Catholic programs and had been thrown out. Verne Henderson directed programs of basketball in the church gym, did drug counseling in his rooms, and took kids camping in upstate New York. He was young and handsome, and the kids liked his programs. Nearby merchants were thrilled and supportive.

Margaret Wright was and is a very fine singer. She sang at church services and special occasions, a tremendous contribution. She also had an excellent career. When she was on television, Judson watched every show. When she had a solo on stage, we all went to opening night. We were spellbound and will never forget her in *As You Like It*. Katherine Hepburn was also in the cast.

Many students participated in church programs and they were always welcome. There was no line between church and students. The staff cared about all of them and were very proud of them.

ALICE SPIKE
lives in El Paso, Texas.

Paul Spike

Paul Spike, a son of Robert Spike, wrote the following letter in October 1976 on the occasion of Howard Moody's twentieth anniversary as senior minister at Judson Memorial Church. It is one of several letters exchanged between Paul and Robert Newman. Bob Newman's letter on the same occasion is included in the section on "The Judson Student House." Both letters are reprinted here by permission of Paul Spike and Robert Newman. ⎯⎯⎯⎯⎯⎯⎯

My first memory of Judson is the way it used to taste: a musty, plaster-laced, damp grit somewhere up on the back of my tongue. I must have consumed several pounds of Judson as I learned to walk on those linoleum floors, to roll down the marble steps on West 4th Street and slide down the banisters inside the lobby. Then I remember the way the gym used to smell on Friday afternoons in the winter after the NYU basketball team finished a week of practice. What was basketball? Whatever, it smelled pretty lousy. Next I remember the view from our apartment on the second floor of the Student House. Especially Frank's barber shop on the other side of Thompson Street which was always full of well-dressed Italian gentlemen who often arrived in Cadillacs which they left double-parked in the middle of the street. They never seemed to get any tickets. And the green shanty on the corner of Thompson and West 3rd where an old man sold the best lemon ice in the Village. Next door was the strip joint with its pictures of girls who seemed to have silver shoelaces sprouting out of their breasts. I think it was my mother who told me that these silver shoelaces were called "pasties" and were New York City laws. The strip joint didn't really open until long after my bedtime. But on a hot summer afternoon I would pass by its open door, bound for a lemon ice, and the stale beer fumes would make me dizzy on the sidewalk.

MACARTHUR AND MCCARTHY

I remember watching General MacArthur's parade arrive in Washington Square from the roof of the Student House. None of us on the roof were supposed to cheer. And I have a weird memory of waking up at 5:30 a.m. and turning on the television thinking I was going to see another Department of Agriculture filmstrip on the Modern Farmer. Instead I got a fuzzy picture of plumes and sashes and swords. Then this enormous diamond crown was lowered onto some girl's head: Queen Elizabeth. There was the night when I wasn't allowed to stay up with my parents and their friends to drink beer and watch Adlai Stevenson win the election. I didn't want to miss all the fun. In the morning, I knew I hadn't. Later there was somebody named McCarthy on television every afternoon—was he the same guy we'd watched from the roof?—who didn't seem to cheer my parents up at all. I didn't begin to fathom McCarthy, but I knew for sure that Ike was a jerk. And all my teachers at St. Luke's knew I knew it too.

STICKY BUNS AND FRIED BOLOGNA

The Student House had a cook named Betty who was the color of worn cordovan and very nice. She cooked delicious sticky buns but my favorite was her pineapple upside-down cake. We didn't eat with the students but upstairs in our apartment. My mother was a good cook and I especially liked her fried bologna which we were allowed to have for both lunch and dinner. On Sundays my father would cook western omelets, after we got back from church. Except for one Sunday every month which was "pot luck": everybody in the congregation would bring a macaroni casserole or some cold cuts and we'd eat off paper plates in the back under the balcony. The congregation in those days was around forty persons, quite an improvement from the eight or nine persons who used to come when we first arrived.

I was one of the few kids around Judson in those days. Later more families started to join and at times there was even a Sunday school, but it never lasted very long. The kids were too many different ages, too snotty, and volunteer teachers were not all that easy to find. I remember Doris Todd as a very fine Sunday school teacher who used to let us run around in the gym with a basketball that we didn't know what to do with and couldn't have if we had.

A FUNNY SERMON

At one time, for a few months, there were two sisters who used to come to church every Sunday although their parents never attended. I was captivated by the elder sister, she was about nine (I was six). We used to sit together in the front pew during the service. I only remember because of one morning when my father began his sermon with a joke. It must have been a fairly good joke because the entire congregation went a little haywire for several minutes, laughing like they were at a party. I could tell that this response had pleased my father. (It had also impressed my girlfriend.) Unfortunately, I concluded this was the best way to show one's appreciation for a good sermon. As my father tried to wind down from his opening joke into the relevancies of that morning's text, each time he paused at the end of a sentence, the silence was filled with the hysterical guffawing of his son. I hadn't gotten the first joke, though I had laughed like hell. There was no reason to think I should be getting all these other jokes as well.

My father didn't seem to notice but he did cut his sermon short and announced the next hymn. As the first strains of whatever it was began to rise in a crescendo of hungover voices, my father stepped out of the pulpit and, leading the singing, came forward until he was standing above me. "Shut up!" he hissed. I have never been so surprised in my life. I think he was afraid I was going to whoop right through all the prayers.

BUMS IN BROOKS BROTHERS SUITS

My father's office was a good place to visit after school, if the door was open. If it was shut, it meant he was working, "counseling" it was called. I would wait outside and talk to his secretary, Evelyn Poole. Her husband Bob was actually Santa Claus and visited the Student House every Christmas Eve. When my father's door eventually opened, I would hurry inside and waste no time suggesting that what he really wanted was a Good Humor Toasted Almond bar.

He usually agreed and would send me into the park with enough money for two. But sometimes my own panhandling would be interrupted by the appearance of a shabby representative of the Bowery. Standing in the doorway to my father's office, these old men would begin to whimper, shuffle their feet, and mumble what was left of their stories. I doubt if it has changed much even today. My father would listen and then take them back into a room which was full of old clothes. Donated by a previous generation of wealthy Washington Square Baptists, there were piles of worn Brooks Brothers suits and thick overcoats from Saks, many of them in perfect condition. In fact, my father always wore an overcoat selected from this pile. For years, Judson dressed the bums on the Bowery in true Madison Avenue style.

The Judson Youth Center was the headquarters for the toughest, craziest kids in the Village. My father spent a good many of his mornings down at the Centre Street courts testifying about their characters and arranging their bails. In return, these kids taught me how to make a proper fist and how to shinny up No-Parking signs. I passed this second lesson on to my brother John, who was so good at it he couldn't pass a No-Parking sign without immediately climbing it to the very top. Unfortunately, it took him a little longer to master the art of climbing down. I remember some anxious family scenes with my brother, barely three, growing panicky and tearful clinging to his No-Parking sign above my mother's outstretched hands.

I remember the Rouault exhibition which [Robert] Newman and my father organized in the church. They had ripped out all the pews and built plywood and plasterboard stands to display the somber prints. A television crew arrived looking for filler for that evening's news and later I was absolutely amazed to see my father's head growing inside the lighted box as he told the interviewer that, no, he saw nothing "sacrilegious" about transforming a church into an art gallery. As I recall, there was some anxiety in our living room that evening as to whether or not the Baptist City Mission Board would agree.

Finally, I have a vision of my own room in our apartment on the second floor of the Student House. It had once been a dentist's office in the old Judson Clinic and the floor still had the fittings for the dentist's chair which made it spooky enough. But then I remember all the nights I lay in the dark listening to the nightmare sirens and the squealing tires and the voices of angry drunks on West 3rd Street. And all the nights I spent trying to catch my breath as my father held my head over the hot steam of the vaporizer. I had pneumonia four times in the Student House; twice they had to call an ambulance and take me to St. Vincent's in the middle of the night. And I remember bad dreams about someone trying to stick a bomb under our apartment door, about prowlers outside my window on the fire escape, about hypodermic needles wrapped up in an old rag and jammed behind a radiator in the church. I don't think I could say that I had a happy childhood at Judson. For one thing, there were hardly any other children and all my friends were, like Newman, many years older than me. We were always poor; everyone was. That didn't bother me, but it bothered my parents, and *then* it bothered me. I was happiest when I was surrounded by adults, when people were drinking and laughing and flirting, like the time the entire congregation (about 25 people) got together to paint the church and everyone got loaded on gin and Tom Collins mix. I still remember how good that awful sour Collins mix tasted and how I understood that such a taste was incredibly special and bound to make you giddy. Little did I know that some of my friends that afternoon were soon to be described as "beatniks" in *Time* magazine. Little did I understand that it was gin, and not Collins mix, which made everyone else act silly. So little did I comprehend that I actually thought I was an adult, too, not a child. Twenty years later, it makes me sad.

PAUL SPIKE
is a writer and makes his home in London.

Norman O. Keim

Norman Keim worked as a minister to students at Judson from 1955 to 1958.

W hen I came to work at Judson Memorial Church, the Student House was a coed co-op of some thirty-five students, of whom about one-third were overseas students. Half were undergraduate, half graduate students. They represented all the schools in the metropolitan area.

The students were expected to help in the kitchen and in the maintenance of the house. If the walls of the hallways are still green, it is from a paint party, with the paint contributed by a kind contractor.

We had a Sunday evening forum where we would have distinguished professors and guests from the community. Probably the most famous guest we had was Pete Seeger, who came down to us hopping mad after his afternoon concert at the Museum of Natural History was canceled at the last minute because of his leftist leanings. He sang for us until the wee hours of the morning.

WINTER STUDENTS, SUMMER STUDENTS

The 1950s were an exciting time. We had a couple of Gold Coast students in the house, and when the Gold Coast achieved its independence in 1956 we had a grand banquet of goat meat and toasted the Queen. The African students brought down their drums from Columbia, and we had a great demonstration of "talking drums." There was also the war between Israel and Egypt in 1956. We had both Arab and Jewish students in the house, and the war led to lengthy debates.

Probably the most famous student living in the house at the time was Eva Hesse, who went on to become quite a cult figure in art circles. Not so long ago a friend sent me an article from the London *Times,* which reported that one of Eva's sculptures in an auction was valued at between $400,000 and $600,000. We used to have her art hanging all over the house. Eva died very young from a brain tumor.

There were at least three marriages that came out of the house. The only couple I have kept in touch with over the years are Sally Lem and Bob Simon. They now live in County Clare, Ireland. We visited them in their house that they built right on the ocean. He is a retired psychologist.

During the summer we had a different group of students living in the house. They came to New York to attend the Church in Urban Life program. During the day they held jobs in the city, and at night and on weekends we had distinguished people coming to speak to the students: politicians, union organizers, artists. One name that comes to mind is Gus Tyler of the ILGWU. Bill Rogers, campus minister at the University of Georgia, was leader one summer; during another summer it was David Mitchell from Trinidad, graduate student at Union Theological Seminary. They lived with their families in the corner basement apartment off the kitchen.

One night we had Art Blakey, the jazz drummer, playing for young people in the gymnasium. As we were cleaning up, Thelonious Monk walked in, and we all went over to the Student House for a couple of beers. We had a jazz symposium at the church and had our planning meetings in the lounge. The panelists were Marshall Stearns, Rudi Blesch, and the jazz pastor at Saint Peter's Lutheran Church.

In my student work I worked closely with the NYU Law School. We were able to establish the Clarence D. Ashley Lectures in Law and Theology. Again, we had some of our planning meetings in the lounge. Our first lecturer was Bishop James Pike, and during the second year we invited Paul Ramsey of Princeton University. His Judson lectures provided two chapters in his book *Nine Modern Moralists*. William Stringfellow was a great help in getting that lectureship established.

The lots across Thompson Street were then tennis courts, and on the corner of Third Street was a soda fountain that apparently was a drug trafficking point. The police used the bathroom at the Student House as a surveillance point and would bring in young people to frisk them in our hallway.

As director of the Student House I was on a committee of the Protestant Council of directors of Protestant residences in the city. We once had a meeting at the United Nations, where Eleanor Roosevelt addressed us. Mrs. Roosevelt, of course, knew Judson well. She lived right across the park, and during the 1956 presidential campaign she and Tallulah Bankhead addressed a political rally in the church.

The *Village Voice* of July 31, 1957, described that year's Urban Life Project as "an unusual group to find gathered in a church." We *were* pretty radical, trying to learn from jazz and Bishop Pike how to make Christianity relevant to urban dwellers.

NORMAN KEIM
lives in Syracuse, New York, where he is chaplain at Syracuse University.

Bernard D. Mayes

Bernard Mayes was director of the Judson Student House from 1958 to 1960.

I n 1958 Robert Spike and Robert Newman returned to New York from shooting material for a film about experimental parishes in Great Britain. They had visited Leeds, where I was working as an Anglican priest in the "house church" movement. One of the results of their visit was that Howard Moody and the Judson Board invited me to be the director of the Student House. I had never been to the United States, and the visit changed my life and that of many others.

I arrived on Labor Day. After twenty-seven years in a Britain depleted first by depression and then war and burdened with its crippling class structure and its homophobia, racism, and antisemitism, New York presented me with an entirely new world, splendid, vigorous, open. Within days of my arrival, the *Village Voice* interviewed me and asked me to write about my first impressions of America. The editor told me he agreed with Howard that things were going wrong, and he was interested in my objective view of things. These were things I still knew nothing about, and my enthusiastic article on behalf of America was inevitably rejected.

STUDENTS, FAITHS, SEXES

At the Student House I found a curious collection of undergraduate students, most attending New York University. They represented many faiths and several sexes. One student appeared to be a princess from India. She refused even to talk to another Indian student because he was of a lower caste and belabored me for doing so; that I was the director seemed to her to reinforce her complaints. Homesick for her entourage, she would commandeer the phonograph, upon which she would play never-ending Indian ragas. For this she would wear a purple and green sari shot with silver while sitting cross-legged on a silk cushion.

Another student was an angry, uncooperative Jewish atheist with whom I had endless arguments while we both stood in the corridor clutching plastic glasses of wine. Our intellectual positions were both so convincing that in the end we seemed to have exchanged them—he for Christianity and I for Judaism.

There was also a white student who was very much in love with an African-American woman whom he was determined to marry, despite the times. I saw nothing wrong with this and was surprised to learn that everyone feared for their safety. The woman had a friend who was keen to show me the real world, and together we drove to Washington, D.C., only to discover that, because my companion was black, none of the better restaurants would let us through their doors. I was appalled and demanded entrance. She kept pulling me away. "It's I who will be punished, not you," she told me, "anyway, I am hungry and I want dinner not the police."

My apartment in the house consisted of a couple of large rooms painted blood orange. It was no doubt this repellent color, combined with the fact that the walls contained large bulges suggestive of buried bodies, that had caused the rooms to be known as the one-time bedroom of Edgar Allen Poe. It was here, in the midst of the Village fleshpots, that I was able to entertain the first gay friends and lovers of my life. When Howard learned about it, he waxed philosophical. "Why should I prevent you from making love in church property," he said, "when we make love in it, too?" In those days, that was something, and it showed how revolutionary Judson was, as well as what a great leader Howard had become.

LEARNING AMERICAN VALUES

Unexpectedly, it was food rather than love affairs that occupied the minds of most students. They seemed able to eat anything and everything at all times. We had a common refrigerator into which they stuffed open cans, open bags, and open bottles. People took whatever they wanted. Some of the cans looked so poisonously old that I feared for my charges' health, and I put up a notice "Open cans must not be left to rot." The following morning I found that someone had scrawled a swastika on the message. Americans, I was told, object to words like "must." Even in matters of life and death, one should say "please." It was another lesson in American values. Judson had broken through my priggish, prudish upbringing and was determined to teach me about life as it was meant to be lived in the Village.

Taking my cue on Halloween, I went all the way and dressed in full but unconventional drag. I went as a witch, complete with broomstick. Another Judsonite joined me as a six-foot-two *femme fatale*. Together we toured the Village, stopping traffic. On returning to the house, I was met by our Indian princess, who demanded penance by way of two hours of ragas.

SNOW AND THE PARK

One New Year's morning, I woke up to a strange silence that seemed to have descended upon the house and the streets alike. On getting up, I found that I was unable to open the front door to Thompson Street: It was blocked by two feet of snow. Manhattan had become a fairyland decorated in a brilliant white blanket that shimmered beneath a sky as blue as a cornflower. What cars had been left out could be detected only by the humps in a snowfield that stretched way up Fifth Avenue from one side of the street to another. After I had pushed the door open wide enough to get out, it was only to be half buried in a sparkling drift (the wind blows around that corner!). Beautiful though the winter scene was and seemingly ideal for snowballs, not a soul was outside and I soon realized why. After no more than 100 yards up Fifth Avenue, I was hiding in doorways, my face frozen solid. The temperature was around zero. Snowballs were out of the question. I staggered back to the house, where everyone was gathered around the burping steam radiators. Later that day we held a dance in the kitchen.

In the spring of 1960 Governor Nelson Rockefeller, aided and abetted by the local Residents' Council, was planning the takeover of Washington Square Park by private developers. Accordingly, the students and I quickly found ourselves caught up in a demonstration to "Free the Square." We were met by riot police armed with helmets and truncheons. It was a hint of the sixties to come. The press took pictures of us being manhandled. But we won, and the park has been free ever since.

A TRIP TO THE SOUTH

At some point, the Judson Board arranged for me to reconnoiter the South. I was told that the Judson congregation was eager to learn what was happening on the frontier. Because I was in New York, the BBC had invited me to report back to America, and accordingly I broadcast to Britain every week. If I was going south, why not begin by interviewing the new explorers of outer space being trained in Virginia? That was certainly a new frontier. After that, I could move on to Koinonia Farm in Americus, Georgia, and interview the Jordans, who were running the only racially integrated farm in the United States. The night before I left, Judson's students bought me my first American pizza and wished me luck. Some thought I would never return.

At Langley Field in Virginia, where America's first astronauts were training, I was put inside a space suit, whirled around in a centrifuge, and strapped inside the very space capsule itself. I even interviewed Gus Grissom (in the shower of all places), the astronaut who was later burned to death. The Cold War was well on its way and, naive as I was, even I could see that space itself might become the battlefield of the future. It was a heady experience with all the world breathlessly looking on.

But the Jordans (pronounced Jerdans) were also risking their lives. Americus is a small town famous for its nut trees. It sits in the midst of dry Georgian plains surrounded by nut orchards and hay fields. I was met by the patriarch of Koinonia Farm, Clarence Jordan, who warned me, with much shaking of the head, that regularly every week, the farm buildings were invaded by the Klan, whose trucks drove around the farm buildings firing shotguns through the windows. I could hardly believe such a wildly western story. To an Englishman, the Ku Klux Klan seemed more an American throwback than a force to be reckoned with. As I was to learn, the fact that blacks and whites all worked and dined together at Koinonia Farm made it a very dangerous place to be.

At the Jordans' invitation, I joined the work force, picking and packing pecans (a nut I had never seen before). I made friends with the pickers, black and white, and had long discussions about the strange southern states. At night we all dined together. One evening we could hear in the distance a honking of horns accompanied by raucous shouts and war-whoops. I thought it must be a party some-where, but as if in a World War II raid, everyone in the room dived under the tables. Jordan pulled me down with him even as into the farm area came trucks, roaring and skidding around the farm build-ings, shotguns exploding, glass smashing, the shouts and whoops suddenly near and terrifying. Under the tables, children and some women were crying with terror while all the menfolk looked hag-gard and somewhat sheepish but also furious at wanting to do some-thing but fearing to be lynched. Then the trucks roared away, and we climbed back to our meal.

Clarence Jordan had warned me not to go near the local Baptist church because it was the Klan's headquarters, and their welcome was unlikely to be warm. Not believing that self-respecting Baptists could actually be members of the Ku Klux Klan, I took off on a blaz-ing hot Sunday morning for the worship service at the pretty salt-box church surrounded by a white picket fence.

FANS AND BATS

Inside the little wooden building the air was stifling, but the long white pews of pine and cedar gave off a warm, friendly scent. The congregation was clearly a farm crowd. The men were tall or round, dressed in well-worn dark suits, their faces lined and solemn. The women were either large or thin, with old-fashioned hats of straw wrapped in muslin. Throughout the service everyone fanned them-selves with wooden Egyptian-style corrugated fans decorated with advertisements from the local undertaker. The pastor, surrounded by his deacons and solemnly robed in puritan black and white, deliv-ered a Bible-thumping sermon in which we were all threatened with hell fire and damnation if we did not mend our ways. After this, suit-ably chastened, we sang several choruses of "Washed in the Blood of the Lamb." The pastor then delivered a blessing and left the church, standing by the front door to greet his congregation.

As we rose to leave, I was quickly surrounded by the endlessly fluttering fans and by broad welcoming smiles: Who was I? Where did I come from? They were all very eager to know. But I had no sooner told them that I was staying at Koinonia Farm than the smiles turned to stone and the gestures of welcome were withdrawn. In seconds, the church had emptied, leaving me alone. Outside I could hear murmuring and raised voices. Collecting my recording equipment, I slowly made my way past the empty pews and down the aisle to the door. Hot sunlight streamed through it as if from an open oven.

Outside waiting for me stood the deacons, not in their robes but in open-necked shirts with the sleeves rolled up: six large men each grasping a heavy axe handle. A shrill woman's voice from somewhere behind them cried out, "Go awn, Elmer, yew show im, yew show im!" One of the deacons moved close to me, his head a good deal higher than mine. He lifted his axe handle. The others moved in, their weapons also now coming up at the ready. Their leader's large face was blotchy and contorted. My knees shook. I was clearly about to be bashed to bloody pulp, an experience Judson had ill prepared me for. He snarled at me that I was a "nigger lover" and a "dirty Commie" and must now "take what's coming." I could see the pastor, sitting on the gate swinging his legs. In a moment's inspiration, I shouted to him. It saved my skin. Reluctantly he came over, his deacons making way. I was asked, ordered in fact, to come to his house. He talked for an hour as he explained to me why "niggers don't go to heaven" and therefore should be kept separate. I was then shown the door.

As I tottered toward my car, feeling rather as if I had been scalped, another vehicle swooped in from the road and squealed to a stop behind mine. It was the local sheriff. He walked toward me, fat, smooth-faced, and slow, gun at the ready. He had heard, he said, and I still cannot believe this, that I had arrived from a "Commie submarine off the coast," and unless I went back to where I belonged he would run me in. Not knowing how to argue with such misinformation, I was in no mood to take on the Georgian police force. I hastened back to Koinonia and then drove back to the comparative safety of Judson House.

Back at the house I told them my story. It was scarcely believed. Were things down there really as bad as all that? The Judson congregation seemed disappointed. Perhaps they had hoped for a martyr's death, or was it that their worst fears were confirmed?

The Indian princess wanted to console me. She was scornful of America. There was no racism in India, she told me. She then asked me if I would like to meet Pandit Nehru, who had arrived in New York on a visit to the United Nations. Of course I accepted, and soon a little party of students and I were sitting cross-legged on a carpeted floor while the great man told us of India's problems. He was glad, he said, to see Indian students in New York but he pleaded with them to return to their homeland once their studies were finished. Later I asked him whether he thought they would take up the challenge. "No," he told me sadly, "once they have tasted of America, they can think of nothing else."

THE EARLY 1960S—THE CALM BEFORE THE STORM

I found the Student House to be curiously unpolitical. Apart from our battle of what we considered "our" park, the students seemed apathetic. But then we learned that a presidential candidate was coming to town. The park was crowded. No one could tell us where the candidate, whoever it was, would speak. Surely not the fountain! Then, suddenly a tall figure moved onto the balcony of the new university union building right next to the house. It took us only a few moments to realize it was John Kennedy. Taller and younger than the politicians we were used to, with a face that was splendidly tanned, he looked immensely healthy and rich. His Boston accent echoed over the hundreds of people below him, many of whom were hanging on every word. Most of the women students clutched each other in ecstasy, and even the men looked unusually respectful. Was the New Age he promised right around the corner? It seemed that way.

So it had long seemed at Judson. Sitting on the balcony at Judson Church or in the gymnasium watching local boys being taught how to box, visiting with local artists intent on a new art form called "Happenings," I would talk with other Judsonites as well as students. Whatever the reason behind Judson's Student House, it was clearly in the midst of a growing American maelstrom. Living there was unsettling. The place had no rules, no preconceived expectations, or it seemed to have none. It was a sanctuary for explorers coming in out of the cold. But unknown to us, its tiny rooms were incubators from which the new youth of America would soon erupt. It was the quiet time before the storm.

In 1990, **BERNARD MAYES** abandoned Christianity. He is currently an academic dean in the University of Virginia and Fellow of Brown College.

Beverly Waite

Beverly Waite was the manager of Judson House from 1959 to 1968. _____

In 1959 my husband, Ralph, left his ministry in Garden City, New York, to become an actor. He talked with Howard Moody about the job replacing Betty Murphy as manager of Judson Student House. Howard interviewed me, and I got the job I wasn't looking for. We moved our three little girls and all our belongings to what would be our home for the next nine years.

Those years were intense in every way. Greenwich Village in the sixties was "happening." I made the acquaintance of more foreign students than I can remember and made many close friends. We had great times partying in the Lounge. I think of Chuck Gordone and Jennie Franklin calling my white-girl twist "cute." My girls produced several plays, graciously attended by our residents.

Our oldest daughter, Sharon, developed leukemia and died in 1964. I'll never forget Howard Moody's supportive presence during her illness and after her death, nor the truly memorable memorial he orchestrated for her. Howard read a letter Sharon had written to her dear friend Jennie Franklin, who was serving in Mississippi that terrible summer.

Ralph and I separated shortly after that. There was a great deal of pain during those years but also much joy and laughter. When I think of laughter, I think of Julie Kurnitz, Paul Richter, Jack Matlaga, and of course Jennie. I remember the blackout of 1965. Returning from my girls' dance class, I found that the only lights in the Village were coming from my apartment. Jack Matlaga had collected every candle in the house and was holding a dinner party there.

I remember the march on Washington in 1963 with Susan Stern Moore, when we were part of the throng that heard Dr. King's famous speech. I remember the snow storm that turned New York into a village of light, with nothing moving but snowballs and happy people. I remember the sickness in my gut over the assassinations of Jack and Robert Kennedy, Dr. King, Malcolm X.

I remember with joy Ed Brewer's taking Sharon to see the Nutcracker. A few years later, Kathleen and Suzanne were dancing the Nutcracker, which was also one of my great joys.

I remember Jon Hendricks's demonstration for peace in the garden when I totally freaked out as he started to cut a limb from our only tree. The crowd thought I was part of the show.

I remember Lee Guilliatt's unforgettable rendition of "Don't Think Twice" and Al Carmines's beautiful artistry.

I remember rats in the subbasement and charming inspectors out of citations.

I missed a lot of the Judson experience because I was extremely busy with my personal life. But I did attend a memorial for Lenny Bruce and a happening in the sanctuary when green paint was thrown on someone. In the Student House I became involved in a suicide attempt, Haitian guns hidden under a bed, a benefit for one of Harry Koutoukas's creations, a TV crew invading my living room for a segment of a report on Judson Church. I remember Carman Moore chasing a thief who was making off with the possessions of one of the students. We entertained the Living Theater at the Student House. There is nothing like expanding the mind, and Judson House certainly encouraged that.

During my final year, in 1969, I was on the staff of the runaway program. Under Art Levin's benevolent direction I worked with Michael Parker, John Maige, Bob Lamberton, and Nancy Katchel to help redirect the messed-up lives of the scores of teenage runaways. From them I learned a great deal about living honestly and courageously. I have a special thanks in my heart for Mike Parker, who helped me to see things differently.

During a time of spiritual confusion, my years at Judson House helped me to see what in the world God was doing.

BEVERLY WAITE
lives in Hawaii.

Joseph and Judy Pickle

Joe and Judy Pickle lived at Judson House from 1959 to 1960 while Joe was an assistant minister in charge of students. _____

I n the summer of 1959 we came to New York City after one year of marriage with a sense of adventure, excited to be living in Greenwich Village, looking forward to cultural lights, and fascinated by the chance to work in an "experimental church." I had sought the opportunity to work with Howard Moody because I had known him earlier through the Baptist Student Movement, and we knew of Judson as a model of a vital engagement of the church with urban life. I had been assigned as an intern assistant minister to Judson Church.

The internship was part of my ministerial program at the University of Chicago. Howard interviewed us in Chicago, fed our growing enthusiasm, and left us puzzled by his question, "How can you stand it here? It is so quiet." We caught on after spending July and August in his house on East 18th Street, and by September we were more prepared for the noises of the Village.

THE CHURCH IN URBAN LIFE

That summer we got acquainted with Judson House by sitting in with the Church in Urban Life Program. We saw what a residential teaching center in the middle of the Village could mean to students trying to understand what life in the city was really about and what Christian service in the city might involve. The lively conversation, fascinating visitors from many walks of life and cultures, and friendships nurtured by common experience provided models for what we attempted during the next academic year.

Judson House had a main entrance on Thompson Street leading up a couple of stairs to the first floor, with an apartment, recently taken by associate minister Bernard (Bud) Scott and his wife, Gisela, on the right. There were stairways to the basement and to the second and third floors straight ahead, and a hallway to the left leading past two small rooms to our apartment. In the basement, at the south end under our apartment, was a kitchen with tables and benches for up to twenty-four people, a room with coin-operated washer and dryer, and, under the Scotts' apartment, a lounge where most of our discussions and meetings were held. Next to the lounge was a small area that had become the Judson Gallery. Both the gallery and the kitchen had outside entrances from stairs down the Thompson Street sidewalk.

Our students lived in small rooms on the upper two floors: women on the second, along with Betty Murphy, the church's business manager, and her family; and men on the third. We had that year only about eighteen students, half of whom were international students. Most studied at New York University and a few attended Cooper Union or the New School for Social Research. A few were actively interested in Judson Church, but most students lived at Judson House because of the low cost, fewer dorm restrictions, and interesting housemates. They were not very close as a group, but we all got to like each other.

My internship included several specific responsibilities. As resident director of Judson House, I was to be a counselor to the students, deal with crises, and interpret what the Judson community was all about. As part of that work I was to serve as a member of the interfaith campus ministry at NYU. I was also to assist Howard Moody and Bud Scott, sharing some preaching duties and sit in on committees.

Everything we did at Judson taught us more than we could fully understand at the time. We learned from the congregation, from friends outside the congregation, from the city, from Howard especially. We learned about politics, art, theology, life, and tragedy. We learned about ourselves and what it meant to be the Church. We learned about sin (indirectly?) and about grace (directly). We were truly at home. Any other church experience we have had since then has had to meet a nearly impossible standard.

LIFE AT JUDSON HOUSE HAS ITS CHALLENGES

Coming to Judson was great for me, but it was harder on Judy. Enthusiastic as she was, moving meant giving up her teaching position in Chicago and applying for a one-year appointment near the city.

Judy found a job teaching at the Woodmere Academy out on Long Island. Her hours and mine did not mesh. Judy had to get up early in the morning to catch a train on the Long Island line out to Woodmere. That meant she had to be up and out of our apartment no later than 6:30 a.m. Unfortunately, hot water did not come on at Judson House until 7:00 a.m. So I got up before 6:00 each morning, boiled water for her to wash, made breakfast, helped her get her stuff together and out the door. Then I went back to bed!

My day did not really begin until about noon. Students might be up and about, but if so they were on their way to class or work. The time for meeting with them was usually around supper time and into the evening. And so my workday continued till midnight or later. Judy, on the other hand, came home tired and needed to grade papers and prepare for the next day. We recovered on the weekends. Still, at times we felt like ships passing in the night.

Not that we had much passing room. Our apartment consisted of one room with ominously sagging plaster walls held up by burlap "wallpaper" and a Castro convertible. An opaque window with metal grillwork (protection from burglars?) faced onto Thompson Street. It was our only source of cross-ventilation in hot weather. The window was just above the heads of passing pedestrians and people could not really look in, but we could hear them talk as they passed. There was a tiny little kitchen behind a wall on the opposite side of the room. It had a two-burner plate, a sink, and a refrigerator, enough room to stand, and a small window onto West Third Street. Most of our really fancy cooking was done in an electric skillet. We did have a huge bathroom, bigger than many of the students' rooms. It had a window with clear glass looking out on the Judson garden.

It wasn't much of a garden, but everybody thought, "Someday we will have a garden." Nothing much came of it while we were there, but even so, it had a tree. There was room to park a car, but in those days nobody had a car.

ROACHES AND RATS

The rhythms of Judson House as a student residence were set partly by the academic calendar, partly by the disappearance of most students on the weekends, and partly by kitchen work and maintenance. At first, we hesitated to report the appearance of cockroaches (surely, we haven't been lax about cleaning?). When Howard and others stopped laughing at our midwestern naïveté, we learned why we saw so many cockroaches in the middle of the week: Wednesday was spraying day. Rats were not often seen on our floor, but they appeared regularly around the kitchen. One of the women students from Queens had a practical New Yorker's approach to such vermin. One day, she was sitting in the kitchen happily talking with a handsome young resident from Spain on whom she had an obvious crush, when she saw a large rat run past. She yelled for the young man to bring a large pan of water to a boil. She found a broom and began to chase the rat. When she had finally cornered the rat in the laundry room, she told him to bring the pan of hot water, with which she quickly doused the rat. The tenderhearted young man was appalled. The woman lost the boyfriend but she did get the rat.

For us, life in the Village centered on Washington Square and the larger university area. We got to know the coffeehouses, the folk music clubs, and something of the predominantly Italian neighborhood south of Judson. We remember restaurants where you could bring in Coke specials (red wine in Coke bottles) and play bocce in the back. But it was the gauntlet of bars and strip joints on West Third that reminded us we were in the big city. Judy remembers one poster advertising the delights within—a scantily clad woman with flaming red hair named Tempest Storm.

NAKED WOMEN!

One night, while Judy's parents were visiting us from Chicago, her mother heard a loud voice from the street yelling "Wow! Naked Women!" My mother-in-law sat bolt-upright in our Castro convertible (Judy and I were sleeping in a small storage room) and quickly covered herself with a sheet, thinking the voice was referring to her! Judy's parents weren't so sure about our seedy lifestyle.

In spite of roving teen gangs, the Mafia, and pervasive heroin, we felt safe on the streets. We had a sense of the beat culture. Cramped little bookstores were everywhere. Poetry was spoken openly on the streets. Poets and painters and playwrights and musicians were everywhere.

But the heart of our life at Judson House was the Judson Church community. We were taken in immediately as family; we had never felt so at home in a church. And what a church it was—people who loved to spend time together, share each other's causes, argue. For us, it was a transforming experience to be intimately involved in the life of an intensely engaged, intellectually vital, passionately committed congregation.

HARVEY COX AND FATHER DIVINE

The style of my work with the residents of Judson House was set by the ethos of the church. Programming was minimal and fairly informal, and emphasized conversation and discussion of current topics, but mostly hanging out. Sometimes we brought in interesting speakers to give talks in the lounge on intriguing issues. I remember in particular Amon Hennessy from the *Catholic Worker,* Harvey Cox, Peter Berger, and Dan Wakefield.

What we did teach a lot was existential theology. We saw films filled with angst and pathos (Ingmar Bergman) and talked into the wee hours. I did little formal Bible study. This was based partly on a realistic sense of who the students were and partly on my growing resistance to fundamentalism. (I remember being deeply shocked and offended when one of the students in the Church and Urban Life program had found a job selling expensive Bibles to poor people who were to be persuaded that they absolutely had to have beautiful Bibles.) But mainly, my thinking was informed by the thoughtful theology of engagement that Howard Moody embodied and that was the Judson ethos.

In the summer of 1960 Judy and I directed the Church and Urban Life program, building on our internship experience. Now we were the old hands. The project gave us an opportunity to take students to other churches and community centers; to deal with students as they sought employment in the city; and to learn and share the resources of the city. We took trips to a mental hospital on Long Island, to Riker's Island, and even to Father Divine's center (called a "heaven") in East Harlem, where we were well fed and inspired by the no longer physically present Father and Mother Divine.

Additional dimensions of my internship, beyond the outreach to students, were the engagement in local politics and discovering the gritty spirituality of the arts. The extended ministry to students was a "going out" sort of ministry. In the fall, I spent a great deal of time attending meetings and assessing various approaches to working with students in an urban center. By the middle of the year it became clear that one of the key areas we should be working in was the black students. African-American students were just beginning to emerge as a distinctively self-conscious community at NYU and at Cooper Union. Several of us in the campus ministry worked closely with a new campus branch of the NAACP, advising on organization and trying to put black students in contact with supportive resources in the larger community.

THE EARLY MOVEMENT

By the spring of 1960 sit-ins had begun in certain parts of the South. Black students and many of us who were supportive of their cause decided to conduct a sympathetic boycott of the Woolworth's at 42nd Street, across from the New York Public Library. Members of the church joined with a group of students from NYU and from Judson House to march in a silent picket line in support of the southern sit-ins. All of the picketers were told to dress in good clothes; look neat, clean, and respectable; and not to respond to taunts. We had been instructed in the tactics of nonviolent resistance. We were vilified, cursed, spat upon, and occasionally encouraged. One white-haired, well-dressed man whispered obscenities in Judy's ear as he walked along beside her in the picket line.

In a related effort, I spent some time trying to get students from Africa engaged in a dialogue with African-American students. It was painful to watch African students distance themselves from African-American perceptions of what it was like to be black. The African-American students were hurt and frustrated by this distance when they desperately wanted to find connection.

Politics was a way of life in the Judson community. Within weeks of our arrival we were distributing leaflets for the Village Independent Democrats, learning through Howard and other members of the congregation (Sue Harwig and Gretel Commings come to mind) about the needs of the community and being urged to engage the community in creative ways. At the 1959 Democratic Precinct Election, at which we hoped to unseat Carmine DeSapio, I was a

VID poll watcher even though I was not registered to vote in the city!

The Community Service Program ministry to troubled teenagers led to a growing concern about drug addiction, the need for alternative treatment for drug addiction, perverse laws and prison conditions, and a growing sense that abortion laws had to be changed. Other activists were committed to the Fellowship of Reconciliation and antinuclear movements such as SANE. The Caryl Chesman execution was the occasion for an impassioned challenge to capital punishment. We saw the world through the eyes of C. Wright Mills, Franz Kafka, and Samuel Beckett. But ours was not the politics of alienation but of engaged conversation. We hosted and encouraged labor reform movements and groups such as Fair Play for Cuba. We were determined to move out of the McCarthy era, and we saw Judson Church as a catalyst for resistance to conformity and spiritual vacuity.

THE JUDSON GALLERY

Another part of Judson's ministry was to the arts. Bud Scott took particular responsibility, but the centrality of the arts program was clear to the congregation and was strongly supported by Howard Moody. The Judson Gallery allowed artists to have a small place in the Village where they could put up shows at no major cost and without having to deal with gallery pricing. We opened the basement stairway down into the little room below the Scotts' apartment, and it became a working gallery for a lively group of artists such as Claes Oldenberg and Jim Dine. Some of the earliest performance art presentations ("happenings") were at the Judson Gallery.

Little did we realize at the time that we were witnessing the transformation of pop art. I vividly remember running the ditto machine to run off early copies, in purple ink, of Ray Gun comics drawn by Claes and Jim. (I'd sure like to find my copies of those smudged art works.) Scott edited, with Daniel Wolf, a quarterly magazine, *Exodus,* which contained poetry, visual arts, and a "worldly spiritual vitality." The constant presence of artists in the Judson House intrigued our students. This presence, and the issues posed by the artists about the meaning of creativity and of spiritual meaning beyond the materialism of the age, touched us all deeply.

More than a building, Judson House was a living body in the heart of the city. Like Judson Church, of which it was a vital organ, it engaged its environment. Its many forms and mutations kept it in living connection with the Village, the city, and the world beyond.

We used to say of the Church that it was like a living cell with permeable membranes: drawing the world *in* for nurture in worship and community, and sending *out* its nurtured spirit in mission to transform the world. So, too, with Judson House. We drew people into the house as a place of growth, rest, reassessment, recovery, and learning. But we did not stay inside. We went through the membranes back into the world, confident that our life inside the Church was worth sharing more widely. We read, we talked, we argued, we explored because we had learned that one must both be nurtured in the fellowship of Christ and witness to that fellowship throughout the world. In all of its permutations, Judson House has been the place where people came and went, not from one world to another but from one dimension to another within a shared world full of risk and blessing.

JOE AND JUDY PICKLE
live in Colorado Springs, where Joe teaches in the Department of Religion at Colorado College.

Al Carmines

Al Carmines was Judson's assistant minister from 1961 to 1964 and
associate minister from 1964 to 1981.

My experience with Judson House began before Judson hired me. I used to come to the art gallery showings and the parties they had in the lounge in the Student House before I met Howard or anyone. Steve André, a classmate at Union Theological Seminary, was connected with a lot of people at the house. They had happenings in the gymnasium or in the gallery. The parties often lasted till three in the morning, and then I would have to get up at 6:30 to do my field work on Long Island or in Yonkers. But I got excited about avant-garde art—Claes Oldenburg, Allan Kaprow, Jim Dine. This was 1959–1960.

I graduated from Union in 1961. I had my interview with Howard Moody because I wanted to stay in New York and get a Ph.D. I had never composed or thought of composing or writing or anything like that. Anyway, Howard told me the church wanted to hire me for two years to start a theater program and also to work with artists. I was happy to take that position.

The summer before I came to Judson in September 1961 I lived with Lyle Guttu and someone else in an apartment on Washington Place. I worked in the library at Union Theological Seminary, probably the most unfortunate job I have ever had. I had to vacuum books. My supervisor was a Chinese man who would say, "Al, if you do it right the first time, you do not have to do it again. Now you have to do it again." (My vacuuming skills have never been great.)

In the fall I would have an apartment in the Student House, and Lyle also needed a place to live in the fall. Lyle and I have been close friends for over forty years. So I went to Donald Birt, who was acting minister at the time, and asked him if it would be all right if Lyle lived with me in the apartment in the Student House. There had just been a scandal in the church. A former associate minister had told the congregation that he was gay. This was 1961, and the congregation was terribly upset. So Lyle moved into a place on Avenue A.

MY FIRST APARTMENT!

I moved into the Student House on the first floor, on the corner of Thompson and Third streets, and I lived there my first three years at Judson. I was thrilled. I had my own bathroom. I had never had my own bathroom. At home we had five members of the family, and sometimes seven when my two cousins lived with us for a while when their father died. I also had never had a shower—I grew up with a tub. I had my own living room, my own kitchen, my own bedroom for the first time. I could not believe it.

BETTY AND WILLIE MAE

In 1961 the Student House was dominated by two people. One was Betty Murphy, who was the controller of the Student House. She was a lovely woman with a youthful face but prematurely gray hair. She lived there with her husband, Richard, who attended medical school.

At the Judson board meetings, which Betty attended, Howard would say at the end of the meeting, "Betty, what did you have to give them this month?" Betty would say something like twenty dollars or thirty dollars. For months, I had no idea what they were talking about. It turned out that Betty was slipping the sanitation men— this was when Robert Wagner was mayor—some money so that they would pick up all the garbage promptly without letting it build up into a terrible situation. I was shocked when I found out, but Howard wasn't at all.

The other person was Willie Mae Wallace. She was the cook, a black woman. She cooked two meals for the students and then took over the job of cleaning my apartment. Willie Mae was a fabulous lady. She would make wonderful meals, very good and very fattening, Southern cooking like I was used to. She and I would always gather in the morning. In those days I usually stayed up till four or five in the morning and then sleep till eleven or twelve, because my job was to go to bars and cafes and to meet artists and playwrights. The doughnuts for breakfast were delivered around six in the morning, and I would try and stay up till then. I would have a couple of doughnuts and a couple of cups of coffee or maybe seven cups of coffee and then go to sleep till about twelve to go to the office and meet with Howard.

INTERNATIONAL STUDENTS

At that time the Student House was a residence for foreign students at New York University. I remember some of them quite well. My closest friend was Kala Pant, an Indian girl. She came from Puna. She was a Brahmin and her grandfather was a maharaja. Back home she had become pregnant, and her entire family took her to the gates of the city and left her. Her lover paid for her to come to New York and to enroll at NYU. Kala Pant typed my graduate papers for Union Seminary.

Another good friend was a Pakistani guy named Said Said. He and Kala Pant would not eat at the same table, because he was Muslim and she was Hindu and there was great strife between the Pakistanis and the Indians at that time. It got so I would eat my evening meal one night with Kala and one night with Said—lamb and rice with Kala and beef and rice with Said. The cow was sacred to Indians, and of course there was no pork for either.

There were people from every country. It was a wonderful environment. A lot of things changed for me in that year. There was a man from Nigeria who gave me a robe when he left. There were people from Germany, from Italy. There was Marjorie Saunders (who still calls me every six months from Spain, where she now lives). Her father was the headmaster of the Peddy School in Hightstown, New Jersey, and he persuaded Howard to accept Marjorie as an American student, even though the Student House was really for foreign students. There was another American, Bob Sergeant, a North Carolinian. I was very close to him.

Juell Krauter and Beverly Bach lived in a commodious apartment. Chuck Eaton, who worked in the drug program at Judson, also lived in Judson House.

During my first year, Bob Nichols and I ran the theater together. We founded the theater and did plays, and I acted in all of them. I had acted before in college and in seminary. In fact, a producer offered to set me up in an apartment in New York if I would study acting. He thought I would be a great actor.

I BECOME A COMPOSER

A year later, we were doing a play that needed incidental music. Larry Kornfeld, who directed the play, said, "Al, just write some incidental music that we can have between the dialogue." The play was called *Vaudeville Skit,* and it involved three bums in a Becket-like play, so I wrote what I thought was Becket-like music. Jerry Tallmer, who reviewed the play for the *Village Voice,* went ape over the music and wrote something like, "A new composer has been discovered. He writes like no one else writes."

That's how I began my career as a composer. I did not have a piano in my apartment, so I worked in the Student House lounge, which had an upright piano and a recordplayer. I would listen to Bessie Smith and Mozart.

Beverly and Ralph Waite came to the Student House and took Betty Murphy's place. Beverly was another fabulous woman. Ralph was an actor and a UCC minister. They divorced while they were there.

By 1964 Judson House had become predominantly a residence for artists. Many artists lived there: Larry Kornfeld, Marty Washburn, Charlie Adams. It was a vibrant place with painters, sculptors, dancers, filmmakers, students of Merce Cunningham, students at NYU, students from the New School, people who studied with Jimmy Waring.

AN EVEN BIGGER APARTMENT

In 1964 the Judson board decided to take me on full-time as an associate minister. Lew Pressler, who was the head of Judson's personnel committee, took me to lunch. We went to Rocco's, which was down on Thompson Street between Bleecker and Houston. We had a couple of drinks. He was kind of hesitant, but finally he said, "We want you to be our associate minister and the board has decided to offer you a salary of $3,500 plus an apartment, a bigger apartment in Judson House. We want you to bring up your piano from Virginia, and we will pay for that." I was overwhelmed: $3,500 is like $45,000 now, plus the apartment. I said that I could only give a tentative yes, because I really wanted to pursue a Ph.D. I wanted to study with Paul Tillich.

I moved down to the other end of the house and now had two bedrooms, a big living room, and a nice-sized kitchen directly above the gallery.

A STRING OF SECRETARIES

At the church my first secretary was Shirley Cantrell, and then Juell Krauter worked for me for a while. Juell was a good secretary, except that she would get involved with these bums who would come in off the street and ask for money. I was always terrified, but Juell was very sympathetic. She would listen to these long, drawn-out stories about why they needed the money. The bums never frightened her until one day, when I was up in the sanctuary and heard Juell scream. I ran down, and there was this man who had removed Juell's shoes and was sucking on her toes. Juell wanted him to let her toes go. He would not let her toes go and was moving up to her ankle. I called the police—I did not know what else to do. They came and literally had to pull the man off her legs. The police said, "Don't you know who this is? This is So-and-So, the well-known foot fetishist."

For a brief period I had a male secretary, Søren Agenoux. His mother was Danish, his father French. He did absolutely nothing. He was very aesthetic. He read scripts all day long. I got scripts by the hundreds once the theater was established, and Søren never wrote any of my letters. All he did was read scripts. He would give me ten that he thought worthy of my attention, and he discovered Irene Fornes. I kept putting her off and had not read any of her scripts. Finally Søren said I must read this script, which was the first act of *Promenade*. So I did, and I was absolutely bowled over, and we did *Promenade*.

Kathy Jacobsen was my next secretary, and she was the first full-time secretary just for me. She was wonderful. She lived with the Moodys at Grace House on East 18th Street. One night she asked me to dinner there. I loved going to Grace House, because Lorry is a fabulous cook. Lorry left us alone, and all of a sudden Kathy began to cry. She told me she had to quit. "What do you mean you have to quit? I am very satisfied with your work." She said, "Al, don't you understand? I am pregnant." And I said, "But you can still be my secretary." No, she said, she was going back to Iowa to have the baby. And so she did. When she was ready to come back, she took up her nursing career again because the pay was much better.

I was desperate for a secretary, and that's when Joan Muyskens came to work for me. This was in 1969. I had a terrible time remembering Joan's last name. John Tungate finally hung a sign in my office that read: "Your secretary's name is Joan Muyskens." (He made another sign with the drawing of a woman, underneath which it said: "There is a bomb in Guilliatt.")

LOVE ENTERS THE PICTURE

In 1967 I had my first love affair with a man, Jeffrey Apter, while *In Circles* was being done. Jeffrey was Jewish, small, a poet, dictatorial, impossible, but I loved him very much. I cast him in the shows I did. He had a tenor voice that was fairly good. He and Ira Siff would do tenor duets. I never thought of living with him; it never crossed my mind. He had an apartment on Sullivan Street and I had the apartment on Thompson. Then one morning, Jeffrey showed up. He brought suitcases with him, and clothes and books and records. He spent all day carting his stuff over. And something inside me said, "Let Jeffrey live with you. It will be a lovely experience. But you keep paying for Jeffrey's apartment." I don't know why I thought that in the back of my mind, but I was terrified for some reason.

CAST PARTIES WITH PUNCH

We began having parties in my new apartment for every play—opening parties and closing parties. These parties became wilder and wilder. There would be eighty to a hundred people. I had done a play by Harry Koutoukas called *Pomegrenada* for which I had also written the music, and I had created a punch in Harry's honor called the Pomegrenada Punch. It was a very famous punch. It was champagne and cognac and strawberries and sometimes blueberries. I had no idea it was so powerful.

Albert Poland came to see *Peace* because he wanted to produce it, and I had no idea who Albert Poland was. After the show he wanted to attend the party, and I said great. At that time I stored my liquor in a closet in the church office—I don't know why. I asked Albert to help me carry the liquor to my apartment, and Albert said,

"I am not a livery boy, you know, I am a producer." I said, "I know you are not a livery boy. Now you take this box and I'll take the other, and we'll go to my apartment and make the punch." Albert had an appalled look on his face, but he did take the box over.

The parties were usually wonderful. Everybody came: church members, actors, actors' friends, actors' enemies. There was a good fight at almost every party. There would be fist fights over who got to spend the night with whom. At one party, someone locked herself in the bathroom. Someone else knocked on the bathroom door to be let in, and when the door did not open after a while, this person began banging and using force, knocking the door to smithereens. Willie Mae came the next day to clean up. She said, "Al, what happened to your bathroom?" I said, "Some people got a little carried away." She said, "It looks like the whole party got carried away." She was very upset.

JUDSON DANCE THEATER

The Judson Dance Theater started because of the Judson Poets Theater. The Theater did *What Happened* in 1963, and we used dancers in that play. When the dancers saw the space, they were thrilled and asked if they could start a dance theater using Judson Church. They also wanted to take the name of Judson Dance Theater.

The Judson Dance Theater gave its first three concerts in June. I was terribly nervous. I had been watching their rehearsals in the gymnasium, and I could not believe what they were doing. They were standing still, they were running, they were grabbing people from the audience to join them, they were climbing ladders. They had tape recorders on with moans and groans and sometimes high whistles and flutes and sometimes electronic music. The audience loved it. The dance theater was far in advance of anything else that was happening.

In 1966 Yvonne Rainer and Bob Morris did the famous nude dance in the sanctuary of the church. Howard and I were both called upon to go to the American Baptist Convention and explain the use of church space for nude dancing. Howard loved a good fight. I wrote a paper that Howard could use in defense. In the paper I said that in Victorian times people used to hide the legs of a piano because it was thought that the legs might excite men and women too much.

Howard met with the Baptist people and we were exonerated or at least we were not thrown out of the convention. The Judson Dance Theater flourished enormously, as did the Judson Poets Theater.

CATWALKS AND A SUNKEN TUB

In 1970 my apartment was renovated. Bruce Mailman, who produced *The Faggot* and who owned the theater where we did *Peace,* took a great interest in me as a person. He told me, "You should really have something done with that apartment. It is wonderful space, but it is so old-fashioned. See if the church will give you a couple of thousand dollars to redecorate." So I asked Howard about it, and Howard said that it was indeed old-fashioned and the church would give me the money.

I planned to be away anyhow to do *In Circles* at Stanford University. I was going to drive all the way, since I was not flying in those days, so I would be gone all summer. I told Bruce everything had to be done by September. Bruce asked, "Are you giving me carte blanche as to how to do everything?" And I said, "Yes, I don't care what you do." Bruce said, "I am going to make it state of the art. You will be in *Time* magazine, *House Beautiful,* everything. I am going to turn this place inside out."

I went to California, and after two months returned home to New York. I opened the door to my apartment, and it was like opening a door into space. The first thing that happened was that I fell. Bruce had built platforms, catwalks, all around the edge of the place, and I now had a sunken living room, which Bruce said was very chic. This huge, sunken space was surrounded by cubes that were covered with gray industrial carpeting. My grand piano was in this space. When I opened the door to the bathroom, there was a sunken tub. I was used to taking a bath in a regular tub. I was never good with my feet—I was never a dancer. I fell into the tub every time I took a bath. I stopped taking baths because I could not get in and I could not get out. Luckily there was still the shower. Once a week I would take a bath and fall in and fall out.

The apartment gave one an Alice in Wonderland feeling, and people were struck by it. No one complimented me, though, which upset me a lot. People would say, "Oh, your place looks so interesting." But they never said that it looked nice. At first, visitors thought that the gray cubes were temporary until the real stuff came, but they weren't. I never had any furniture other than those cubes. They were very uncomfortable to sit on.

The master bedroom now had a sunken bed. That sunken bed saw more activity than you can imagine. As people would get drunk on the punch, they would fall forward into the bed. They would go into the bedroom to smoke marijuana or something, and they would collapse into the bed. And then, around two in the morning when I got ready to go to sleep, there would be ten people lying on my bed, out of their minds. I would have to wake everybody up and get all except a few people to leave.

At some point the church decided I needed more space, and the space that used to be the gallery was added to my apartment, with a spiral staircase joining the two.

ILLNESS AND SURGERY

One other event that must be mentioned is my aneurism, because that happened in the Student House. At that time I was close to a student at Union Seminary, and he often came to church. We were doing a play, and after one of the shows we had gone to the McBell's restaurant on Sixth Avenue, and he came home with me for a final drink. All of a sudden I blacked out. The student became terrified and called up Paul Rounsaville. Paul came over right away. An ambulance took me to Saint Vincent's. The people in the emergency room determined that I had been drinking too much and told me to go home and sleep it off. For the next three days I was totally out of my mind. I remember nothing except thinking weird thoughts.

I was taken to Roosevelt Hospital, and when they asked me there how old I was, I said twenty-one and John Kennedy is president. Larry Kornfeld, who had taken me, said to the hospital staff, "He is crazy as a loon. He has lost his mind. I hope you realize that." They put me in a bed. After two weeks I was operated on, and that was the beginning of my closure with Judson.

AL CARMINES
is pastor of the Rauschenbusch Memorial Church in New York City.

Ed Brewer

Ed Brewer was Judson's music director from 1964 to 1968. ⸻

Writing about Judson House more than thirty years after the fact is a bit like playing the game "Telephone," where one whispers into a neighbor's ear some secret sentence and then waits for the garbled answer to come out at the other end of the line of people. Filtered through the ears of the intervening players and through the aging eyes of someone who wonders if he has grown up yet, these memories are naturally a bit suspect.

My residence in the house began in the fall of 1964. The mid-1960s were the days of flower power and miniskirts, of all-night radio on WNCN when Bill Watson would play the passions of Bach twice in a row, a time when our federal government saw fit to send its young men to fight a war in the heroin haven of Vietnam, a period of major changes in the structure of our society, a setting for dancing in the rain on Thompson Street after a Sunday service.

The Student House was the setting where lots of things happened, not necessarily by design but because a lot of different people lived there and had a chance to mingle. The environment was conducive to activity. My memories of that time are unrelated to any grand scheme. There was none; the play was unscripted. However, the composite of these elements made for a way of life that thrived at Judson. The Student House was a focal point where ideas germinated and grew, often finding their way into the larger Judson community and beyond.

Judson House provided accommodations for some members of the church staff and for a wide variety of students pursuing various disciplines at institutions throughout Manhattan. It was in my capacity as music director of Judson Memorial Church that I came to have an apartment in this stimulating place. The permanent residents, such as myself, enjoyed complete apartments. In spite of this we spent much time in the communal living areas, all of which where on the lowest level of the building. The most popular of these areas, the kitchen, was adjacent to my apartment. The lounge, to the north of the kitchen, was the site of frequent parties, and to the north of the lounge was the gallery, where during the week Al Carmines and Jimmy Carter were often heard playing Mozart late into the night. The tempos seemed to increase as the liquid refreshment flowed.

Other staff members besides Al who lived there during my time were Beverly and Ralph Waite and Chuck and Ann Eaton, both couples serving at different times as house "parents." Ro Lee, the office administrator, lived in the apartment upstairs from me.

THE COOK AND THE KITCHEN

Willie Mae Wallace cooked the communal supper every day, leaving it on the stove for us to help ourselves when our schedules succumbed to our appetites. Supper and its aftermath provided the focal point for activities into the evening; it was the spawning ground for much of the activity of the house. Later in the evening, other people would drift through, often after theater rehearsals in the Meeting Room.

One such person I remember very fondly was Susie Pardue, also one of the few New Yorkers in this complexity of invaders. A dancer who had had considerable success on stage during her childhood, she had a deep appreciation of people. Her spirit was infectiously cheerful. Her contacts in the music world included some of the major composers of the time. Many people remember her performances as Roo in Al's *Sing Ho for a Bear*. Al would often come over with the director Larry Kornfeld, who also lived at the house for a while. Everyone knows that the best part of any party takes place in the kitchen.

Bull sessions of the type found most often in college dormitory rooms took place in the kitchen as well, with people hanging around after supper before heading out for the evening. Kent, a law student, had a particularly lucid rationale for the nonexistence of God, based on the premise that the logical conclusion one must draw, given the brains that we have, leads to a denial of the existence of God.

The lounge was the site of Friday night dance parties. These occasions provided the opportunity for me to learn to dance again, what with rock 'n' roll having taken over the dance floor. The madrigal group, made up of some members of the church choir augmented by a few other singers, met there. The lounge was also a place to hang out during the week, providing a change of venue from one's own room, and it tended to be quieter than the kitchen.

The gallery was a space with as many purposes as the church's Meeting Room. Not only did it house the art shows that its name implies but it also served as a small lecture/recital hall. Here is where I held my weekly lecture/demos, where I discussed the structure of the preludes and fugues of Bach and played them on the harpsichord. Kate Millett and Yoko Ono, to name but two, sat there many days during their one-person shows.

APPLE WINE AND A HARPSICHORD

The bedroom of my apartment, aside from providing direct access to the garden and being the location of several maturing gallons of apple wine I made one year, became a workshop in which I built my first harpsichord. The construction took many months, and the completed instrument became an integral part of the Judson Chamber Concerts. The space I worked in was desperately cramped, and the only available power saw was in the community center at the church. I made endless trips to the saw to shave a hair's width from one part or another to ensure a proper fit. The most intoxicating and toxic part of the building was in the finishing, when I sprayed a lacquer base paint with all the lack of ventilation a basement room affords. Although I had a large door opening to the garden, there was only one small window opening onto the street to provide any amount of cross-ventilation. Twenty minutes into the job I was close to legally intoxicated. It was on this instrument that I played my debut recital in the Meeting Room at the church in 1966. The apple wine, by the way, tasted more like vinegar than wine, and it produced a most god-awful hangover I can remember to this day.

Charlie Adams was one of the icons of the house. More than most people I knew at that time, Charlie personified the caricature of how many people saw the sixties. Older than most of us, he participated fully in the dropout culture. By affection an artist, he helped with the custodial duties required by any community. His paintings reflected the tripping common in the sixties and to which he was no stranger. When the historic Roosevelt organ in the church needed a lot of repair, Charlie spent endless hours removing the old, dried-out leather from countless valves and replacing it.

The many social events at Judson House were interspersed with moments of solitude. One Christmas day—probably my first year there—I woke as was my custom late in the morning and wondered how to spend the rest of the day. Since the house was always so active, I had assumed that sooner or later someone would surface and I would find some company. This did not happen. I kept listening for footsteps somewhere, but the house seemed empty. I recall hearing a few footsteps coming from the apartment directly above me, where Ro lived, but lacking confidence I did not go upstairs and knock, not wanting to intrude. We compared notes at a later time and found we had both spent a lonely Christmas.

A close friend of mine who lived at Judson House when I first moved in was Lurline Purvis. My relationship with her was more personal than with the other residents in the house. One of the profound influences of the house, although seldom verbalized, was that it made this type of relationship possible. One of the few native-born New Yorkers at Judson, Lurline challenged me emotionally, and even with her lack of formal musical training she knew much more about the emotional content of my performances than any of my teachers had discussed.

The front steps of Judson House had their regular occupants. In those days they were called winos, and they seemed to help keep the street safe. They were regulars who knew the people on the block and caused little or no trouble except from the minor inconvenience of having to step over them to get into the house. My private entrance to the subterranean level at the corner of Third and Thompson had a continuation down the stairs to a subbasement, and there were occasional visitors to these realms.

The vacancy created by the departure of Ro Lee from the overhead apartment was filled by Thom and Joan Kilpatrick. Thom, a writer on scientific issues, went to Vietnam as a reporter for an electronics magazine and came back trying to figure out how to tell a story he had seen that the manufacturers of electronic military gear did not want to hear.

DEATH AND LIFE

One of the clearest memories I have is the reaction of the kitchen crowd to the news of Jimmy Waring's suicide. The house seemed to be in shock. Although I was stunned by his death, I did not understand the deeper despair that pervaded the atmosphere. For many of the residents life was a fragile entity, and the line between life and death a thin one indeed. For my part, I was so engulfed in the richness of the life I was experiencing in New York and in the Judson community that the death of a contemporary was a tragedy but it was not a threat to my own future—death was not staring *me* in the face. Life was my friend, and death was something that happened to others. It took me a long time to comprehend the emotional impact of this tragedy on the community.

THE BLACKOUT OF 1965

Several other events have left sharp memories. One was the blackout of November 1965, when the only lights on the street came from motor vehicles. Another was the transit strike on New Year's Day in 1966, which forced people needing transportation to trust strangers in cars and which ushered in a temporary reign of human warmth and compassion in the cruel streets of New York. Then there were the assassinations of Martin Luther King, Jr., and Robert Kennedy in 1968. I vividly recall David Johnson sitting on my couch in shock over King's untimely death.

MUSIC WITH VIRGINIA

One Sunday morning in 1965 marked the beginning of my current stability (?) and happiness. The horn player of a woodwind quintet that was supposed to play at a Sunday service had fallen victim to Saturday night overindulgence and never showed up. However, Virginia Bland, the oboist with the group, did. We later got together to read through some music for another service. The rehearsal did not last long, since everything just fit together so easily. Virginia joined the choir (that seemed to be one of the major ways to get my attention in those days), and when her lease expired in the spring of 1967 she parked her stuff with me before departing for Italy for the summer. Upon her return she moved in, and in November 1968 Hugh Pickett showed up at our new apartment on 104th Street along with Thom and Joanie Kilpatrick, the best man and matron of honor.

Two of the lasting results of that Student House meeting in 1965 are Barry and Diana, our son and daughter.

Judson House and Judson Church have been inseparable for as long as they have existed side by side. The programs of each have moved with the needs of the day and the interests of the people who use the space. I am often reminded of Howard Moody's statement on the mission of the church—and this applies equally to the Student House—to bring God to the artistic community. The church invited the artists to come in and use the space, and when the time came to bring God to the artists, the church community discovered that the artists had brought life to the church.

The success of the Student House must be measured in its relevance to its participants. I can testify to the success of the Student House as a place where I found new meanings in life and personal growth.

ED AND VIRGINIA BREWER
live in Leonia, New Jersey.

Larry Kornfeld

Larry Kornfeld was involved in the theater at Judson for many years.
During some of these, he lived at Judson House. ─────────────

T oward the end of 1960 I decided to leave the Living Theater, where I had been working as general manager and assistant director. A close friend of mine, Joel Oppenheimer, told me over dinner one night that Judson Church was starting a theater, and they wanted to do his play, *The Great American Desert*. Joel wanted to know if I was interested in directing it because he loved my work. Would I do this at the church? My initial response was, "No way. They won't let you do this. The play is filthy." And Joel said, "The Judson Board said they would do it, and I have their support." I said, "I can't believe it's a church, Joel. It has the word 'fuck' in it many, many times, and other words, too." We had gone through this with the Living Theater just a few years before with the premiere of a play by Paul Goodman, which was the first time the word "fuck" had been used in a theater openly. We had been expecting to be arrested but nothing happened.

Anyway, Joel reassured me that the board of the church had said they would support the arts program with no censorship, and he said he believed them. So I said I would do it, and that was the first real production that Al Carmines set up. The theater had been started earlier by Al and by Bob Nichols, or it may have been Bob Nichols and Howard Moody. They may have done a production of Faust. But the first theater *season* started with *The Great American Desert* and a translation of Apollinaire's *The Breasts of Tiresias*. This was around December 1961/January 1962. Well, I came to do that play, and it turned out very well. Howard told me the story that he or someone on his staff was hanging out in the hall at the end of opening night when some high Baptist official and his wife came down the stairs, and this person overheard the wife say to the husband, "George, that's the best fucking play I have seen in years." The story may be apocryphal but it is wonderful.

That's how I came to Judson. I did another play and then another. Very quickly I became the resident director, whatever that meant. There was no way of becoming artistic director, with Al's position as the arts minister. I did about half the plays.

I MOVE INTO JUDSON HOUSE

I lived in Hoboken at the time. My upstairs neighbor there was George Dennis, the poet, playwright, novelist, and social critic, now dead. Both he and Joel Oppenheimer died of lung cancer, both ferocious smokers. George was a good friend of mine. We lived in this old building. George always wanted to open his apartment up, so he kept knocking walls down over the couple of years that I lived there. One night the whole ceiling came down while I was asleep. The stuff buried everything. I had become more and more tired of living in Hoboken, and the day after the ceiling fell on me, I gave my cats away to friends, I gathered some books and things that I had, and moved into Judson House. Before I came to live at the house I had already spent a lot of time there, playing bridge and going to a lot of parties. Howard offered me a place there.

I had a room on the third floor, directly across from the stairs. I don't remember who my neighbors were. Al had the big apartment downstairs. I brought in a bookcase and a painting of Julian Beck's called King Lear, and I had a rug. It was very pleasant. I may have had two rooms. I took my meals in the kitchen. That was the arrangement because now I was staff. The church paid me a small stipend of about $50 a month, but I spent all my time in the theater, so I was allowed to have free meals. The arrangement allowed me to leave teaching. My time at the Living Theater had been a high-level apprenticeship. When I came out of that monastery and went out into the world—I am speaking in medieval terms—it was Judson and the Student House that allowed me to develop my skills over ten years. I lived at the house for two years until 1965 when Margaret Zipse and I got married, and then we moved to Brooklyn to a house that Lee Guilliatt found for us.

Willie Mae Wallace was the cook for the house. I don't know where Willie Mae lived. I know she came in and she cooked wonderful meals, twice a day, lunch and dinner. She was more than a cook, she was the housemother. She was raucously funny, a strong woman.

I was very fond of her. We took things for granted. We were all staff, paid and unpaid, it was not so much staff as it was community. It was the sixties, and I did not explore who paid whom. Beverly and Ralph Waite ran the place. In hindsight, the Judson Board obviously put up money for it and supported it.

I GIVE UP BRIDGE FOR MARGARET

There were always lots of interesting people in the house, in addition to the people who lived there. There was Julie Kurnitz. She was the light of the world. I remember Paul Goodman coming to visit often, sitting in the kitchen. At that time Paul was one of the great figures in American radical politics. He loved the young people at the house and engaged with them.

There were bridge parties. Al Carmines was my partner. Al, Julie, Jack Matlaga, and I used to play bridge. Margaret and I played bridge, too, when we were first married, but I found myself getting very nasty, and I decided that if this marriage was going to last, I had better not play bridge anymore, so I gave it up.

After I moved out I kept my position as resident director of the Judson Theater, but, of course, I did not spend that much time at the Student House any more. I would occasionally drop in, certainly at rehearsal time. But I had my own home now, and then I had a child.

THE CAGE AT THE GALLERY

One of my favorite events at the Judson House took place at the Judson Gallery. Kate Millett had organized a happening that involved waiting outside in line before you could go into the gallery. Margaret and I went inside where there was a big wooden cage, beautifully sculptured, and they squeezed a lot of people into it and then they were able to close it. There were maybe fifteen or twenty people in it. Lights started flashing, there were incredibly loud noises, and of course you did not know what was going to happen. It was like a torture box. I hated it, so I broke the box and got out of it. I thought, "The artist is going to hate me for this." Already she came running over and said, "You are the first person who has resisted." I occasionally tell this story because for me it was a sign of how passive the avant-garde had become. This was 1967. The artist was waiting for people to respond, to tear it apart, but they went in and did nothing.

There was a flow in and out of people at Judson House. You did not ask what people did, why they were there. Some were related to the theater, some to the church, some of them were just there. There were hayseed types who would move in for the summer.

The garden was wonderful. When the weather was nice, we would sit outside late at night. I have a drawing that Jon Hendricks did of me when we sat there one night. He picked up a piece of cardboard and a stone and he made scratches with the stone on the cardboard. Then he picked up some dirt and rubbed it into the scratches and did the portrait.

Jon Hendricks and I were good friends. Actually, Margaret and I were able to get married because of Jon's parents. I had never met Jon's parents, and Jon and I drove to Vermont to visit them, wonderful Quaker people. We spent a weekend with them. They were elderly people, or what seemed elderly to me then, and it was wonderful to see two people who had been married many, many years, with a lively intellectual life. It was an example to me of how a married couple could still maintain a friendship after all those years, which I had not seen much—just wobbly marriages, divorcing marriages. Jon's parents inspired me to get married myself.

That was part of the community at the Student House. It was not just what we did at the house, but how it gave us a base for growing up. It was a safe haven. For me, it was also very important that I met so many people who were not New Yorkers. There were people from Ohio and Iowa! I barely used to think those people existed. I am an old New Yorker, born and raised here. My parents grew up in New York. The contact really broadened my outlook. And for those people it was the first time they lived with a real New Yorker. It was a reciprocating community.

LARRY AND MARGARET KORNFELD
live in Brooklyn, New York.

Ro Lee

Ro Lee was Howard Moody's secretary in the mid-1960s. ──────────

There was a time when the only thing that made sense in my life was my work at Judson Church. The world certainly didn't. President Kennedy had been assassinated and my mother had married her third alcoholic husband. The psychotherapist I was seeing had broken my trust. Howard Moody's suggestion that I move into Judson House was probably based on his astute observation that I was very much alone and just a babe in the woods of the big city.

Shortly after I moved in, a hippie girl I had befriended put some LSD in my coffee one night without telling me. Even though the dose was not strong enough to cause a "trip," it turned out to be the best thing that could have happened to me as it blew the lid off the repressed demons that had haunted me and started me on the path to break free of them.

Even so, I still had many problems, especially in dealing with people I did not know. Howard asked if I would like to get some competent psychiatric help. He knew a psychiatric diagnostician connected with Mount Sinai Hospital, which had a pilot program where one lived at the hospital for up to three months but could keep one's job.

It sounded perfect, and once I knew I was in trustworthy hands I was able to unravel the tangled web of events that had been my life up to that time. This was the time of President Johnson's "Great Society," and health care was available to anyone who needed it. I would never have been able to afford the help on my own.

I remember reading once that Greenwich Village was the place where young people came from all over to rewrite their identity, and that was surely true for me. Judson's beacon of sanity was exactly what I needed. It was the first church I had experienced that felt like my idea of what a church should be. When I asked Howard what was necessary to become a member of Judson, he said that one simply had to believe in a higher being.

My four years at Judson were the beginning of a life that has turned into one of service. As the poet Kahlil Gibran says, "What are your joys but your sorrows turned upside down." All the terrifying experiences of my early life are now put to use in understanding and relating to those who come to Erehwon Retreat, the healing center I established in 1992. And true to the axiom in psychotherapy, one's experiences once understood become the tools to help others turn their lives around.

I thank everyone at Judson who has helped me to get from there to here.

RO LEE

changed her name to Rosa Lee to mark her journey from an incomplete to a whole being. She lives in Rock Hill, New York.

Arthur A. Levin

Arthur Levin has never officially been part of Judson's staff, yet he
has run more programs than any other person alive. ————————————

When I first became involved with Judson Memorial
Church in the early 1960s, I don't think I even knew
that there was a Judson House filled with resident students. The only part of the building I knew was the Judson Art Gallery, which occupied the northeast corner of the building and had its
own entrance.

Although I had known Howard Moody through reform democratic politics, my immersion in Judson took place through the arts,
primarily the Judson Dance Theater. After college and a stint in the
U.S. Army, I returned to New York City. Through friends I had come
to know a number of the dancers who eventually formed the core of
the performers at Judson. For several years I put up with the crowds
and bad sight lines to watch dance history unfold. Sometimes I even
became involved in performances—usually at the back of the house
but a few times as an "extra" in performance. I also viewed all the
art shows at the Judson Gallery.

In 1966 I left the world of business and came to Judson to run a
pilot project aimed at the hundreds of teenagers that crowded Mac-
Dougal Street on weekend nights. Howard, Al Carmines, and I conceived of a storefront arts project that would use Judson artists and
performers to teach kids from the street five evenings a week. The
Judson Teenage Arts Workshop, around the corner from Judson
House on West Third Street, was one of the first of its kind using art
and artists to serve the teenage street population. Unfortunately, it
was too new a concept to attract funding, and after about six or
eight months the program had to close its doors.

I next volunteered to help reorganize the administrative side of
Judson Church. The office was overwhelmed with the demands of a
hyperactive arts program, a growing church community, and the as-
sorted civil liberties activities that became a hallmark of the church's
work in the larger community. As a result, I continued to be involved

in the Judson arts programs. I even designed lighting for a few plays and helped out where needed—and even when not needed.

As I became friends with some of those who came to Judson to fulfill their conscientious objector (CO) status and lived in the Student House (Jon Hendricks and Reathel Bean, among others), I actually became more familiar with the building and its history. At about this time, Judson Church was deliberating whether to continue the housing of students or whether the space at Judson House might be put to meeting other needs.

RUNNING WITH THE RUNAWAYS

In 1967 Howard and I were approached by a consortium of progressive charitable foundations who wanted to support some safety-net activities for the growing youth culture that had flocked to the Lower East Side and who were hanging on the every word of Abby Hoffman and Jerry Rubin. Judson's history and Howard's reputation were an attraction to the foundation directors, who enjoyed being part of the hippie culture but who worried about giving money directly to Abby and Jerry.

Howard and I worked on a proposal that incorporated several programs. The first was to be a crisis center for teenage runaways. It would be only the second of its kind in the country and would use Judson House as its base. (The other, Huckleberry House, was located in San Francisco's Haight-Asbury section.) The second program would be a free medical clinic for teenagers and young adults to be housed in a construction trailer and relocated several times a year throughout the Lower East Side.

After Judson received a sufficient commitment of funding from the foundations, Howard and I went about planning for the opening of the runaway house. This meant first ending the student residence program. We then started preparing the house for its new function. At the end of the school year in 1968, the last students moved out and we began to prepare for the crisis center's opening. The project hired Nancy Katchel to work with me and we hired a few more COs as well.

Howard and I visited the police commissioner of New York City to inform the police department of what we were doing and to plea for some flexibility so that we would be able to work. We wanted to

The modest sign of the Center for Medical Consumers in a window of Judson House, 1999. Photo by Alice Garrard.

be able to assure runaways that they were in a safe place when they came to Judson House. Our commitment to the police department was that we would work to resolve whatever problem had caused the runaways to leave home.

Judson Church had once again been able to move into an area of need and construct a programmatic response. Judson House took on all of the colorations—literal and figurative—of the 1960s, including bizarre repainting of spaces. For a variety of reasons, not the least of which was Judson's tradition of not making programs into a permanent agency, the runaway program ended after a few years, and so did my involvement with Judson House, that is, until 1978.

CENTER FOR MEDICAL CONSUMERS

In 1976 Howard and I had started the Center for Medical Consumers. We housed it in available space on East 62nd Street, where I was administrator of the Center for Reproductive and Sexual Health (CRASH) on behalf of the church. After two years, after the decision to close CRASH, we moved the Center into Judson House, using the renovated space that had been occupied by the Moody family during the renovation of Grace House. I found myself back in the space where the office of the crisis center had been located and where I had slept every other night during the runaway program. The rooms on the upper floors were still covered with graffiti and symbols of the 1960s.

Maryann Napoli joined me soon after the opening of the Center. The Center for Medical Consumers still occupied the space twenty-two years later.

BRICKS AND MEMORIES

My head is filled with a variety of images of all that has gone on within the walls of Judson House and in its garden. I helped organize and carry out the laying of used brick in the garden. Amateurs all, we somehow constructed something that lasted to the end. The bricks are only one of many memories. People who lived in Judson House as students still stop by just to look around and tell us of the wonderful experiences they had when living there. Perhaps we should offer a garden brick to each and every person who lived, worked, attended meetings, or worshipped at Judson House as a tangible reminder of all the communal activities that took place in this space for almost a hundred years.

ARTHUR LEVIN
continues to be involved in the work of Judson Memorial Church.

Joan Muyskens

Joan Muyskens kept Al Carmines organized as his secretary from 1969 to 1977. She lived at Judson House from 1973 to 1977. ───────────

My first experience with Judson House dates to 1967. I had come to New York on vacation and stayed with Alice Bosveld, with whom I had gone to college. Alice took me to Al Carmines's apartment in Judson House for the first reading of *In Circles,* for which Alice planned to do the lights.

In 1969, when I moved to New York, Alice told me that Judson Church was looking for a secretary for Al Carmines. I applied, and Howard Moody and Arlene Carmen gave me a typing test. I had never typed on an electric typewriter and did not know how it worked. None of the keys seemed to be functioning. After a while, Arlene returned to see how I had done, and I explained that all the keys were stuck. She then explained that I had to turn the machine on first. Howard and Arlene were willing to give me another chance because they were desperate. I was hired even though I typed only thirty-five words per minute. (By the time I left Judson, I had increased my speed to 110.) Al never interviewed me.

In Circles introduced me to Gertrude Stein. I had never read anything by her. Actually, that was the worst part of working for Al: typing Gertrude Stein scripts. You could never tell if you had left out three words or three lines, and I always had this terrible fear that I had left out three pages.

THE (IN)FAMOUS CAST PARTIES

One of the attractions of performing at the Judson Poets Theater was getting to go to Al Carmines's famous opening and closing night parties. During the years I worked as Al's secretary, one of my duties was to go over to his Judson House apartment half an hour or so before the show ended, straighten up a bit, pop a canned ham in the oven, pour bags of pretzels and chips into bowls, and put out various other finger foods (all of which would be consumed within the first twenty minutes of the party). At the exact time the curtain would come down, I'd put frozen strawberries and peaches in two large punch bowls and begin opening bottles of champagne, which Al would then use to make a very lethal punch. Bowl after bowl after bowl of this punch would be consumed by the hundred or more people squished into Al's apartment.

These parties were the great social occasions of the theater, and as the majority of those attending were single people in their twenties and thirties, they marked the start of many a romance. Al delighted in observing all the pairings and took credit for any that ended in lasting relationships. He was less amused when someone would become fixated on him (this was a not uncommon occurrence) and not want to leave his apartment at party's end. Perhaps the most disruptive of these fans was the woman who locked herself into the bathroom about midway into a party and refused to budge, even though dozens of champagne-drinking partygoers were pounding on the door pleading for entrance.

After pouring the last of the champagne into bowls and mixing up his brew, Al would sit down at the piano and begin to play and sing—first his own songs, then some hymns or sentimental show tunes, and then always the blues. Conversation would cease, we'd each find a spot on the floor (Al's apartment contained one sofa, bookcases, a much-abused baby grand piano, and about a dozen carpet-covered cubes designed as seats and extremely uncomfortable) and escape into this incredible music for about an hour or so. When Al would finally wind down, we'd slowly leave.

AN APARTMENT IN JUDSON HOUSE

When Howard Moody heard that I was apartment hunting in the spring of 1973, he asked if I would like to live in Judson House. I could have the small basement apartment on the south end of Judson House for $125 per month The space was in terrible shape, and I would have to renovate it at my own expense. I had been working for Al for about four years. I worked not just days but also three or four nights a week ushering or house managing for the Judson Dance Theater and the Judson Poets Theater, so I jumped at the chance to live next door to the church. When I moved into Judson House a few months later, the only other occupants were Al, John

Tungate, and Mr. Jones (who surely had a first name, but I believe I never heard it used).

My apartment was on the basement level—right on the corner of Third and Thompson, down a half-dozen steps from the street. It consisted of four rooms: a 12- by 15-foot living room; a 12- by 7-foot bedroom; a similarly sized kitchen; and an L-shaped bathroom. It was a small apartment with a surfeit of doors. The living room had three: the front door opening onto the stairway up to the street, a door to the kitchen, and one to the bedroom. The bedroom sported the door to the living room, one to a closet, and one to the bathroom. The kitchen had a door to the living room, a door to the bathroom, and a door to a room that was always referred to as the "old kitchen," a large basement room that in 1973 served as John Tungate's workshop. My refrigerator sat in front of the door to the old kitchen. My bathroom also had three doors: the one between it and the kitchen, one to the bedroom, and one opening into a sunken area off the Judson Garden.

I have many fond memories of life in Judson House: John Tungate raising tomatoes on the roof and sharing them with the rest of us in the building; warm summer nights in the garden nattering with whoever happened to stop by; watching the garden squirrels, whom John had trained to eat out of his hand, go to work each morning and return each night (they religiously climbed a tree, leapt onto the House roof, over to the fire escape, down it to Thompson Street, and on to Washington Square Park for the day, and returned at night for John's handouts). There was Al's period of cooking—several months when he would appear almost nightly at my door to borrow an electric mixer, a casserole dish, eggs, milk, whatever. For someone who kept forgetting how to turn on the oven he whipped up some amazing and wonderful things. Mr. Jones sometimes knocked on my door late at night having forgotten his keys and needing to go through my apartment and the garden to the unlocked back door of the House.

A BURGLAR AND THE WINOS

Then there was the night I returned from vacation a day early. Exhausted, I dumped my bags in the living room, put on a nightgown, and fell into bed only to hear a clamor in the kitchen. I jumped up to investigate and upon throwing on the kitchen light discovered John Tungate perched atop my refrigerator in his underwear with hammer in hand. He muttered an apology, crawled down, and disappeared through the door behind the refrigerator into the old kitchen, leaving me to spend the night wondering why he had staged this bizarre appearance. The next morning he explained that he had heard my gate (it had a distinctive squeak), seen a light go on in my apartment, and, believing I was out of town until the next day, thought someone had broken in. To catch my robber in the act, he entered my apartment the only way he could without breaking in himself.

Generally congregated in front of my apartment, leaning against the fence and gate by my front door, were a group of homeless men— what in the 1960s we termed "winos." These men lived between the liquor store on the corner of Bleecker and Thompson and Washington Square Park. Before I moved into Judson House, they had tended to use my front door as a urinal. The regulars and I soon got to know each other, and when I'd go in or out, one of them would usually open the gate for me and give a little bow. I'd smile, say thanks, and go my way. This polite live-and-let-live relationship went on for a year or two, until the morning that I ran into Cornbread Givens on the sidewalk between my apartment and the side door of the church.

Cornbread, a tall, attractive black man, had been the previous "occupant" of my Judson House apartment. He had never lived in it, but he had used the rooms as a temporary office. If my memory is correct, Cornbread was involved in getting assistance for cooperative farms in the South. At any rate, he had been gone for several years when our paths crossed that morning. Upon seeing me, Cornbread called "Joan," ran to me, picked me up, spun me around, an gave me a big kiss. We chatted for a while, then went our separate ways. The next morning, as I walked from my apartment to the church, one of the winos yelled "Joan," grabbed me, spun me around, gave me a big kiss, put me down, and doubled up laughing. This ritual went on for several weeks, much to the amusement of the other hangers-out.

TIME AND AGAIN

Because my windows were at street level, I had little privacy; on the other hand, I was privy to all the conversations on the street (I had no air conditioning and my windows were open a lot). Listening to the winos was an education in how the legal system worked. They had all been in and out of jail so many times that they knew exactly what their rights were and which Legal Aid lawyers were best. They referred to various judges by first name. I also overheard many an amusing conversation at 4 A.M. when the Raspberry Freeze, a jazz bar on Third Street next to the church garden, and the lesbian bar across from it closed and the two groups of patrons collided.

My favorite sound, though, was that of horses' hooves echoing through my bedroom early each Sunday morning as New York City's mounted police went to work. A fan of *Time and Again,* I would listen to the passing horses, then slowly open my eyes to see if I would be in a different time—if perhaps I might find myself in a just-opened Judson House in the city that Edward Judson knew and loved. Alas, it never happened. But early each Sunday morning as I lay in my basement bedroom, I'd have a fresh chance to dream.

JOAN MUYSKENS PURSLEY

lives in New York City.

Arlene Carmen

Arlene Carmen died in 1994. The following chapter was written by Abigail Hastings, with help from people who knew Arlene well during the twenty-seven years that she worked at Judson Memorial Church as its administrator.

It was a rare lunch with Arlene that I did not leave with the same impression: After what could be a lengthy conversation, there I was feeling naked, so to speak, while it seemed she still had her coat on. I mention this because I knew from those encounters that Arlene was a private person. Only in the period of collecting remembrances of her days in Judson House did I realize how private. There was not even strong consensus about when she moved into the house—somewhere in the early to mid-1970s. These fuzzy recollections must delight her. I find Arlene's stealthlike occupation of Judson House a fitting likeness to her furtive presence in the back of the Meeting Room during Sunday services.

Arlene was not new to the Village when she moved into 237 Thompson Street. She had lived in an apartment above a fish restaurant at Jane and Hudson, and before that and somewhat prophetically—as she would probably not have said—she had an apartment on the corner of Bedford and Carmine streets, the very corner where Judson's predecessor church, Berean Baptist, had stood years before.

Arlene moved into Judson House as it was undergoing yet another incarnation—from student and runaway house to staff housing and a home for the Center for Medical Consumers. By all accounts, she enjoyed her twenty years there, joking from time to time about how difficult it was to get "the landlord" to attend to repairs.

Living and working in close proximity may have heightened Arlene's need for privacy, the instinct and inclination to create a place of sanctuary for herself. Still, her apartment was open for the occasional pledge dinner or a brunch for new church members. Apparently, her kitchen was not a hotbed for cooking, although she did get involved in the "Eat Club" and managed to come up with a casserole of her own making, of which she was quite proud. But the story

I love, which may be apocryphal but so captures the spirit of Arlene, is the chicken story.

CHICKEN SOUP FOR THE SICK

Perhaps because she was Jewish and was presumed to know such things, Arlene was asked by someone in the congregation for instructions on how to make chicken soup. Arlene's knowledge of cooking was not vast, her primary source book being the *I Hate to Cook Book,* but somewhere she picked up the conviction that for a good chicken soup you have to use the feet.

So it was when Arlene set her mind to making chicken soup for a sick friend. She knew she had to start with a *live* chicken. Fresh poultry—really fresh—was available for many years from a dim if noisy shop further down on Thompson Street. Arlene went and picked out two chickens, had them killed and plucked, and brought them back to her small kitchen to make a soup of healing properties, fortified no doubt by the inclusion of those feet. Sources that are normally highly reliable confirm that Arlene was so grossed out by the innards that she threw everything away and let her friend remain sick.

SECURITY AND SANCTUARY

Arlene was a fastidious monitor of Judson House security. Both Arlene and Roland Wiggins were on the case of unlocked doors, lights in the garden, or unannounced guests in the house. At the same time, Arlene recognized those emergency situations where the use of the house and its hospitality were more important than the rules and regulations generally enforced.

Over the years, Arlene created sanctuary in the apartment not only for herself but also for others who needed a place of protection and acceptance. She opened her home to the working women who sought safe haven, some of whom had decided to leave the life of prostitution and others who needed an in-between place to sort things out. A small guest room off the living room welcomed the women and others over the years in a quiet gesture of hospitality. The apartment was sometimes a venue for young people in the church to gather and graduate from bubble gum to adult conversations with Arlene. The apartment was also the site of a series of "flashers" meetings—a gathering of women, and at least one man, where issues of menopause were explored at a time when "the change" was rarely discussed so candidly.

There was the time during Judson's involvement with Central America in the 1980s that a call came from a lawyer about a woman refugee who had been smuggled into the country. She had been brutalized and raped in a prison in El Salvador, and with her was a baby from that rape and a nine-year-old. The lawyer needed a secret place to take her deposition and hide her for a few days. Arlene did not hesitate for a moment, and the woman and her two children were put up in the guest room next to Arlene's apartment. Arlene made a "safe home" for that family until they were able to move into a more permanent safe environment.

Arlene was not always alone in the apartment. For many years she had the companionship of Maxine. Max was a beagle who late in life developed a pronounced and raucous respiratory pattern (a dog only Arlene could love, someone said). Arlene also took in one of the babies of a Lee and Essie brood, a kitten named Butter. Butter was named not for the color of her coat, as I had imagined, but for a prostitute Arlene had known.

In so much of what Arlene undertook, it seemed as if she was intent on teaching us the meaning of *chutzpah,* a quality she often demonstrated in the choices she made in her life's work and in her attitude toward life. Seeing her one Sunday morning with a bruised-up face was a reminder of the courage and fortitude that living on Thompson Street sometimes required. There were frequently those who lingered, loitered, or simply took up residence on the 237 stoop, and one such regular, perhaps in a bad way that night, shoved the heavy metal door into Arlene's face. It is said that he later came to apologize, but Arlene bore the mark of the incident for quite some time.

If the rowdy parade of urban life—with the all-night singing, drug exchanges, car alarms, and drunken brawls—tormented Thompson Street, then the antidote was out the window on the other side of Arlene's apartment. She loved the Judson garden, tended it, fed birds there, set out wind chimes, and kept flower boxes in bloom. She was known to sit in the garden when the choir was practicing in the Long Room, listening for the sounds she loved coming from the open sliding doors. In the summer, on those Sundays when she did not quite make it down to the service in the garden, she still listened from her narrow and hidden side balcony, a stream of cigarette smoke the only sign that gave her away.

I was in Arlene's apartment only a few times but I remember its comfortable feel. I remember thinking how the working women must have felt to be welcomed into a place that was so unpretentious and accessible. I think about her books and her bamboo furniture, the elegant pantsuits hanging in her closet, and the oxfords she loved to wear. As with all lives well lived, an imprint is made, vivid and enduring. Little wonder that sitting out in the garden, it was hard not to think you still heard her wind chimes by the flowerboxes, or think you just saw a glimpse of curling smoke escaping from that second-floor balcony.

Roland Wiggins

Roland Wiggins has been the custodian of Judson Church and
Judson House since the mid-1970s. ────────────────────────

Ifirst came to Judson in September 1973. A friend of mine named
Susan Marshall asked me to come. It was an Agape Sunday. I
looked around and said, "What kind of church is this?" And she
said, "O, you know, it's a theater and it's a church." Well, I was used
to churches with preachers and pews. We sat down, and everyone
was singing and eating peanut butter and stuff. So I started coming
regularly. At the time I was working for Vincent Lippe. They were
wholesalers of Christmas decorations on Fifth Avenue and 26th
Street. I donated a lot of stuff to the Judson Bazaar.

Eileen McNutt was the first person I met at Judson. She introduced herself and said she was having a party at her house, and
would I like to come. I have never forgotten that.

At the time there was a young woman named Lola who was in
charge of the agape meals. She was on her way to California to
make a movie, and she asked me if I could fill in for her until she
came back. She never returned and I am still here, waiting for her to
come back.

The job at Judson developed slowly. First, all I had to do was
open up on Sundays for the service and close the church again. Then
Arlene told me about this fellow Cesar, who got arrested for making
bootleg liquor. He had been the custodian. Arlene wanted to know if
I was interested in the job. I said I could do it at night and still keep
my daytime job. Then my job with the wholesalers folded, and I
came to Judson on a permanent basis.

MOONSHINE ON THOMPSON STREET

In September 1982 I moved into the apartment in Judson House
where Joan Muyskens and Cesar and two other fellows had lived before me. Arlene preferred me to live in the house for security rea-

sons. Cesar had had this sideline, where he made liquor in the bathtub. On Saturday night he would take a table from the church and set up outside on the corner of Thompson and West Third and sell the stuff. I had never seen a bathtub that was so white and spotless. Cesar also had a lot of alcoholic friends who would stay the night in the Garden room and other places. That was another reason why he had to leave.

Before I moved in, I had to scrape the paint in the rooms. They were covered with sixties drawings of naked women and stuff. I also had to fix a few things, but otherwise the place was okay.

Living where you work is good in one way and bad in another. People know you live there and will bother you for things day and night. They don't make appointments. But it's good when it is snowing. I got used to the noise on Thompson Street, especially on the weekends.

DRUGS ON THOMPSON STREET

Life on Thompson Street has gotten a lot better. Back in the 1980s, it was very bad. The winos would hang out on the Judson House steps. They would drink and get into fights with broken bottles. We still have drug addicts. The pushers don't hang out. They come because they know their customers are here, but then they move on. The drug addicts stay around because they want to use what they just bought. Most of the users are New Jersey people, but some are from right around here. Also, you would be surprised to see how many cabdrivers come here, early on Sunday morning, five or six o'-clock. Most of the stuff that sells here is crack and pot. Cocaine is too rich for the people down here.

It used to be even worse. Now that we have a surveillance camera on the corner of Thompson and the park, the users have moved to either Sullivan or LaGuardia Place. I also keep telling everyone, keep walking, man—the pushers and the customers, street people, everybody. You have to be careful with the street people. It could be anyone. People remember what happened to Arlene. She tried to enter the building, and one of these guys would not let her. As she opened the door, he slammed the door in her face. Her face was messed up for weeks.

Street people often come to Thompson Street with a lot of garbage, and when they leave, they don't take their garbage with them. The worst spot now is Third and Macdougal. Even some people from NYU are selling dope. They busted a security guard with seventeen years on the job.

I got a part-time job with the laundry here on Thompson. The guy that owns it asked me to be around because the people that use it feel safer that way. That way, you stop trouble before it starts. There are no more street people hanging out there.

I don't know many of my neighbors. It used to be that you knew people ten, fifteen, twenty years. Now people rent for a year or two and move on. There are mostly small apartments, so when people get married or have a baby, they have to move. Every two years you see all new faces.

This has been a good job for me. I like working with my hands. The building is not in such bad shape now as it was in the early eighties. The building was rewired and the plumbing is all right. We still have trouble with the heat because it comes from NYU. Sometimes they shut it off, and then we have to complain. Mark Rubinsky did a lot of work here in the eighties when he and Lee Hancock lived here.

I have met a lot of good people. I must say I have never met a bad person at Judson although I may not agree with everyone. I have a lot of good memories of this building and especially the people. Some are still around, others have moved on. One thing I miss these days are the parties we used to have at Judson. Boy, Judson people could party. The parties at Al's place were something. A lot of people have gotten older now and they no longer live nearby. The younger generation, when they get to a certain age, they move on.

THE SUNDAY SCHOOL KIDS

One thing I have always enjoyed is the Sunday School. I knew these kids from when they were babies, some even before they were born. And then you see them grow up and go off to college. I remember all of them. Blaine used to give Arlene a fit when instead of being in Sunday School he would be in the gym with a basketball; Josh Wolff would give Arlene a hard time, too. There were the Deakins kids, the

Craft girls, on and on. There was a group of kids, and then it seemed to stop, and now we have just girls in Sunday School. As a matter of fact, there have always been a lot of girls. You can count the boys in the last twenty years on your hands.

When you have been here this long, you can go on talking forever. I'll miss this place.

ROLAND WIGGINS
continues to be the custodian for Judson Memorial Church.

Lorry Moody

Lorry Moody and her husband, Howard, have been connected with Judson since 1956.

This old house has been home to us, both literally and figuratively, for over forty years. When Grace House was in the process of conversion from a one-family brownstone to a luxury duplex (1975–1976), our family was housed in what is now the Center for Medical Consumers. Every time I walk into the library I can picture our living room and bedroom in that space. The French doors opened to the small roof area (over Roland's bathroom), which was just big enough for two to enjoy alfresco dining in the summer. What is now Arthur Levin's office was our dining room and Dan's bedroom combined. (Deborah was away at college.) What is now the front office was our kitchen.

We loved having Arlene Carmen as our upstairs neighbor. At the least provocation we would join forces for a late evening icecream "smorgasbord" and hash over the events of the day. It was also very reassuring to have John Tungate and Roland Wiggins living there and taking care of the building inside and out. And with Paul Rounsaville and Al Carmines across the hall, we could not have asked for a more congenial and stimulating place to live.

C&C AT C

It would be impossible to highlight the hundreds of events that were held at Judson House, but among the more memorable were Al's cast parties and Champagne and Carmines at Christmas (C&C at C), when Al would give his unforgettable performances in his apartment. At C&C at C in 1976, our son Dan, who was sixteen at the time, and a friend were recruited as waiters to mingle among the guests with champagne refills. The guests were shoulder to shoulder, with holiday cheer flowing freely. The boys must have decided that when a bottle got too low to pass again they would "clean it up." By the end of the affair they were hors de combat—a true learning experience. Dan has never touched champagne since. The aptly named punch Al served at his other parties became almost as famous as Al himself. Many guests also found this brew instructive, including our daughter, Deborah, who became an unwitting student on one occasion. Being the designated caregiver, I of course did not benefit from this educational experience.

When Howard retired in 1992 we helped with plans to get the apartment ready for Bill and Laurie Malcomson's stay. When Peter Laarman arrived and the Malcomsons went back to Seattle, we were privileged to be under the Judson House roof again. It has been the ideal living situation, especially for Howard's activities. Once more we enjoyed the most delightful housemates. First, Arlene, of course, then Andy Frantz and Garp, Louise Green, Maureen Wallin, and Hannah upstairs, Roland Wiggins on the corner, and weekday greetings and celebrations with Maryann Napoli and Arthur Levin at the Center for Medical Consumers across the hall.

THE PEACE OF THE GARDEN

I cannot separate memories of the house from reminiscenses of the garden, our private refuge from the busy street. Sunday morning worship, weddings, plantings, parties, greetings, and farewells all start to blend a bit, with one exception. In my mind's eye I can still see Reathel Bean at the BBQ, bless his heart. (Shouldn't he have a plaque or something?) Our pets have loved having a safe place to run and play, watching the birds and chasing the squirrels. The garden is a mini almanac, telling us the weather and the seasons out our window.

I will be forever grateful for all the ways in which Judson House has supported and enriched my life and for all the dear friends who shared with me in its history.

LORRY AND HOWARD MOODY
divide their time between New York City and Santa Barbara, California.

Lee Hancock

From 1981 to 1985, Lee Hancock served as assistant and associate minister at Judson Memorial Church. She and her husband, Mark Rubinsky, and eventually their first daughter, Hannah, lived in Judson House.

The unassuming metal door never revealed the secrets that were inside. The door opened to a multitude of hospitalities that often collided, confusing those who entered: a residence for some; for others, a place of learning, of group interaction and argument, of decision and celebration. Over this threshold, people came to investigate a health problem, attend a study group or board meeting, or, like Arlene Carmen with her signature quart of milk and us, find home. It was the site of the Center for Medical Consumers. Art Levin, with his maniacal grin, presided with an eager quip, barb, or joke. His sidekick, Maryann Napoli, always the foil, was perpetually amazed by his foolishness.

It was not always easy adjusting to multiple activities. The desire for refuge, to escape from city life, was often denied. Judson House was a collision of public and private that challenged the practiced urban art of ignoring one's neighbors.

THE B AND T CROWD

Weekdays were heavy with the traffic of the church and its various ministries. Weekends were rife with the presence of what Roland Wiggins poetically termed the "bridge and tunnel crowd from 'Bohoken.'" Thompson Street was the shortest distance between two points: the beer store and Washington Square Park. The smell of vomit, urine, and beer on Sunday morning always created a unique context for church, especially during those hot summer days when worship was held in the garden. Roland, always a firm believer in the virtues of water, would throw gallons of it—hot, sudsy, and cut with ammonia—over the steps and into the stairwells to neutralize the souvenirs of Saturday night revelries.

One Saturday evening in the early spring, the crowd was renewing its energies as the trees in Washington Square Park began to bud. I was downstairs in our apartment doing laundry. We had just installed our first bourgeois accouterments, a washer and dryer brought in by sturdy Sears employees from the outer environs of New Jersey. As I bent over the dryer, a member of the B and T crowd jumped over the grate into the stairwell to relieve himself. Startled by the noise, I turned and met him eye to eye with less than three feet between us. Here I was, playing the role of the suburban housewife, maintaining the order and normality that come with folding laundry, when the intruder entered my stairwell to pee. The abrupt encounter jarred us both. With youthful braggadocio, he let fly word and gesture designed to mask his dismay at my unexpected presence. I, in the role of matron, and he, the aspiring Village punk reminded of the world he inhabited before entering the Holland Tunnel, were caught in the dance of an unexpected rendez-vous. This colliding and crashing of worlds and roles and expectations shaped the very life of Judson House.

HANNAH ARRIVES

The advent of Hannah in 1985 added another layer of texture. I vividly remember the mother of all surprise showers pulled off in the garden literally under our noses. It was beyond our wildest imaginings to be feted with a shower so grand that the child to be born received more presents than baby Jesus himself. Then there were the careful preparation and decorating of the nursery, a room once dedicated to late-night revels and assignations, now transformed into a vessel of innocence in yellow and white.

During the summer of 1985 while on maternity leave, I would stand in the nursery window on Sunday morning overlooking the garden, holding my infant and watching worship. I would listen to the words and sounds of Judson being Judson at its best, in the songs and prayers and truth telling called worship. I would sway and rock with Hannah in my arms, and ever so often a stray eye—from Sue Harwig, Kae Lewis, Dan Shenk, David Johnson, or others—would glance at the nursery window to embrace the infant in our midst.

Then there was Roland Wiggins. Roland was the sentinel, keeping watch over the property. Nothing escaped his vision, eagle-eyed yet friendly. He was our protector, not self-proclaimed but always steadfast. Roland brought a sense of quiet security to the place. One moment invisible, the next he would pop out of nowhere, green eyes flashing smiles for baby Hannah bundled up for a park excursion. Roland adored babies, cooing and flirting with her while deftly maneuvering an awkward stroller down the steps of Judson House.

LIFE ON THOMPSON STREET

Glancing down Thompson Street, your eyes were always met by those of another inveterate watcher: Billy Soto, who owned and operated the newsstand on the corner of Thompson and West Third. Between Billy and Roland, our block was always covered. Nothing got by, nothing was missed, not the antics of the drunken Indian man who, more than once, poured out his story of woe on the naive ears of an earnest associate minister.

The top floor of the building, long in disrepair, was downright spooky. Beyond Arlene's apartment and up a flight of stairs, ghosts of other lifetimes inhabited tiny rooms with chipped paint and windows painted black, adorned with an occasional abandoned peace symbol. In his characteristically enthusiastic but low-key way, Howard, the dreamer of dreams, would sporadically take us up to the top—Art, Arlene, and myself—to discuss the prospect of resurrecting the space, hoping against hope that it just might not be impossible to find the necessary energy. In its silence, this floor stood as an odd monument to history, its uninhabited status in direct contradiction with the lower floors, which burst with activity.

The lounge of Judson House held its own mysteries. It was inhabited with furniture that provided equal opportunity discomfort. The couches were comic: frighteningly low but unquestioned, since they were neither purchased nor in ill repair. One had to sink very far down to hit bottom. Getting up was always a challenge; others seemed to master the art more gracefully than I. But comfort did not matter. The intellectual querying, the sparring and sparking of the imagination, distracted from immediate fleshly concerns.

The walls and stairwell of the basement floor had the feeling of catacombs thanks to their dank and musty ambiance, not to mention leaks from the bathrooms upstairs. In those low spaces, history was made in art and revolution, and in the human heart. Witness and creativity wound round each other in acts of resistance and imagination and love that brought life to those who, gathered into community, breathed in its heady and aromatic Spirit.

LEE HANCOCK, MARK RUBINSKY,
and their two daughters live in Upper Nyack, New York.

Mark Rubinsky

Mark Rubinsky and Lee Hancock lived in Judson House during Lee's tenure as assistant and associate minister at Judson from 1981 to 1985.

"It needs a little work," said the tall guy with the sharp, short hair and a perceptible glint in his piercing blue eyes. Today those words would make me want to hide under the bed and cover my ears. In 1981 it was a symphony: 2,000 square feet of limitless opportunity. In those days, "it needs a little work" meant that anything was possible. Besides, I had spent many hours renovating other people's apartments—and this would be for us.

It was with these thoughts that I first "met" Judson House and the place where the newly called assistant minister, the Rev. Lee Hancock, and I would soon take up residence. It meant a new era in our lives, for Lee a job at one of New York City's most exciting and controversial churches, and for us an apartment in Greenwich Village.

The measuring, designing, and dreaming began immediately. Then followed several weeks of packing, which was surprising, since the move itself took one day in a loosely packed, modestly sized truck of a professional mover. When the truck pulled into Thompson Street, it blocked traffic. We did not pay attention to the alternate-side-of-the-street sign. Even though the movers unloaded the truck in less than three hours, a particularly obstreperous neighbor called the police, and we split the $50 ticket for obstructing traffic with the movers. We were officially welcomed to the neighborhood.

Exhausted, we unpacked a few boxes, unrolled our futon by the window, and lay down, bathed in the light from the streetlights through the bare windows as we watched a full lunar eclipse perform for us over the Village rooftops.

AL CARMINES'S OLD APARTMENT

The next morning we surveyed the scene. As you opened the apartment's front door, you were immediately confronted with three steps going up to a three-foot-wide runway that ran to the far end of the room where the kitchen was located. The wall to the left was completely covered with shelves made from construction-grade two-by-tens. Usually found under floors and used as joists, they certainly made for strong, if relatively crude, bookcases. A little further to the left was a small bedroom with a pit in the middle. The pit was the shape of a mattress. Again down the runway, also to the left, was a bathroom that at first blush seemed standard: sink, toilet, sunken tub, except that it wasn't really a sunken tub. A raised floor with a weird shaggy black carpet made it look sunken. Past the bedroom was the small but serviceable kitchen, also raised from the original floor level. At the end of the main room to the right of the runway a large squared-off platform created a dining area. The long, thin space to the right of the ramp was the living area. All of this area was covered in threadbare, stained, smelly, dusty, formerly gray but currently scary, industrial carpet, acres of it, climbing the side of the runway and draping the steps. We were not inspired to take our shoes off.

But the space did not stop there. Down a fairly treacherous (at least after a few drinks) spiral staircase was another room. We were told it had been a gallery space. This space with its illustrious past was now dark because a wall covered up one of its windows. The ceiling was crumbling. At the end of a short hallway there was a toilet that had not been used in decades. On one side of the space a door led out to iron steps up to the street, and on the other side there was a munchkin-sized door to the fabulous garden in the rear.

(Yup, it needed a little work, glint, glint.)

But the possibilities were endless. So we got a dumpster and a bunch of friends. We even remembered to order it on the right alternate-side-of-the-street parking day. It was the biggest dumpster we could get: twenty cubic yards. We wanted to be sure to have plenty of extra space. We removed one of the front windows and built a ramp from the window to the top of the dumpster. A few hours of hard work, and we would be rid of the smelly, moldy industrial carpet. We would get rid of this runway, too.

The runway had a rich history. During a discussion with my electrician at the off-Broadway run of Russ Treyz's *Cotton Patch Gospel* I heard a little more of the legend of 237 Thompson Street. Admittedly, this is hearsay, but my electrician claims to have been a participant and he was relatively sober the day he told me the story.

HOW THE APARTMENT WAS ORIGINALLY RENOVATED
(ALTERNATE VERSION)

It was five or fifteen years ago (this should set the stage in terms of credibility), and Al Carmines was opening another show. Because he was a loved and respected genius of Off Broadway and because it was his birthday (or Christmas or just because), a group of folks decided to surprise him with an overnight renovation of his apartment at Judson House. While Al labored next door at the Judson Poets Theater, this crew would effect a magical transformation of the apartment. An unnamed set designer drew up plans, and a flock or gaggle or bunch or mob (you choose, but remember it was off-Broadway in the 1960s or 1970s) of stagehands descended upon the premises for an orgy of renovation and managed to have the place complete by the time the curtain came down and the opening night party began.

I have the utmost respect for professional stagehands. I work with them often. They are truly loving, loyal, honest, talented craftspeople. I have also worked as a carpenter and electrician for off-Broadway theater. We, too, were caring, loyal, talented, and honest, but the craft part was variable. Many of us were just learning. I would have to surmise that the assault on Judson House that fateful day was a learning experience for many. It certainly was for me, those many years later, on that day of the dumpster.

YARD AFTER CUBIC YARD OF DEBRIS

Soon the carpet was in the dumpster and barrels of just plain trash were being lugged out. It was now time to demolish the runway. Crowbar in hand, we began to pry at the plywood. With a mighty screech it began to loosen. It screeched because it had been assembled with an evil nail called a resin coated box nail. This nail is coated with the same resin a violinist uses. As the name implies, the nail is meant to secure wooden boxes that will see rough use. It is meant never to come out, and it lived up to its reputation.

We were finally making headway, and the top of the runway came off. It was like opening a treasure chest. Would we find a time capsule of keepsakes? Maybe some old playbills? Would you have guessed all of the construction debris from the renovation? If plaster weighs around 100 pounds per cubic foot (just a ballpark figure), a conservative estimate would run to a minimum of three tons. It looked more like twenty, and it was topped off with (and this is absolutely, unequivocally true) a pair of dirty socks, some underwear, and half a Blimpie sandwich still in its bag (no, we did not open the bag but it felt rather intact). At least we now knew why things always smelled sour and gritty, like an overflowing ashtray the morning after a good party.

(It needs a little work, he said with a glint in those steely blue eyes.)

Garbage can after garbage can went into the dumpster. In a fit of youthful optimism, we had procured a floor sander, and someone started sanding the exposed floors. They looked like the boards of an old dock that had been exposed to the elements for decades. There was so much dust you could not see the wall at the far end of the space, but by the time the sun was setting the floors had been sanded, the runway was memory, and the dumpster was filled to the rim. It had been quite a day. We served beer and pizza to our faithful friends (thank you) and then took showers in the bathroom with the black shaggy carpet. The water leaked into the community room below. I am sure we slept soundly that night, although I can't remember where.

Several months later I was spending my days renovating and my nights at the Majestic Theater as the stage manager for the show *Agnes of God*. Things were slowing down on the Mr. Fix It front, so we did the logical thing: We decided to throw a party. That would inspire us to move ahead. It was to be Arlene Carmen's fifteenth year at Judson, and a surprise party was in order. In the spirit of earlier renovations, we stayed up all night gluing parquet tiles to the just finished curved steps to the dining area as we vacuumed sawdust and removed construction debris. We finished around 3 p.m. and people started arriving at 4.

It was a great party. At Judson House it always was.

MARK RUBINSKY AND LEE HANCOCK
live in Upper Nyack, New York.

Bill Malcomson

Bill Malcomson spent twenty months, from the spring of 1992 until the end of 1993, as interim pastor at Judson Memorial Church. This was the period after Howard Moody's retirement and before the arrival of Peter Laarman in January 1994.

When Laurie and I arrived in New York, many people told us how fortunate we were to live in a large apartment at Judson House. We had not lived in apartments since college days, so we did not consider it that good a deal. However, we were grateful that we had a place to live so close to everything. I enjoyed being next door to the Meeting Room and just inside from the garden. Laurie was close to where she found work, at Saint Joseph's, over on Sixth Avenue. We also loved Washington Square Park, where something was always going on.

What we did not like was the noise. Living on the first floor, we were often painfully aware of what was going on just outside our front door. On weekends, folks from New Jersey came over and used the front stoop as a place to gather, drink, use dope, and be loud. Cars with rap music booming from huge speakers seemed to be coming down Thompson Street nonstop. It sometimes felt as if we were living in the middle of the street. Our bedroom was on the floor below the living room, and fortunately the sounds were more muffled there. Incidentally, we enjoyed sleeping under an old tin ceiling.

On weekends, a young man would park his bike in front of our building and entertain his friends. Laurie got to know him well, but it soon became obvious that he was a drug supplier. He was nice to us because he did not want us to turn him in.

One time we noticed that a pigeon was spending a lot of time outside the window of the first floor bathroom. We realized she was sitting on eggs. Every time we used the bathroom we checked to see how things were progressing. Finally an egg hatched. Arlene Carmen thought we were a little nuts getting excited over a baby pigeon, but we enjoyed observing nature up close in the midst of city dirt and grime.

It was fun to realize that our apartment had witnessed a lot of makeovers and a lot of history. We could tell where major renovations had been done in the past, not excluding Al Carmines's installation of a "stage" on which to perform. We used it as a dining area.

All in all, Judson House turned out to be a great place to live in spite of the noise, dirt, and drugs. We lived in the middle of a great city and in an incredible village inside that city. We were participants in history. We continue to look back on that time in our lives with real fondness and warm feelings.

BILL AND LAURIE MALCOMSON
live in Seattle.

Paul Chapman

Paul Chapman used Judson House as his base for the Employment Project. ─────────────────────────

In May 1994 I meet Peter Laarman for the first time and talk about the employment crisis: Our economy is eliminating jobs, disposing of people, sending jobs overseas. People are working longer, yet wages are stagnating. What happens to us when there are no more jobs? I tell Peter about the Employment Project, which I started in Vermont, where I am living at the time.

In December 1994 I have a question for Peter: The year-old project needs to relocate to an urban center. Does Peter have any ideas? His answer is: "We have some rooms in Judson House. Contribute some sweat equity, and the space is yours. Your project will be independent of Judson, but the Judson community will get behind you."

In January 1995 the Judson board agrees, and on February 1, 1995, I confront the second-floor mess: two rooms at the end of the corridor on the West Third Street side and about 200 square feet of storage space. There is one room for my office and one room for associates and eventually for job seekers, where they can practice their computer skills, compose and print their resumes, access the Internet in their search for jobs, and know that Judson supports their efforts.

The graffiti we find are nothing very original, by-words of an era: Sex, Love, Peace, Pot. Death Is Out There, Home Sweet Home. "Anna" and "Carlos" are scrawled in lipstick red on the black-painted walls. Someone created a white peace symbol with paint so thick it ran.

The dark walls make the rooms look even smaller than they are: 9 by 10 feet, with a bare light bulb in the ceiling and a few crude shelves nailed to the wall or hung with wire from the ceiling. Each room has a 3 by 3 closet. Some walls are glued with burlap to prevent the plaster from crumbling further.

DUMPSTERS FULL OF TRASH

First, the trash must go. It takes two dumpsters to remove the junk that has accumulated since the rooms were abandoned and the pigeons took over. There is almost nothing to save. Then follow the long hours of tearing out, plastering, cleaning, and painting. Five gallons of plaster and three coats of white latex are needed to cover the old wounded walls and dark paint. Still, some of the lipstick graffiti leaks through, still legible: "Anna."

We replace the ceiling with sheetrock and paint it. (Later, the leaking roof stains our new ceiling.) We remove the closets but save the sturdy two by fours. It's hard to find straight two by fours like these. New windows are installed and the offices are equipped with new wiring to run office equipment. We install air conditioning. The bright morning sun shining over the Catholic Center is a joy year around, but it gets hot in the summer, warns Art Levin. A month later the carpet is laid and in come two telephone lines, the fax machine, the copier, the computer, the file cabinet, and the old cherry rolltop desk (19 cubbyholes, 11 drawers) that goes wherever I go.

On July 31, 1995, Bob Herbert, a columnist for the *New York Times,* writes about Judson Memorial Church and the Employment Project. We are now on the map. The column gives rise to dozens of telephone calls from people facing an employment crisis.

NO MORE JOBS

We begin our Wednesday night meetings in September 1995 in the Judson House Lounge. Every week we see people without work, people who want to change jobs, people in their twenties who cannot figure out how to get the required experience no one will give them, people in their fifties who have been either downsized or replaced by younger, cheaper workers. There are people who have been let go from jobs after many years: executives, cooks, buyers, doctors, administrative assistants, waiters, school teachers, managers. Others come because they cannot handle the long hours, job insecurity, and hostile environment of their jobs: nurses, editors, drivers, warehouse workers.

They come to express their anger, uncertainty, distrust, depression. *I am so angry at the way they made me leave. I had given so much to that company—my life—and they pushed me out like flot-sam. An hour to clear my desk while security watched.*

People describe their crises at home. It is hard to get started in the morning. The children are embarrassed. The bills are piling up. The spouse is getting impatient and irritable. There is no longer health insurance. Friends do not want to hear about it. *Where did I go wrong?*

Six different versions of their resumes are out there. Sometimes there is the encouraging interview, followed by days of waiting, hoping. The phone finally rings. *Sorry, we are looking for someone else.* There is temp work, a few days here, two weeks there (but no benefits). People dream of starting their own business, becoming a graphic designer. But there is so much competition out there.

Some people do get new jobs, decent jobs. Others come back to the group after a year because things did not work out. *I was doing well. They said they liked me. I don't get it.*

Since March 1995 the Employment Project has published a monthly newsletter, *No More Jobs.* We print it on pink paper, to make the connection with the new workplace reality (the dreaded pink slip) and send out 1,200 copies. We want to deepen the awareness of the religious community to the economic crisis in the lives of their members. We remind churches and synagogues of their biblical mandate to work for economic justice, to assure equitable distribution of the Earth's resources, with special concern for the least among us: welfare recipients, minimum-wage workers, the millions of children who grow up in poverty.

How do we live responsibly in an economy that favors the privileged few and marginalizes the majority? How do we live responsibly in an abusive economy? How can we be a sign of hope and of God's love?

Carlos? Anna? Have you found a place in this world after leaving your 9 by 10 Judson home? Have you found your Home Sweet Home in this hard world? We are still here and the door is open.

PAUL CHAPMAN
continues his work as director of the Employment Project.

Andrew Frantz

Andrew Frantz, Judson's Sunday School coordinator, moved into Judson House in 1995.

I should probably begin by telling you that I do not believe in ghosts. This position is not ironclad, and if you, dear reader, happen to come from the great beyond, please take no offense and feel free to show up at the foot of my bed, rattling your chains in the middle of the night. It's just that in an age where angels seem to be hovering 'round cash registers everywhere, and with a generation of X-filers at the start of a new millennium, their heads filled with supernatural conspiracies far beyond Area 51, I remain the doubting Thomas. Call me stubborn. Call me obstinate. Call me Ishmael, I don't care. But if you are looking to consult with the occult, then call me a cab. Where some see spooks, I tend to see kooks. Of course, leave it to Judson House and the late Arlene Carmen to shiver the very timbers of my apparition opposition.

In the spring of 1995, Judson's Congregational Life Committee asked me to coordinate the entertainment for a party to be held that May in the garden. I had been up in front of Judson's congregation before, serving as liturgist, leading the Sunday School children in singing, and once having spoken on Father's Day. But this was to be my first time to lead the congregation in anything, and I was anxious to do my best.

For this particular evening I chose the music and put the song-books together. While the songs may have been a little predictable, everyone seemed to enjoy singing them, especially out under the moon and stars, or whatever passes for stars in New York City. I led the Sunday School children in Woody Guthrie's "Mail Myself to You," and I sang "I'm Dating My Dog" for the first time at Judson. What everyone seemed to enjoy most was a spoof I had written on Georges Bizet's "Carmen," entitled "Laarman," marvelously sung by Margaret Wright and Robert McNamara, which told the story of Maxine Phillips, former head of Judson's Pastoral Search committee and a devout Socialist, and how she came to choose Peter Laarman, a former union organizer who looks suspiciously like V. I. Lenin, to be Judson's new pastor. To wrap up this long (and incredibly egocentric) paragraph, I received lots of pats on the back and congratulations on a job well done. But none meant as much to me as two little words Arlene Carmen uttered later that night as she hovered over my bed surrounded by thousands of shiny reflecting lights. "Good job!," she said. Coming from someone I respected and cared for as much as I did Arlene, and, of course, coming from someone who had died the previous fall, the simple compliment meant a lot to me.

THE GHOST OF ARLENE CARMEN

For many of the twenty-seven years that she worked at Judson, Arlene lived in the Judson House apartment I now called home. She was a wonderful and compassionate friend and someone to whom I looked for guidance and advice as I began my own sojourn as a member of Judson's staff.

Seeing Arlene again was simultaneously gratifying and terrifying: gratifying in the comfort and joy I felt in being reunited with such a dear friend, terrifying because, well, she was the *late* Arlene Carmen. Arlene was smiling as she spoke to me and when she finished, she slowly drifted away. As for me, I sat bolt upright in bed, shaken and in a pool of sweat. I just knew this could not have been a dream. It seemed so real that I got up and searched the rest of the apartment for any sign of Arlene's presence. Finding none, I returned to bed and thought, uh oh, it has finally happened. I have become one of those people everyone always makes fun of: a slow-talking Southerner claiming to have seen a ghost or a UFO. If Judson House was a mobile home and my name was Earl, I'd fit right in. As in biblical days of yore, I told no one but pondered these things in my heart.

Professing to be an anti-apparitionist may seem somewhat incongruous for someone who lived at Judson House. Judson House may not have been haunted but it was nonetheless alive with the ghosts of all who passed through its doors: shadows of runaways who found safe haven here, or the specter of youth left behind by a few of Judson's present members who once called this building home.

Be still and sense the spirit of the many whose hope was and is to make a difference in our community and in our world: workers in the offices of the Employment Project, Religious Leaders for a More

Compassionate and Just Drug Policy, or the Center for Medical Consumers.

OTHER VOICES, OTHER ROOMS

Listen and you will hear the voices of those long since departed who call out to us from the archives. Hear the laughter of today's Sunday School children. Men's groups. Women's groups. A cacophony of sound from the thousands of words spoken in hundreds of committee meetings: Congregational Life, Social Concerns, Buildings, Finance, Personnel, the Board, Ordination, Sunday School. Through the reflective meditation of a study group, the belligerent wailing of drunks on the stoop, or the soulful blues wafting through the walls of Roland Wiggins's apartment, Judson House served as a repository for much of Judson's song.

ME AND MY DOG

In the invitation to write something for this book, I was asked to describe my life at Judson House and to describe "any outrageous parties" I may have had. I am sorry to disappoint, but I am not the outrageous-party type. Aside from Arlene's appearance, it has mostly been a quiet life, or as quiet as living in the Village and around the corner from a firehouse can be. It was just me and my dog Garp, along with my neighbors Howard and Lorry Moody when they were in town, Arthur Levin working in the library, and Roland Wiggins. About the only time things got outrageous was when Garp unexpectedly decided to attend a committee meeting in the lounge. On those occasions, Judson sounded positively pentecostal as Garp (part golden retriever, part kangaroo) raced around the chairs and leapt in and out of the laps of shrieking committee members.

I will miss Judson House dearly. But what I will truly hate to have lost is the garden, and you don't have to have lived at Judson House to appreciate such a precious resource.

THE SACRED SPACE OF THE GARDEN

As Judson's Sunday School coordinator, I am rarely able to attend Sunday services. At most, I can be found standing in the back of the

Meeting Room for a few minutes, trying to gauge how much longer the service will run before releasing the children to eat all the coffee hour cookies and run back and forth between the outstretched wings of the bas-relief angels above the baptistery. But in the summer, when the services moved to the garden, I was usually able to steal away, stand on the back porch, sing a verse or two of a hymn, and maybe even catch a sermon now and then.

To me, these summer services were what makes Judson so special: to be outside, and yet cloistered away from the city, with tall ailanthus and sycamore trees providing shade from the sun, surrounded by the greenery of the ivy growing against the Judson House walls; to sit amid petunias and impatiens, bright red geraniums and hot pink begonias; to sense the breeze against your face; to feel as if nothing separates you from the God of whom you are singing; and to listen not just to the ordained but to regular Judson folk talking about their lives and the wonders of the Spirit.

In this garden I heard Lee Guilliatt speak passionately of her art. I listened to David Blythe reflect on what it was like to grow up as a preacher's kid. I watched Peter Laarman rally the troops before a Gay Pride parade.

In this garden I hid Easter eggs for the Sunday School children so many times that they all knew where I was going to hide them. I watched Charles Heist-McNamara plant tulip bulbs and found myself in the middle of snowball fights, severely outgunned.

In this garden I balanced paper plates of pasta on my knees, drank a little wine, swapped stories with Miriam Corbett, listed to Reathel Bean sing and play his guitar, and sung a song or two myself with the gifted Emmy Bean.

I know that the sum of Judson is more than old buildings and gardens, and I understand the material needs we have as we face a new day. But to me, the spirit of Judson was found in this garden more than in any other place. From the open air we breathed to the very dirt that lay between the bricks that made up the garden floor, Judson's spirit lived here, among the echoes of our laughter, the joined chorus of our singing, and the still silence of our prayers. The knowledge of losing this sacred space to a building chills me to the bone and will haunt me the rest of my days.

When I think of the garden and of Judson House, I think of Arlene Carmen. She was an enormous presence here for so long. I still refer to the apartment I live in as Arlene's apartment. Several months after her "visit" at night, I stumbled upon a large picture of Arlene, taken at her twenty-fifth anniversary party, that was taped to a credenza in the church office. There was Arlene, smiling just as she did that night she visited me the spring before. The shiny reflecting lights I had seen that night came from the reflection off the silver dress she had worn to the party. Though I could not recall having done so, I must have seen this picture before and buried the image in my subconscious. Perhaps there was no ghost after all.

My first reaction upon realizing this was to shout out in joy. I wasn't crazy, at least not where ghosts were concerned. But my joy was short-lived, and I soon found myself overcome with sadness to the point of tears. The things and people we love often disappear too soon. Somewhere deep in my heart I treasure the notion that a friend of mine who was gone had come back to spend one last moment together. That thought alone is enough to make me want to believe.

ANDREW FRANTZ
is the Sunday School Coordinator for Judson Memorial Church.

THE CHURCH IN URBAN LIFE PROJECT

From 1950 to 1965 Judson Memorial Church ran an annual summer program for Baptist college students from outside New York City. Students applied from all over the country, and a group of between fifteen and twenty was selected to spend a summer in New York City.

The program was run by various directors who were not on the regular Judson staff, although the senior minister was involved in setting up the study program. Each program had a different theme, but all related to the church in an urban setting. The students lived at Judson House. Upon arrival in mid-June, the first task was to find a job for the ten weeks each would be in New York. The evenings were filled with reading and discussions and lectures by well-known people. On weekends, the students took advantage of New York's beaches, attended plays, and hung out in coffeehouses and jazz bars.

The Judson archives contain reports for the institutes of 1955, 1956, and 1961. From these reports and from the testimonials that follow, it is clear that the Urban Institutes left a lasting mark on the participants.

Bernice Lemley

Bernice Lemley was a participant in the 1954 Church in Urban Life project.

S omewhere in the dusty corners of this retired archivist's home, I should have found an account of my misspent youth in wicked New York at the age of twenty-one. That sentence is accurate except for the words "misspent" and "wicked." Nothing is misspent, and "wicked" is a phenomenon of perspective. Alas, the facts of much of my personal history appeared to have bowed to the exigencies of a migratory professional life, disappearing with several personal libraries. Many faces and images survive from that summer student institute at Judson in 1954, but memory alone, without names except those of Bob Spike and Marcus Barth, must supply both history and perspective.

The life-changing force of my first encounter with New York City forty-five years ago had the asteroidal character of collision, which invariably occurs when country meets city. Had my collision with urban life in its quintessential form not been cushioned by a parachute with attached oxygen tent called Judson House, I might not have survived the landing. That I returned safely to West Virginia from this "coming of age" classroom and lived to tell the tale is pure grace, incarnate in the caregivers who uniquely congregate in urban churches such as Judson. With the help of that parachute, I lived to experience the happy convergence of country-bred ideals and energy-infusing urban realities.

I brought with me to New York a worldview born of a West Virginia farm community near the Ohio River in the Great Depression. As one of eight children whose father was an American Baptist rural pastor and whose mother was completely devoted to caring for her large household, I ate the religious values of the time with my food. The primacy of work and education were deeply grounded in Baptist traditions that were strongly embedded in Scottish Calvinism. Lacking money, the people in the area had taught themselves, with occasional and unreliable evangelists providing a religious dessert. At last, they chose one of their own, my father, to study for the ministry and be their pastor. My father was the Protestant equivalent of the worker-priest. Factory work and farming fed his family; pastoring was his endowed role in community life.

We moved to town, where in grade school I learned about poetry, music, and art. As I hung the clothes and hoed the corn, my imagination yearned to follow the roads beyond the hill behind our house. In my high school years, to know where the roads led became an obsession.

In 1951, a recruiter from Alderson Broaddus College came from beyond that hill, plucked me from my reveries, and set me down in a work-study program at the Myers Clinic Hospital in Philippi, West Virginia, along with dozens of other students from the hill country. For five years, American Baptists were my caregivers, winter and summer.

College study turned from nursing to my first love, music, and in the summer of 1952, I became an American Baptist ambassador to three states, singing in towns and mountains to find others like myself and bring them Baptist help. In the summer of 1953 I joined a team project at the Weirton, West Virginia, Christian Center, two blocks from the belching bessemers of a steel mill, doing community research and running recreational programs for neighborhood residents.

In 1954, a brochure and application from Judson Memorial Church suggested that I might be ready for the big city. All else defied that suggestion. At twenty-one, I was burned out. My professors at the college wrung their hands over a dutiful P.K. (preacher's kid), once open and adventurous, now withdrawn and sullen. I had sunk into a typical college crisis: (1) a change of focus from nursing to music (self-serving enjoyment over sacrificial service); (2) the destruction of my early worldview by religious teachings at variance with my upbringing; and (3) the inevitable rebellion and flight from the confusion into bittersweet romance and poetry. The wayward and the lovelorn are inseparable twins: They are blind, deaf, and dumb to pious advice.

So began the quest, not for the Holy Grail but for the pot of gold at the end of the rainbow that would solve all problems, answer all questions, and clothe me in a persona I could like. Only years later, when I began to recognize myself in the young of later generations, did I begin to understand how universal the questions are and why heaven keeps silent at that stage of life.

I had never seen my mother cry except at funerals. Tears flowed silently that day in June 1954 as I packed a bag and accepted $24.00 for bus and subway fare and food to reach a place called Washington Square. Everyone but my mother and I knew it was the home of the beatniks. But Judson Church was American Baptist, so it was OK.

The Judson House staff had their priorities in order: "Find a job. Then we'll talk about God." No longer would my benefactors hand me jobs. I had to find them on my own. They would protect me while I learned but the assignment was mine. I hadn't a clue about how one finds a job in the city. Like a cold plunge in alpine rapids, nothing awakens a dead spirit quite as abruptly as the necessity to survive where nothing and nobody looks or sounds familiar.

Before I had finished congratulating myself that I had actually taken a subway, got off at the right stop, and even found the church at the end of it, I was back on the streets. That first day the silent guardians of fools and children followed me all over Manhattan as I looked for work. The dangers of getting lost or meeting life-threatening situations never entered my mind. What did what the overpowering smell of fish. No fishmarket in the world smells like a fishmarket on the Avenue of the Americas. We had fish for dinner that night.

Judson House's KP team fed me that night. KP duty is a sine qua non of summer projects and a blessing to the student. It is a predicta-ble function that endows a sense of the familiar in the midst of multi-cultural shock. Common work promotes generosity among strangers.

Marcus Barth, the leader of the Summer Institute that year, was a kind spiritual caregiver who shared our shocks and dilemmas without judgment there in the basement lounge. The theological ex-ercises of the mind in that intimate setting have over the years be-come the truths of the heart. We shared our encounters in the city, both on the job and in our evenings together. Together we visited Harlem and the Bowery, Fifth Avenue churches and storefronts on the Lower East Side, the United Nations chapel and the offices of the *Village Voice*. What lessons each carried home were probably, like mine, what each most needed to learn. From a kind theologian we absorbed by osmosis the spirit of a church that simply responded to need as it encountered it.

We learned about the world's need from a safe place. We learned how important houses of safety are in all human experience. Being "saved," as a spiritual truth, was transformed from the notion of fleeing from sin into one of finding faith in a "safehouse" in the midst of physical and spiritual desperation.

In those dazed first weeks when I was absorbing a hailstorm of human experience, I was unaware that I was learning what Marcus Barth taught us. I was too busy wrestling with Objective Number One: Find a job. In and out of employment offices, I mastered the art of job hunting slowly. I made a false start in my efforts. I took the first job I was actually offered, in a sleazebag handbag-cleaning warehouse, because I panicked. Twenty-four dollars does not go very far after buying bus fare from West Virginia to New York and job hunting all day, even back then.

After three weeks, the IRS closed the place down, and I did not get my last paycheck. Job hunting again, I was telling everyone I was looking for a temporary job, and no one wanted me. I had an interview at the Sloan-Kettering Institute for medical transcription. It was the perfect job. Lost in upper Manhattan, I took a taxi to the interview, and the driver took the long way around through Central Park. After I paid him, I had one dime left. He swore at me for not tipping him. I threw the dime at him and fled. I was so upset I flunked the typing test. Weeping, I told the interviewer what happened. She offered me the job, but I was defeated already. Convinced I would not be able to handle the job, I walked the sixty-eight blocks back to Thompson Street. I had no job and no money. On the way down, I stopped at the warehouse, demanded my last paycheck, and got it. A bank refused to cash it because I was not a depositor. Back at the house, the housemother rescued me and also invited me to babysit for her.

On Independence Day, I was far from independent. I poured out my woes to a fellow student at the house. He took me to a free concert in Washington Square Park, to a ride on the Staten Island ferry, and a sunset over the Statue of Liberty.

At the sweatshop I had become the unwitting object of hate without saying a word to the poorest people from the ghetto. In their eyes, I was one with the white supervisor who could have been a field boss on a plantation a century earlier. Not until the civil rights era of the 1960s did the warehouse experience help me understand why all things white draw automatic anger from those who are at the bottom of the economic heap. For a brief moment that summer, I was at the bottom, too. What I did not understand was that I had a way of escape.

The weekend was soon over, and my friend encouraged me to look for jobs again. I met an employment agent who taught me, first, that I had skills people needed, and second, that city economics are different: "You are here for three months? Lady, you are permanent." The agent sent me to a dentist who had offices on Madison and 42nd Street. He did not ask about my permanence, and for the next two and a half months I was happy earning money as his dental assistant and accountant (more skilled as the latter than the former). By the end of the summer, I repaid Judson's faith in my power to carry my weight in the community and took home $35.00 to my mother. She deserved every penny of her $11 profit; she had heard from her prodigal daughter just twice.

I returned to school in the fall a new person. Judson House and urban life had corrected the wildly spinning gyroscope in my brain and spirit. Judson supplied the safe nest from which I learned to fly.

In my retirement I have discovered the relaxing pleasures of baseball, and I have discovered baseball writers. George F. Will, in *Bunts,* says that "opportunity is purchased with the coin of risk." All I can say is "Risk all your coins. The quest is worth it."

BERNICE LEMLEY
lives in Philadelphia after a long career as archivist for the University of Rochester Medical School and the American College of Physicians.

Juell Krauter

Juell Krauter was a participant in the 1959 Church in Urban Life
project. She was also Al Carmines's secretary for several years.

I grew up happily in a small central Texas town, with a nice balance of achievements, rewards, and romances. In 1959 I received a bachelor of arts degree with a major in English from the University of Texas at Austin. During my last semester I lived at the Austin Christian Faith and Life Community led by Joe Matthews. I was beginning to suspect that something was amiss. I had not found the man to marry, and my spiritual life was confused.

I wanted to spend the summer after graduation in a large city and had applied to several projects. I was accepted to be part of Judson's Urban Institute. I arrived by bus on a Saturday morning at 2 A.M. A taxi took me to Thompson Street. At first, we could not find what looked like a livable building. Eventually I rang the bell at 237. Steve Andre opened the basement door and let me in. We had coffee and had the most wonderful conversation on aesthetics. I had just completed John Silber's aesthetics course, and Steve was writing a paper on the topic. We walked around the Village and even down to the Hudson piers. The intelligence and openness with which he talked gave me an exciting first impression of New York City. I was sure all Village people were like that.

Judson House was a beehive of activity. Below the window of my room I could see artists exhibiting their paintings. Across the street was Café Jolie, a strip joint. Night life flourished within the house. Even the preachers and our project leaders could be found in the back yard at all hours discussing some stimulating subject. I began the process of getting my New York teacher's license. I could not imagine returning to Texas in September.

Howard Moody offered me a part-time summer secretarial job at the church, which I readily accepted. (In 1965 I would become secretary to Al Carmines.) Our project leaders, a handsome young couple, were students at Union Theological Seminary. Our program was filled with unique activities—a wonderful foundation from which to learn about New York City and to explore all the theological questions that plagued me. I reveled in the exposure to liberal intellectuals, modern religious writers, and the various forms of New York culture. We studied Paul Tillich, Erich Fromm, Martin Buber. Each night we had speakers or discussions or went to plays or movies (there was a foreign film theater around the corner). One unusual event was a banquet at Father Divine's church in Harlem. (His followers, who considered Father Divine to be God Personified, did not believe in marriage, and all the young girls, "Rosebuds," had a V on their uniform, for Virgin.)

After the summer, three project members—Barbara Bailey, Margaret Underwood, and myself—decided to stay in this Fabulous City and got an apartment on 16th Street. We had a constant stream of visitors and we talked late into each night. It was a wonderfully expansive experience. (A year later, Margaret and I teamed up with Beverly Bach, who had been part of the 1960 Urban Institute, and moved into the large apartment in Judson House that was later occupied by Al Carmines.)

The wondrous summer of 1959 punctuated the end of my innocent childhood and was the springboard into a deeper, although more painful, level of existence. I began teaching at a girls' junior high school in Harlem but discovered I could neither teach nor control these streetwise girls. Over the next year, I experienced bitter defeat for the first time in my life.

I fell in love with a black teacher. It was an ambivalent romance that could only end badly. When he decided to marry someone else, I lost control over my emotions. My journals of these years give a clear picture of breaking down piece by piece until nothing was left.

For ten years I lived in New York City, and Judson Church remained my community center. With therapy and by regaining confidence by becoming a social work supervisor, I had a year of relative rest in Berkeley, California, where I became a masseuse. Back in Texas, a man with six motherless children gave me a family, to which I added my son, my only non-ambivalent relationship. We divorced after six years. After one other failed relationship, I returned to my hometown in Texas in 1991. I could go home because I had finally learned to cope with negative tensions, both internal and external.

JUELL KRAUTER BROWN
lives in Comfort, Texas.

Robert A. Yangas

Robert Yangas was a participant in the 1959 Church in Urban Life project.

The year was 1959. I had just completed graduate study at the University of Missouri-Columbia and was looking for a way to transition into the world of work. I had a strong religious and social service orientation, which had been reinforced by my undergraduate study at Ottawa University, an American Baptist College in Kansas.

I read about the "Church in Urban Life" project sponsored by Judson Memorial Church in an annual publication titled *Invest Your Summer,* which I believe was put out by the National Council of Churches. Participants were expected to find a summer job in New York City and participate in communal life, study, and daily worship.

I found my job through the *New York Times.* It was a temporary position located at the Labor Temple, a Presbyterian church on 14th Street affiliated with the New York City Mission Society. My responsibility was to lead a work project made up of Puerto Rican and black teenagers. We prepared the pews in the sanctuary for refinishing, that is, we scraped and sanded for eight weeks.

At night and on weekends, the students in the Judson program made field trips to night court; visited Father Divine's Peace Center in Harlem and the Riverside (narcotics) Hospital on North Brothers Island; attended Broadway and off-Broadway shows; listened to and discussed a recording of *Waiting for Godot,* led by Bud Scott; and listened to a surprisingly young Dan Wakefield, who had just authored *Island in the City: The World of Spanish Harlem.* Featured guests were clergy from such churches as the Church of the Sea and Land, Mariners Temple, and the East Harlem Protestant Parish.

When the summer program came to an end, I was allowed to stay in Judson House even though I was not a student at the time. This was crucial for me. Based on my performance at my job that summer, the New York City Mission Society had offered me a low-paying position as a youth counselor at another affiliate, the DeWitt

Memorial Church, a predominantly black church on Avenue D on the Lower East Side. The Student House provided me with furnished low-cost housing and a sense of community, which were essential.

My stay at Judson House during the next nine months was less dramatic than during the summer project, but still it provided plenty of excitement. Of the students who lived there year-round, five or six were foreign, another four or five were Jewish; very few were Protestant. Since I worked in the afternoons and evenings, I was given a house responsibility that I could complete in the morning: I distributed the weekly clean linen to each room. Since it was necessary for me to enter every room, I could not help noticing that on the whole the men's rooms were neater than those of the women students. There were also a number of families in residence: Bud and Gisela Scott, Betty and Dick Murphy, Joe and Judy Pickle, and a musician with a wife and child in the apartment next to the kitchen with the name of Peress. Betty Murphy, the house parent of the Student House, was crucial to its success and touched the lives of a lot of people in a very positive way.

Though there must have been various programs for the students, I don't recall much that happened during the academic year. An exception is the meeting led by the anthropologist Margaret Mead. I also remember a Sikh wedding. There was no television. Life revolved around the kitchen, which also served as our dining room. The cook was a major player in our lives. She regularly played the numbers and once won more than $600 on the combination "237."

I left the Student House in the fall of 1960 when I accepted another position with the Mission Society, this time as director of the East Harlem Youth Employment Service, located on Second Avenue and 112th Street. I remained an active member of Judson Memorial Church until June 1965, when I left for an overseas assignment.

ROBERT YANGAS
lives in Bethesda, Maryland.

Donald H. Birt

Donald Birt was a participant in the 1960 Church in Urban Life
Project, was the program's director for the next two years, and
acted as associate minister of Judson Memorial Church from 1961 to
1963.

M y memories of almost forty years ago of Judson House
are inextricably linked to those of Greenwich Village at
that time. It is hard to separate them.

I first came to Judson as a student in the summer of 1960 to be
part of the Church and Urban Life Project. About twenty students,
mostly undergraduate, took part in this program. Joe Pickle, a theology student at the Chicago Theological Seminary, was the director.
The men lived on the top floor of Judson House, the women on the
second. There were a number of holdover residents on the first floor,
some of whom were working in New York or going to summer
school. One incident that stands out to this day is somewhat Dan-
tean. A bunch of us had gone to Jones Beach on the Fourth of July
and gotten bad sunburns. When we returned to the Village by subway, someone said a good remedy for sunburn was to bathe in vinegar. That night the heat was in the lower nineties, and Bertolotti's,
the strip joint around the corner on West Third, was going full blast.
The Italian kids on Thompson Street were throwing firecrackers
from the rooftops and we were burning up. It took us several days to
recover.

Betty Murphy was house manager at the time. She lived with her
husband, Dick, and their girls in the apartment on the second floor.
She did meal planning and food purchasing. We had a black cook,
Willie Mae Wallace, who did a pretty fair job of cooking for us. She
liked to play the numbers, and "her man" would come by the
kitchen door for collections or payoffs—more of the former than
the latter.

One of the students that summer was a young woman from Indiana University. At the end of the summer, she returned to IU for her
senior year. I returned to Andover Newton Theological Seminary for

my last year. Sometime that fall, Howard Moody asked me to direct the study project for the summer of 1961 and to come on staff as an associate on an interim basis. So I made several trips during that academic year to sort applications and plan the program.

When I returned in June 1961, I was issued the small apartment off the kitchen, which at that time had an exit door to the street as well as to the backyard. We always had security problems, but in the summer the students sometimes left the kitchen door wide open. One day I returned to my apartment through the kitchen and heard a frantic scrambling, as an intruder clambered over stacks of boxes to escape through the back door. The bed had been slept on, but I lost nothing more than two pairs of cufflinks.

By late summer, after the Urban Life students had returned home, I stayed on as an interim associate. My first job was to go through the applications from students who wanted to live in Judson House during the academic year. The house had been run on a cooperative basis in previous years, but by the fall of 1961 students would rather pay additional monies to have food prepared and housecleaning done by someone else. However, the kitchen still saw a lot of activity, especially when some of the foreign students did some specialty cooking. I did some preaching at Judson and participated in the rotation of worship.

Some of my memories from this period are very mundane. I remember having to step over alcoholic men asleep on the landing outside the apartment. There was a mouse that ran across the tops of my books. But that was nothing compared to the rats we got in the house after New York University began excavation for the student union building across from Thompson Street or the vermin we inherited when Bertolotti's closed for a period.

Greenwich Village was a safe place to live in and walk about later in the evening. The folk singing on a Sunday afternoon in Washington Square Park was always great, particularly when Mary Travis showed up to join in. At night you could hear an up-and-coming comedian named Bill Cosby for the price of a cappucino.

Pretty soon it was time to process applications for the Church and Urban Life Project for 1962 as well as for the 1962–1963 academic year for year-round students. Most of the latter attended New York University or Cooper Union, with a few others from the New School and other schools in the metropolitan area.

Then the young woman from IU came back into the picture. In 1962 Shirley Cantrell became Howard's secretary and we got better acquainted. We were married at Judson in April 1963.

By 1963 the drug scene was beginning to get worse. Marijuana, LSD, amphetamines, mescaline, and peyote became more common-place along with the harder drugs such as cocaine. The Judson Poets Theater was breaking ground as well, so there was a lot going on. The gay community was visibly present, and Christopher Street was the place to see flaming queens. But we also had occasion to counsel young men from the hinterlands of the United States who experienced ambivalence about their sexual orientation.

The students of the 1960 Urban Life Project formed a strong bond, and some of us are still in touch. Virginia Seaton now lives in Weston, Massachusetts; Larry Keeter teaches in Boone, North Carolina; Donna Jordan lives in New York City; and Beverly Bach Cassell lives in Los Angeles.

I have a lot of good memories of my time at Judson, but the best is of meeting and marrying Shirley Cantrell.

DONALD AND SHIRLEY BIRT
live in Holly Springs, North Carolina.

Beverly Bach Cassell

I grew up in central Alabama. In the mid-1950s, the ugliness of southern racism worked like a sickness in my teenage soul. My love of my southern homeland and the demons of racism were in an intimate wrestling match.

In the spring of 1960, my last year of graduate school at the University of Georgia, I was invited one evening to the home of a university chaplain who liked the drawings he had seen in a show of my work and who wanted to buy a piece. I took a portfolio of work for him to look over. In the course of the evening he asked me what I was going to do when I graduated. I said I did not know; I only knew that I wanted to leave the South, leave academia, and paint. After a moment he said, "Would you like to go to New York City?"

I had never thought of going to New York. I had only once been out of the South. The chaplain rang someone in New York and handed me the phone. At the other end of the line was Howard Moody. Howard explained the Urban Institute project at Judson Memorial Church, in which, for a small fee, approximately thirty students from all over the country came together during the summer to study social and theological issues and visit different places in the city. Would I like to attend? As I held the phone, I realized that it meant missing my MFA graduation. "Yes," I said.

Standing in a train station in Montgomery, Alabama, my father's face twisted and flushed with emotion as he and my mother watched me leave, I launched the journey from which I would never return, except for brief visits.

During my first taxi ride in Manhattan I tried to hide my drawl among the Yankees. The surprising refreshment of the air of that taxi ride from Grand Central Station down Fifth Avenue to Washington Square still lives with me, and I can still see the variety of faces along the way.

I rang the bell at the funky door of the Judson Student House on Thompson Street. Willie Mae, the cook, stuck her head out the kitchen window at the basement level and told me to come on down.

Next to the kitchen, Allan Kaprow was installing something called a Happening. After dinner I went over to see what he was doing. The Judson Gallery was being turned into a sort of maze that was filled with wadded newspapers and fresh Red Delicious apples that smelled good and apple-ish as we kicked them around amid the rustle of the newspapers during the night of the opening.

In the next few days I met a concentration of genius unlike anything I have ever encountered since. Willie Mae's kitchen was the place everyone drifted into. Chuck Gordone read and reread to whoever was listening his play-in-progress, *No Place to Be Somebody,* which in 1970 won the Pulitzer Prize for drama. The play's feisty digs of fun and anger woke that kitchen up to a fresh black take on Shakespearean brilliance. At the time, Chuck was acting in Jean Genet's *The Blacks,* the first real breakthrough for black theater. The astonishing cast in the little East Side theater included James Earl Jones and Cicely Tyson.

Carman Moore wandered regularly through the kitchen and the make-do lounge. At that time, he was holding forth at the information desk of the New York Public Library on Fifth Avenue, writing poems and composing music in between passing out library information. Like the rest of us, Carman lived on very spare fare. A party at his apartment on the Lower East Side was an experience that expanded beyond a sense of well-being. Listening to tapes of his prolific compositions was a journey of sweet wildness, a gift from the freedom of a gracious spirit. Carman went on to become a well-known composer, receiving commissions from the New York Symphony Orchestra and the San Francisco Symphony, among others.

After the summer project ended I got a job-job and created a variety of studio/apartment combinations over the seven years I stayed in New York, painting. My first place was actually in Judson House. It was the apartment that, later, Al Carmines occupied and, later still, was used by Howard and Lorry Moody. I shared the space with Juell Krauter from Texas and Margaret Underwood from North Carolina. That old brown linoleum floor was great for dancing the twist, and we had some noisy parties. The building was so decrepit that when we danced we all kept sliding over to one corner of the room. One night I woke up with the weird sensation that I was standing up. I then realized that the floor was so slanted that I had slid out of my bed till my feet were flat on the wall.

The old Judson House is steeped with memories for me—rich, warm, and sweet memories of the time I left the suffocating cocoon of segregated whiteness and talked, argued, laughed, and danced with people who came from worlds different from my own. I loved the people; I loved the context. It was a genuine community.

Like an exciting irritant, the edgy avant-garde surrounded me on all sides. I'd stop in the Judson Church Meeting Room to peek in on whatever was happening as I came home late at night. Merce Cunningham offshoots danced mock formalities, stark naked, for straggly audiences. Jim Dine and others, whose names are well known by now, held forth as painters and poets on pieces of crumpled paper attached higgledy-piggledy to the walls of the Hall of Issues. Al Carmines banged away on the piano, playing rinky-tink tunes with show biz/gospel pizzazz and soul into the wee hours of the night.

But it was with Chuck and Carman that I identified as an artist. To me, these two still embody the archetypes of spirit, fire, and genius. Judson was a place of profound bonding as I flailed about to find form in paint to express the presences that welled up endlessly within me. Judson held us in a context vaster than school, nuttier than church, grounded in the history that began with the waves of immigrants for whom the original Judson Church was a mission. We, the members of the Judson community, brought forth our own history. We grappled with the Western tradition of the sacred in the secular context of the sixties. Our sacred path as artists lay in a search from somewhere else than the church as we had known it.

We were community, a circle of motley folk who stood together long enough to feel and absorb the glow and warmth of the creative fires in each of us. Like my childhood, these fires warm me still.

BEVERLY CASSELL
lives in Los Angeles.

Donald R. Ferrell

Don Ferrell was a member of the 1960 Urban Institute.

I am often touched by a sense of irony and fate when I walk by Judson House on Thompson Street in my comings and goings to and from my psychotherapy office on East 10th Street. It is highly probable that I am now working in New York City in part because I had the good sense in 1960, in my junior year at West Virginia University, to apply to the Church in Urban Life project sponsored by Judson Memorial Church. I was accepted and found myself, with other undergraduates from around the country, moving into the Judson Student House in June of that extraordinary summer.

The project was directed by Joe and Judy Pickle, two remarkably able people who guided us into the complex realities of life in New York City and helped us wrestle with the profound questions we were confronting through our immersion in this greatest of all cities.

We also got a taste of the unique ministry of Judson Memorial Church under the visionary leadership of Howard Moody within the dynamic crucible of the cultural, political, and social life of New York. It was one of the most challenging, stimulating, and growth-enhancing summers I have ever lived through. As the end of the summer neared, I had been profoundly changed in ways I could not even fathom at the time.

I returned to complete my senior year at West Virginia University with a deepened sense that I wanted to return to this place and continue to evolve from my Appalachian origins under the continuing impact of an urban culture that, to me, represented the vanguard of a psychospiritual evolution for the whole human family.

And so I did. I enrolled in Union Theological Seminary and graduated in 1964. Seventeen years later, I again returned to New York, after a painful decision to end my first marriage and surrender a tenured position as professor of philosophy and religion, to undergo seven years of training at the C. G. Jung Institute in New York City to become a Jungian psychoanalyst.

Even though I do not owe all of my life to that fateful summer in 1960, it is true that something about working in New York got planted in me then, something I am still practicing almost forty years later.

So I hold that remarkable place and the extraordinary personal and spiritual transformations it has silently witnessed very close to my heart. The loss of Judson House will be a loss for all of us who shared in its life. But I am sure the heritage of Judson House will live on after it has been removed from the landscape. I, for one, shall never forget how Judson House changed my life.

DONALD FERRELL
lives in Montclair, New Jersey, not very far from Manhattan.

Marcia Freer

Marcia Freer was part of the Church in Urban Life Project in the summer of 1960.

My experience in New York City, presided over by Howard Moody and Joe and Judy Pickle, was very influential in my life. The program contributed mightily to my becoming a New Yorker for three years, while my then husband, Don Ferrell, attended Union Theological Seminary.

I still identify myself as an erstwhile New Yorker. Every year I bring ten to twelve college students to the city for two weeks in January for an interterm session patterned after the experience I had at Judson so many years ago. I guess you could say I have become a "bridge person," introducing Nebraska students to various aspects of the city, from living with families in East Harlem; to visiting Covenant House, Fountain House, and Phoenix House; to attending the Metropolitan Opera. I am able to help midwestern students become comfortable in New York City because Howard, Joe, and Judy first extended that possibility to me.

The Judson House memory that occurs to me specifically is of Willie Mae, our wonderful African-American cook, who delighted and cared for us all, cooking for us in good humor and with gusto. I remember one night she served us *tongue*. Of course, she did not tell us what it was until after we had eaten it (it was good!).

Our group went to see *Raisin in the Sun*. I also remember visiting Father Divine's church in Harlem and having a huge family-style dinner there. I also did some research in a nursing home in Queens.

During the day I worked at a firm on John Street in the financial district. At night I went to street dances, ate Italian ices, and hung out in Washington Square Park.

How fortunate I was to make the acquaintance of New York City in this way.

MARCIA FREER
teaches psychology at Doane College in Crete, Nebraska.

Larry G. Keeter

Larry Keeter was a participant in the Church in Urban Life Project in 1960.

J ust how I learned about Judson's Urban Life Project I no longer remember. Somehow, as a senior at Berea College in Kentucky, I heard about it, applied for it, and was accepted. Maybe the program seemed like a good first entry into the big city in preparation for attending Columbia University in the fall of 1960 on a Woodrow Wilson Fellowship in philosophy. Whatever the reason, the time spent in Judson House was a life-changing experience for a small-town boy from southern Appalachia.

In June 20, 1960, my train from Spartanburg, South Carolina, to New York (fare: $34) terminated at the grand old Pennsylvania Station. This crowded, fast-paced station was bewildering and confusing. To the rescue came the most helpful elderly Traveler's Aid lady, who carefully wrote down the directions for my first subway ride to the West Fourth stop. I emerged from the hot, noisy subway station onto the sunny, humid streets of Greenwich Village and carried my luggage the few short blocks to Judson House on Thompson Street. Don and Marcia Ferrell, a married couple participating in the summer project, met me just outside the house and verified that I was in the right place. Joe and Judy Pickle, the resident directors of the program that year, assisted me in settling into my sparsely furnished room on the top floor.

GIRLIE SHOWS

My first night at Judson House was a bit of a culture shock. I got little sleep because diagonally across the street behind Judson House was a girlie show with loud bump-and-grind music playing late into the night. In those days there were three or four strip joints on West Third between Thompson Street and Sixth Avenue. Eventually the coffee shops would put these clubs out of business. Howard Moody enjoyed telling us about the mystified doormen to these joints who used to peek inside the coffee shops, asking whether they had naked ladies in there to attract such good business!

I don't recall losing a whole lot of sleep because of these loud night spots, so I must have quickly gotten used to the noise level—the supporting undertone of urban life. Sadly in later years, my favorite coffee shop, the Figaro, closed to be replaced by a McDonald's.

JOB HUNTING

One of the participants' first responsibilities was to land a job to support themselves during the summer. We were on our own in this matter, seeking whatever advice we could get from our fellow project members. I learned to read the job ads in the *New York Times,* to visit the job agencies, and to deal with the constant rejections from employers since I was only looking for several months' employment.

I was so discouraged that I seriously considered returning home for the summer. I had difficulty riding the subway, I couldn't find a job, and the *New York Times* had no comics. In the end I adjusted. In fact, I became so addicted to the city that even today a week without the *New York Times* is like a week without sunshine. I continue to return to New York City at least once a year to get my fix until my next annual visit.

My first employment breakthrough came when some of the project members discovered that New York City was still hiring enumerators for the 1960 U.S. Census. My first census assignment was a section of Spanish Harlem with part of Park Avenue as compensation. My crew leader asked me to team up with a female enumerator for her protection in the crime-ridden area of Harlem to which we had both been assigned. Pearl Bosco was an attractive Italian-American who attended Hunter College and who actually became my protector and guide.

Pearl took a dim view of me and my feeble attempts at adjusting to the big city until she learned that I had earned a full scholarship to Columbia. Then she became fascinated with the idea of a Southern intellectual in Gotham City. The project members were as surprised as I was when lovely Pearl appeared at Judson House one night after supper and spent the evening talking with a skinny guy from Appalachia.

As a Census enumerator, I immediately experienced the gap between the haves and the have-nots in the city. In Spanish Harlem, I found ten or twelve people living in one room, with hallways and stairwells that were smelly, damp, dark, and narrow. But I met some warm, generous people. One Spanish-speaking family invited me to eat lunch with them. Since I had little spending money and had not yet drawn any pay, I gratefully accepted their hospitality.

Park Avenue—the haves—formed a great contrast with my Harlem experience. I entered luxurious apartments with huge windows that provided a panoramic view of the city that took your breath away. The occupants here were polite, somewhat distant, but usually considerate. On occasion, I was offered a cold drink, which I gladly received.

RC COLA AND HOMESICKNESS

A key to my gradual adjustment to life in New York City and at Judson House was the little newsstand located on the corner of Thompson and West Third. It was run by an Italian woman, from whom I would buy a 12-ounce bottle of RC Cola and the *Times*. I felt peaceful and comforted as I walked across the street in the morning, fresh from a night's sleep, to this newsstand.

What I did not fully understand then, but do now, is that this simple morning ritual connected me with the folks back home, thereby soothing my homesickness. In the mill village where I grew up I used to walk across the street from my house to my Uncle Bill's Greene Grocery Store to drink an RC Cola. In later years, as a seminary student at Harvard Divinity School, I recalled that short walk from Judson House to the newsstand as a significant act of secular communion, joining me in fellowship with the Appalachian folks back home. They might have said: "As often as you cross this street to drink this RC Cola, remember us at home."

HOMELESS RATS

Donald Birt, a fellow project member, told me that New York City had a population of seven million people and eight million rats. At Judson House, we soon met some of the latter.

A building near Judson House was torn down that summer, resulting in a considerable number of suddenly homeless rats. Almost every evening one of these rats would run in from the garden through the open door into the basement lounge, circle the room along the walls, and quickly exit the same way it entered. One night, I positioned myself at the door to the lounge with a blunt instrument (it looked like a hoe with a straightened flat blade) and dropped it on the rat's head as it left the room. To our surprise I killed the rat with one sharp blow. In triumph, I held the dead rat up by its tail as high as I could (in my memory the rat was the size of a small dog). Then we heard the cheering from outside the lounge—the windows at the top of the lounge were street-level—and the Greenwich Village Saturday night crowd were looking in at this sight, sharing our small moment of victory.

A BRUSH WITH GREATNESS

One bright, sunny Saturday morning in Washington Square Park, some of us from Judson House noticed a small crowd under the Washington Arch at the foot of Fifth Avenue. They said they were gathering for a SANE march to protest the nuclear arms race and invited us to join them in their walk up Fifth Avenue to the New York Public Library at 42nd Street, where a citywide rally was to be held.

We walked at the front of the march behind a trailer from which a young man named Ed McCurdy was leading us a singing various protest songs, including one he had written: "Last night I had the strangest dream I ever had before, I dreamed the world had all agreed to put an end to war...." We had just gone a few blocks when a tall, lean man with a banjo came in from a side street to join us. He was greeted with a lot of cheers from the marchers. He walked right beside us and sang with us all the way to 42nd Street. Man, we thought, that guy can really sing and play the banjo. When we arrived at the rally in Bryant Park behind the library, a large crowd from all parts of the city was converging there to hear speeches and to sing. One speaker said, "Now the godfather of the folk music revival will lead us in singing. Please welcome Pete Seeger!" Imagine how delighted we were to discover that this was the man we had marched and sung with all the way up Fifth Avenue.

MY MADISON AVENUE JOB

When my stint with the U.S. Census Bureau ran out in July, I had to find another job. By now I had learned I could not get a job for just a month and a half, so I had to pretend I was looking for permanent employment. A mid-Manhattan job agency sent me to a law firm on Madison and 43rd. They hired me as a law clerk assistant who filed law forms all day long in a room filled with rows of filing cabinets. There were no morning or afternoon coffee breaks, but I had an hour for lunch, which I ate in the nearby Bryant Park. In those days, classical music came out of the loudspeakers at the park at noon.

Since I would not receive a paycheck for several weeks, I packed myself a peanut butter and jelly sandwich those first days and walked the forty-three blocks up Fifth Avenue to the law office. Sometimes I would meet Pearl Bosco on my way back from work. We had long conversations on the streets and in deli shops, where we would stop for a soft drink. After I received my first paycheck from the law firm, I rode the subway to work (the ride was 15 cents), sometimes had a steak at Tad's for $1.99, and might stop for a whole-wheat doughnut (15 cents) and coffee (10 cents) at Chock Full o' Nuts. Looking back, I am glad I walked those two weeks to work. If you really want to know a city, you must walk it.

JFK AND THE 1960 NATIONAL DEMOCRATIC CONVENTION

In the basement lounge at Judson House we gathered around the television set in August to watch the 1960 National Democratic Convention nominate John F. Kennedy to run for President. I was much impressed with the Kennedy mystique. (My parents in North Carolina were FDR yellow-dog Democrats but they did not vote in 1960: They could not vote Republican and they could not vote for a Catholic.)

Just after JFK was nominated, Gail Borchers asked me to assist in the Kennedy campaign in New York City by getting the names of the people living in the high-rise apartment building at One Fifth Avenue. The strategy of the Kennedy campaign, I was told, was to get everyone out to vote on the assumption that most of them would vote Democratic and for JFK. The campaign organizers wanted the names of the people living in this Fifth Avenue apartment to send them mailings to get out the vote.

These names were not available to the public, but someone had arranged for a resident in the building to obtain a list with names of all the residents. From this list I copied by hand the names and addresses of some 300 people. This was my small contribution to the JFK campaign in New York, and I am proud of it. Caught up in the Kennedy charisma, I heard him speak at several stops in the city and shook his hand and Jackie's. I went to JFK's inauguration on that cold, snowy day of January 20, 1961, in front of the U.S. Capitol Building.

BROADWAY PLAYS

In the 1960 Church in Urban Life Project we were encouraged to experience the urban art scene, including the theater. As a group, we attended several off-Broadway plays, such as Tennessee Williams's *Camino Real*. These plays whetted my appetite for Broadway plays uptown, but I was very shy about venturing up there at night. The shorter buildings in Greenwhich Village were more on a human scale, quite comfortable to me. I would stand at night outside the front door of Judson House and look beyond the Washington Arch to the Empire State Building lit up and visible in the distance among all those skyscrapers, yearning yet resisting to go up there at night.

Mary Margaret Carlson, a project member from Dallas, Texas, encouraged me to go with her to see *My Fair Lady*, then still in its first run. For the evening, I dressed up in my best slacks and a while sport coat, the only one I had with me. To me, the theater at 51st and Broadway was a dazzling piece of architecture. You entered into a beautiful, spacious lobby with an impressive ceiling and with ascending stairways on either side to the balcony. *My Fair Lady* must be the ideal first musical to attend. Every song was memorable and well written. I was transported to another time, place, and culture. I was stage-struck. After the play, Mary Margaret and I enjoyed cheesecake at the original Lindy's restaurant. It was a rich, delicious way to top off a most wonderful evening at the theater.

"PSYCHO" AND THE END OF SUMMER

As the Urban Life project came to an end in late August, the members of the group began to leave for their different destinations. I was one of the last people to leave, so to while away the time Gail Borchers and some others and I went to see "Psycho" at a nearby theater. We had the almost universal experience of movie goers then—"Psycho" was a first-rate scary film. After our walk back to Judson House, my bare feet in their rubber flipflops were sooty-black from the grimy streets. I had the classic reaction to "Psycho": I hesitated to shower even in the daylight to wash away the dirt.

RETURN, ALWAYS, TO JUDSON HOUSE

Through the years, I have found myself, like other Judson residents I have talked to, returning to Judson House. That first fall, after my summer residence, I came back to Judson House to visit the cook. I attended worship services at Judson throughout my years at Columbia. I visited other summer institutes at Judson.

When I decided to go to seminary, I came to Judson House to talk with Al Carmines, assistant minister at Judson, and with Howard Moody. Over lunch in a restaurant on Eighth Street, we discussed the schools that had accepted me: Union Theological Seminary, Yale Divinity School, and Harvard Divinity School. Howard and Al shared thoughtful advice with me, being careful not to tell me which seminary to select. Once again Judson House played a crucial role in one of my life-changing experiences.

Over the years since I have returned many times: with my wife, with a class of students, with a youth group, with my son, always back to Judson House.

LARRY KEETER
lives in Boone, North Carolina.

Jim Thacker

Jim Thacker participated in the 1961 Church in Urban Life Project. _____

Although I was in the Judson Urban Life Project in 1961, the first seeds for my being there were planted four years earlier. Immediately after graduation, my high school senior class of thirty-eight, from the small town of Monon, Indiana (population: 1,500) took the train to New York for our senior class trip and spent five days and four nights in New York City—it was later that we realized Manhattan was only part of the city. I still shake my head when thinking about it, but four of us spent two nights at the Billy Graham Crusade at Madison Square Garden. On the second night we sang in the choir, along with George Beverly Shea and hundreds of others.

After the trip everyone in my class said they would be back in New York someday, but as far as I know, I am the only one who ever lived in New York.

In the summers of 1958, 1959, and 1960 I traveled with fellow students from Purdue University to the Baptist student conferences at Green Lake, Wisconsin. It was at those conferences that I first heard of Judson. Howard Moody and Harvey Cox each spoke at the conferences about their experiences in urban ministry and the city. We all crowded around Howard to hear his description of Judson Memorial Church and his ministry in Greenwich Village. After hearing Howard during the second summer, I decided that one day I would live in Manhattan and attend Howard's church.

I applied, and was accepted for, the 1960 Urban Life Project. Unfortunately, my Dad had health problems in the spring, and I needed to stay home and save more money for my last year in college than I would have been able to do in New York. The following year I applied again and was accepted for the 1961 Summer Project.

A friend and I drove from Indiana to New York and arrived a few days before the project began. You can imagine our excitement as we emerged from the Holland Tunnel and headed up to the Village. After spending most of my life in a small town in the Midwest, it was very exciting to be in the city and to know that I was part of a group that would share a unique experience. I had no idea what I would do after the summer, although I was pretty sure it would not be "plastics."

Although my family's lifestyle was modest—my Dad ran a Standard Oil service station and there were four of us kids—I had always lived in a house. It took some getting used to living on the third floor of an apartment building and to hear street sounds at all hours, day and night. I loved living in the Village and seeing the amazing variety of people everywhere.

The church I grew up in—the Monon Baptist Church—was theologically quite conservative and focused on personal salvation with little if any mission activities. The contrast with Judson was dramatic, and I quickly felt at home. During the summer, we read Richard Niebuhr's *Christ and Culture*, Peter Berger's *The Noise of Solemn Assemblies*, and one of Bob Spike's books. We met with Bob one evening to discuss the church in the city. I began to experience the church as an exciting place and an important part of my life. It was wonderful to hear Howard Moody preach every Sunday and to understand and appreciate his role in the religious and political life of the Village. Our group went to many political meetings, during which we met then-Representative John Lindsay and Michael Harrington, among others.

Since I had just graduated from college, I had more opportunity than others in the program to get a permanent job. After several weeks in the city, I was hired as a management trainee for the General Services Administration (GSA), a U.S. government agency that manages federal buildings. I worked for the GSA for five months. I rode the subway downtown to a building on Hudson Street near where the World Trade Center now stands.

The nineteen of us in the Summer Project—nine men, ten women—worked at a variety of jobs during the day and saw plays, heard speakers, went to movies, and discussed books, politics, and everything in between at night. As I look at *The Report of the Church and Urban Life Project 1961,* I am still amazed at the roster of speakers we heard. The list included theologians Paul Lehmann, Will Herberg, and Bob Spike; Chuck Gordone from the cast of *The Blacks;* Bill Stringfellow from the East Harlem Protestant Parish; Sidney Dean of the McCann-Erickson advertising firm; Stanley Tankel of the Greenwich Village Planning Association; Jim Lanigan, a district committeeman in the Village; Bill Ellis from the Manhattan District Attorney's office; and Norman Thomas, John Lindsay, and Michael Harrington, whose book *The Other America* was published that summer.

The plays we saw and discussed included *The Blacks, The Threepenny Opera, A Taste of Honey, The American Dream,* and *The Death of Bessie Smith.*

We had dinner and spent an evening at the Father Divine Peace Mission in Harlem and, at our first worship service at Judson, watched Pete Seeger demonstrate and play with a steel drum band.

My memories of the summer of 1961 include the wonderful Italian ice that we bought at the corner of Thompson and Bleecker, being approached each day by beggars and becoming more callous and less friendly to people I did not know, and getting to hear jazz when I could afford it.

One evening after dinner, when several of our group were in the Student House garden, I heard music coming from a club on Bleecker Street. When I went to see who was playing, I was amazed to learned it was Coleman Hawkins, one of the all-time great saxophone players. Several of us heard jazz at Birdland, on 52nd Street and Broadway. Years later I realized that I was just blocks away when Bill Evans, my favorite jazz pianist, recorded his famous "Sunday at the Village Vanguard" album on June 25, 1961, our second Sunday in New York.

I also remember spending hours in bookstores, particularly the Sheridan Square Bookstore, just a few blocks from Judson House. Although Monon, Indiana, did have a Carnegie library, there were no stores that sold books, so it was a real treat to be living near great bookstores that were open after people in Monon went to bed.

Several events of the summer, unrelated to the Summer Project or the Student House, had a major impact on my life. Jane Jacobs's book *The Death and Life of Great American Cities* was published, and the combination of this book and my summer in the city convinced me to become a city planner. After reading Jacobs's book I took frequent walks to Hudson Street in the West Village to look for Jacobs and the areas she described. In 1966 I returned to New York to pursue a master's degree in city planning at Hunter College.

The second major event, by far the most significant, was the building of the Berlin Wall. In response, President John Kennedy called up many reserves, and I was notified by my draft board in Indiana that I needed to get a physical right away. I did, in the same space and building on Whitehall Street near the South Ferry subway station where Arlo Guthrie got his in "Alice's Restaurant" years later.

In late August, when the Summer Project ended, we all left the Student House, most to return to their last year of college. I recall being surprised that I really had to move, but someone pointed out that the Student House was for students, and I was no longer a student. My plans were not clear. I still had my job with the GSA, but I was making plans to enlist in either the Navy or the Air Force, since I did not want to be drafted.

I moved to a small, ground-floor room at 158 East 26th Street and ate most of my meals at Radowitz Bakery Restaurant, a small, friendly place half a block away on Third Avenue. There is now a big apartment building where the restaurant was.

In November I resigned from the GSA, made a quick trip to Indiana to store my belongings at my parents' house, and left for the Navy's Officer Candidate School in Newport, Rhode Island. I spent a little more than three years in the Navy. For two of the three years I was back in New York City in a building at 90 Church Street.

My summer of living in the Student House as part of the Judson summer project changed my life. I was fascinated by the diversity and excitement of urban life and the variety of people and experiences. During the summer of 1961 the Student House provided a home for nineteen strangers to the city who were making decisions about their futures with many shared values, questions, and concerns. Since that time, I have lived in Chicago, Los Angeles, Brooklyn, and Philadelphia and have been active in churches focused on issues of social and economic justice.

JIM THACKER
lives in Elkins Park, Pennsylvania.

Reathel Bean

Reathel Bean participated in the 1963 Church in Urban Life Project
and returned to Judson in 1966 to fulfill his duties as a
conscientious objector.

I first came to Judson in the summer of 1963 to participate in the
Urban Life Project. This program was intended to give students
an introduction to the city by having us find summer jobs and
living and eating together in Judson House. Our group leader was
Joseph Duffey, then a minister fairly new out of seminary, who later
served in Congress as a representative from Connecticut. His wife
and two young sons were also living in the house, as were Beverly
Waite and her daughters.

We met rather informally at first—usually at dinner—and compared notes on our job search and impressions we had of the city.
Later on, as we all settled into whatever jobs we had found, we began a series of meetings with people who had been asked to speak to
and with us about the Village and the city. Howard Moody was
probably the first speaker. He was certainly one of the most helpful
for a group so new to everything, since he had been in the city less
than eight years and was still able to remember what it was like to
encounter the city for the first time.

Later we heard Paul Goodman and Margaret Mead. Another
highlight was Peter Berger, the sociologist, who had not yet swung to
the right as he was to do in a few years and who had been a sort of
mentor to Joe Duffey. David McReynolds of the War Resisters
League, Harvey Cox (whose *Secular City* had just been published),
and Carman Moore, a year-round resident of the house and a composer, all talked with us during the summer.

Carman and I became good friends over the summer and, this
being the middle of the civil rights era, both had our first experience
of being arrested during an attempt to enter a segregated amusement
park in Baltimore. I suppose that was my most memorable Fourth of
July to date, and Judson House was responsible.

Except for a few visits to Judson when I was a student at Union Theological Seminary (1964–1965), I did not have any real contact until I returned there in the fall of 1966. I had applied for my conscientious objector status and had not heard from my draft board, just as I had written to Judson about doing my alternative service there and had not heard from them. I had come to New York anyway and stayed with a friend, not daring to unpack in case I had to leave for Canada on a moment's notice. I was perhaps being a bit dramatic, but it was an uneasy time. After a week or two, I got a positive letter from my draft board on the same day that Howard Moody returned from vacation and told me I could work at Judson. Since that assignment included a room in the house, all my problems were taken care of at once.

I was given the center room near the staircase on the third floor and received $50.00 a week, both of which were great with me. Jon Hendricks had served his stint as a CO by then, but he had decided to stay on and live and work at Judson. During my first year, the house was used as a residence for artists, and Jon was a sort of supervisor for that program. I was simply living there, my work being primarily that of a handyman and sometime janitor for both the house and the church.

Most of the residents avoided any contact with the church, the one exception being the time some of them were involved in the rescue of chickens slated for execution in a destruction art event. A couple of them presented the chickens in the service the following Sunday and explained why they had interfered with the event. This was in the spring of 1968.

Destruction art was a large part of what was taking place in the Judson Gallery in 1967 and 1968. Since the gallery was located in the same building, the residents were sometimes drawn to the events. One I remember best was staged by Charlotte Moorman, the famed bare-breasted cellist, who invited us to cut her dress into pieces with a pair of scissors. I may remember this largely because some time later Carman Moore presented a number during a concert at the church in which I was cast as a cellist wearing only boxer shorts who was finally apprehended by a cop played by David Tice. It ended with him chasing me around the piano.

The highlight of destruction art, for me, was an event just before Thanksgiving during which a piano was smashed and a chicken killed in the gallery. Jon Hendricks then went to Vermont for the holiday. I got a call soon after telling me that one of the dancers from the Judson Dance Theater had a rehearsal scheduled in the gallery, and I needed to go clean it up. The chicken had been there a couple of days by then. This was the most profound effect that the destruction art movement had on me.

The final phase of my involvement with Judson House had to do with the experiment with runaways. This began in the summer of 1968. The plan was to provide temporary housing, counseling, and other help for teenagers who had left home and ended up in the Village. After a few weeks, though, a pattern began to emerge, with the kids showing up on Friday evening and managing to work things out with their parents by late Sunday. The news was obviously out that Judson was a good place to crash for the weekend.

By the fall, the decision had been made to screen the kids more carefully and set the place up as a more permanent residence with more active intervention whenever necessary. The residents who ended up there that year must have come partly from among those who had come over the summer and from referrals.

Art Levin was active in this project, as was Beverly Waite, who still lived in the house. Mike Parker and Bob Lamberton were counselors, and there was a lawyer who was available for any legal work that was needed. A cook was hired, and when she left I was hired to replace her. My term of alternative service as a CO had ended, but I was living in the apartment off the kitchen, so it was a convenient arrangement.

My menus were pretty limited, which was just as well, since the previous cook had tried a bit too hard. It was difficult to get kids that age to try anything very new—in the area of food, that is; they were ready for any drugs that came along. I remember one of them being brought back one night after he had tried heroin for the first time. It was the sixties, of course, and the counselors walked a fine line trying to maintain some rules and restrictions without being judged too uptight to have any rapport with the kids.

We muddled our way through a fascinating year. My cooking got a little better, and I learned what to keep supplied for school lunches. I think the counselors began to figure out what they were doing. At the end of the year, the project ended and we all moved on.

I often wonder about the kids and hope the experience was as good for them as it was for me.

REATHEL BEAN,
an actor, is still an active member of Judson Memorial Church.
He and his wife, Holly, live in Montclair, New Jersey.

Michael Johnson

Michael Johnson was a participant in the 1965 Church in Urban Life Project.

O pinions differ about when the last Urban Life Project took place at Judson. Some say it was 1964, others 1965. I know my participation in the Urban Life Project took place in 1965, but it is easy to see why there is confusion. Fredrik Logeval, the Vietnam War historian, uses the expression "the long 1964" as a term for the time it took America to choose war in Southeast Asia. Military observers were there in 1963. In 1964 President Lyndon B. Johnson promised not "to send American boys nine or ten thousand miles away from home to do what Asian boys should do for themselves." In 1964 the same U.S. government was already decorating servicemen for acts of bravery in Vietnam. The free speech movement got headlines in 1964. Mario Savio and others who led demonstrations at the University of California at Berkeley were arrested en masse. There were riots over civil rights in most major cities. Martin Luther King, Jr., received the Nobel Peace Prize. By March 1965 the first troops were sent to guard the U.S. base at Da Nang, which stretched the year into the "long 1964." America was committed body and soul to domestic and foreign war.

In January 1965 Johnson was inaugurated President. Malcolm X was assassinated. The Supreme Court ruled in favor of atypical conscientious objectors. The first combat forces were deployed in Vietnam. Antiwar protests began to spring up across the nation. The Unitarian minister James Reeb was beaten to death in Selma, Alabama. Blacks and other minorities across America suffered from gross injustices.

The big brush renders the same picture for both years.

I first heard of Judson House when Howard Moody spoke at the Baptist Student Center at the Universty of Arizona while he was on a short working vacation in Tucson in the winter of 1964. I was program coordinator at the center. Howard spoke to us about "religionless Christianity" and referred to books by William Hamilton, Dietrich Bonhoeffer, and other modern theologians. We asked him about the mission of the church in New York City and had a lively discussion about Robert Moses, heroin addiction, and Judson's arts ministry to Greenwich Village and other Judson programs. Howard made a lasting impression on us.

I applied to the Urban Life Project for 1965 and was accepted. Taking an "express" bus—it had a toilet, instant coffee, and boxed sandwiches—I arrived in New York City only to find out that Judson House was not yet ready for the summer institute participants. For a week, I lived at the McBurney Y on 23rd Street. A group of square dancers in squaw dresses and cowboy outfits also stayed there, and it was as if I had never left Arizona.

Finally, I moved into Judson House for the beginning of the program. We were told to follow all police and fire ordinances to the letter. Judson did not pay bribes to anyone, so we had to be careful not to break any rules or Judson House would be condemned. It was a drought year, and the bathrooms had signs that said "Don't Flush for Everything."

My room was on the corner of the third floor. I remember leaning out the window and watching my Italian neighbors across the intersection. Sometimes there would be hand signs to people on the street that I did not understand. What did they mean? A Judson staffer working in a neighborhood program put word out on the street for gangs to leave us alone.

On weekends it was hard to sleep until the wee hours because of live entertainment from bands in the neighborhood. Sometimes I slept on the couch in the lounge, because it was quieter. My favorite song at that time was "Bleecker Street" by Jerry Landis.

The leaders of the Urban Institute in 1965 were Les and Ellen McClain. They did a wonderful job of coordinating a fantastic schedule of activities. These fell into two categories: "make it happen" events and "let it happen" events. Among the latter was the memorial service in a midtown synagogue for the Jewish theologian Martin Buber, who had died in Israel. Two of the speakers were the sociologist David Riesman and the Protestant theologian Paul Tillich, who himself died later that year.

The "make it happen" activities ran from viewing art films such as "The Bicycle Thief," "The Red Shoes," "Breathless," and "La Strada" to a lecture by Paul Goodman, visits with Jon Hendricks and the Judson Gallery artists, discussions with civil rights leaders, and finding out about Judson's neighborhood outreach program to young people.

My first job in the city was as a laborer at a hospital construction site in Brooklyn. The project was more than a year behind schedule. The superintendent of the site was a European Jew who hardly spoke English and would yell at us in Yiddish if he felt he did not get the respect from the young workers. Here was a cultural gap that I felt I could easily straighten out. When I jumped in to help him, the superintendent got even madder. He rolled up a sleeve and pointed to the tattooed number on his arm. What I understood from the yelling was that he had survived a concentration camp and why did I think he could not handle a couple of punk kids.

After a few weeks as a construction worker, I received a phone call from Howard saying there was a printing job at the Interchurch Center on Riverside Drive, and that is where I stayed the rest of the summer.

The Judson Garden was a cool haven for residents and staff alike. It was OK to talk in the garden, but you could tell when people just wanted to be there. One of these was Larry Kornfeld, the resident director of the Judson Poets Theater. He would stand in the garden after a shower and let his hair dry. If he stayed around after his hair was dry, you could talk to him. Larry helped me overcome my fear of asking stupid questions, so I asked him one day what the word "camp" meant. I was lucky because Larry referred me to an article that Susan Sontag had written on "camp" that year. Larry asked a couple of us to help out with a play that was going to be performed in the balcony of the church. Our role consisted in holding up big muslin flags during the performance and close them between acts.

What little contact I had with Al Carmines I will always remember. Shortly after the project started I returned from work one day to see a large delivery truck in front of Judson House, with Al talking to the driver. They were trying to figure out how to get Al's baby grand Steinway, which he had shipped from his home in Virginia, up the steps and into his apartment. With the help of too many people, we got the piano inside Al's place.

We laid it down on the floor without its legs and pedals. Pretty soon the apartment was filled with the summer residents and some of Al's friends. Al, with a terrific smile on his face, sat down on the floor and began to play. Someone went out for beer. Al started playing Broadway tunes and then asked for requests. He ended by singing Beale Street Mama. I may have left so as to give others a chance to get in, but it was probably because I could not contain my joy.

The summer at Judson had a huge influence on the rest of my life. I finished my bachelor of fine arts degree and went on to obtain a master's of divinity. I studied Japanese and taught religion in Japan for fifteen years and was active in human rights. I have always remained a friend of Judson House, even though I have not often been back. Bertolt Brecht explains my feelings best. The lines are from the poem "The Friends," as translated by Michael Hamburger:

> The war separated
> Me, the writer of plays, from my friend the stage designer
> The cities where we worked are no longer there
> When I walk through the cities that still are
> At times I say: that blue piece of washing
> My friend would have placed it better.[1]

MICHAEL JOHNSON

and his wife live in Chicago. He works as a technical translator in the field of electronics. He and his wife host a religious group at their house each week.

1. Brecht, Bertolt, "The Friends," translated by Michael Hamburger. In *Poems 1913–1956*, edited by John Willett and Ralph Manheim with the co-operation of Erich Fried. New York: Methuen, 1976. Reprinted by permission of the Publisher.

THE JUDSON STUDENT HOUSE

From sometime around 1930 to the mid-1960s, at least part of Judson House served as a dormitory for full-time students attending various colleges and universities in New York City. Initially, the rooms were restricted to the third floor, as the rest of the building was occupied by the Judson Health Center. As long as the clinic was there, until 1950, students entered the building at 81 West Third Street, also owned by Judson Church, and entered the third floor of Judson House from the third floor of 81 West Third.

In 1950 two things happened: the house at 81 West Third Street showed signs of imminent collapse and had to be razed, and the Judson Health Center moved to Spring Street. Judson Church now had the run of Judson House. This was also a time when the church had begun to reach out to the students at New York University and initiated a program whereby students from NYU could live at Judson House at reasonable rates with the understanding that they would devote about four hours a week to community work.

For various reasons the Student House program dissolved in the 1960s. The last students left in 1967. By that time, Judson House was used for other programs: There now was an art gallery and some of the artists lived at Judson House, as did several staff members. For eighteen months, from the spring of 1968 until the fall of 1969, Judson House was home to a resident runaway program. The teenagers trashed the building so thoroughly that most of Judson House could not be used as a residence again.

Seymour Hacker

Both Seymour and his brother Alan lived at Judson House in the 1930s. Seymour is the earliest living occupant represented in this book. ────────────────────

I found out about Judson House because my brother, Alan, moved there in 1932 or 1933 and immediately became part of the Judson community. When I started going to college, which was in 1933, I decided that I wanted to leave home and strike out on my own. In the next year, in 1934, I took a room at Judson House, right across the hall from my brother's. The rent of the room was $2 a week. I stayed there for two years while I was going to City College.

The room was on the third floor overlooking the garden. My brother's room overlooked Thompson Street. The garden was pretty straggly. It was never cultivated much. It was not as large as it is now because the building at 81 West Third was still standing but the empty lot next to it still belonged to Judson.

We used 81 West Third as access to Judson House. That was our address. We went to our rooms through 81 West Third, up to the third floor, and then across to the third floor of Judson House. The lower two floors of Judson House were occupied by the Judson Health Center.

The lower floor of 81 West Third was divided into two apartments. The front apartment was occupied by our Cerberus, Susan Purdy, who was ever watchful. She was the housekeeper. The back room belonged to Iva Wasson, who was the church organist. She was a wonderful woman who was my brother's spiritual mentor. She gave me piano lessons, although I did not get very far.

On the second floor of 81 lived a couple of students from out of town who worked at the Judson Settlement House on Sullivan Street. One was Polly Grover, an apple-cheeked girl from Maine, and the other was Ruth Mabee, a sister of Carlton Mabee, a famous professor of history and sociology at Columbia. On the third floor, on the right side of the stairway, was the apartment of Laurence T.

Hosie, who was the minister of Judson. On the left side was the door to the third floor of Judson House. Larry Hosie was a great man, a Lion of Judah. He was a social action minister par excellence. Howard Moody was in his tradition.

The ladies of the house, along with the ladies who ran the settlement house, formed a cooperative, which we all paid into for groceries, about $15 a month. We all took part in the cooking and washing up, and whatever was necessary. The cooking was done in the basement of 81 West Third. It worked very well. We ate well and it was very sociable and pleasant.

The other tenants were mostly unconnected to the church. They either came in by reference or had the good fortune to come in at the right time. They were usually year-round students. There were not more than ten or twelve tenants. As I recall, my brother and I were the only ones who lived there who participated in church affairs. We went to services and attended meetings of various committees that Larry Hosie was interested in, such as the Fellowship of Reconciliation and the War Resisters League.

Judson House was a lively place. Larry Hosie was the sparkplug, of course. Iva Wasson was a spiritual force, and just her presence was a thing you felt there. Some of the women who ran the Neighborhood House on Sullivan Street were great, too. Willie Wheeler was one of them. She was one of those people that were called settlement house angels at that time. It was a tough assignment working with Catholic Italian kids, whose parents were not friendly to begin with. The kids were not very well mannered. She managed somehow to bring a lot of them along into daylight. There was another woman from South Dakota. She was a gem. She ended up marrying an Italian Protestant boy and lived happily thereafter until the settlement house was disbanded, which was a great shame. The settlement house movement was of another era and could not survive into the disintegration of society that took place sometime back then. Most of the similar settlement houses met the same fate at that time. I used to go to one when I was a kid, the Christadora House.

My brother, who was nine years older than I, was much more profoundly involved in Judson than I. I was too young, really. Alan had been searching for some kind of spiritual home ever since he was a kid. He had gone through junior socialism and other fraternity groups like the Kiva and a few others that were social-minded groups without a specific aim. How he found Judson I don't know, probably through one of the organizations he got into, like the War Resisters League.

Judson became his home, almost instantaneously. He lived there from 1932/3 until 1939. He was a photographer and at some point, about 1937, he got interested in the Southern Tenant Farmers Union through Claude Williams, whom he met. Claude Williams was another great inspirational figure of the time. He was a minister in Arkansas who helped organize the southern tenant farmers and inspired them for many years.

Alan got the idea of going to Arkansas to make a movie about these tenant farmers. He went with Lee Hays of the Weavers, who lived at Judson House for a while. The resulting film has been shown at Judson several times. Alan and Lee had a very hard time. The conditions were really primitive and they were not too well received by the locals. Alan picked up a malignant skin disease down there and he never recovered. It killed him in 1939.

SEYMOUR HACKER,
the oldest congregant at Judson, still runs his art books business
on 57th Street in New York City.

Patricia White

Pat White lived in Judson House for a year while studying at New York University.

In September 1948 I registered for a couple of graduate courses in education at New York University. I also found a part-time clerical job at a magazine conveniently located on Fifth Avenue a few blocks up from Washington Square. After college, I had moved back in with my parents in Westfield, New Jersey, and commuted by train, ferry, and subway to the corner of Sixth Avenue and West Third Street.

My great good fortune was to be introduced to Margaret Wright. Margaret and her husband, the Rev. Dean Wright, had just moved to New York from Oregon to join the staff of Judson Memorial Church. The Wrights lived in a staff apartment at the top of 81 West Third Street, a small historic house owned by the church. Margaret invited me to drop by their place on my way to the subway one day. She introduced me to Dean, and they talked about their work with students.

The Wrights' apartment had a big skylit living room, with a kitchen along the windowless west wall. On the first landing of the staircase ascending to the Wrights' place were two double rooms for women students. At the next landing, a cut through the wall of the building led to the third floor of 237 Thompson Street, which then had a number of single rooms occupied by men students.

My tiny income and student registration qualified me to move into "81" to share a room with Sylvia for five dollars a week. I was overjoyed to skip the long commute and be a grown-up again, as I felt too old to live in the parental home after having been on my own for five years.

A VERY HOT SUMMER

The summer in 1949 was very hot. I remember the women's bathroom, where I showered three times a day and washed my entire wardrobe in rotation (one seersucker dress, two greenish cotton skirts, four blouses, and underwear). Around dinner time, after yet another shower, I put on whatever was clean and walked the few blocks to the Judson men's shared apartment, where Lou had cooked a wonderful communal dinner. We paid Lou weekly in advance for ingredients; he had free rent in exchange for shopping and cooking (who did the dishes?). Lou did fine Italian home-style dinners, of which I especially loved the huge green peppers stuffed with rice and ground beef, then covered with rich tomato sauce and baked. Spaghetti with meat sauce was popular then, as now, but pizza had not yet crossed the Atlantic as universal food.

When we could afford it, we ate out at local restaurants. I especially remember a fish place on Eighth Street, where we often ate what the menu called lemon sole—fish and asparagus in a lemon sauce.

After dinner, walks through the streets of Greenwich Village and Washington Square Park were semi-cooling before another shower and then to bed in a higher-than-body-temperature room. My laundry never included pajamas.

At the end of the summer I was no longer a student and moved to a furnished room on West 11th Street. I remained active in Judson Church, and in the early 1950s I was one of the few women on the Board of Trustees. In March 1950 Bob Newman and Dean Wright set up an exhibition of Georges Rouault's religious works in the church. Dark French Roman Catholicism by Rouault (1871–1958) offended some visitors who expected more traditional Protestant works. I did some volunteer hours of guarding the exhibition and was amazed that people could be so upset they took one look and ran down the stairs to the street.

From October 1955 to February 1956 I served as church secretary. It was a quiet winter as Bob Spike was spending most of the time at his new job while doing the necessary interim work at Judson until Howard Moody arrived.

Right after my wedding on March 7, 1956, I moved to Canada. I was sorry to miss the exciting innovations going on at Judson as they were recorded in the newsletters that came to me in the mail.

PAT WHITE
lives in Victoria, British Columbia.

Mckinley Brown

From September 1954 to June 1955 McKinley Brown lived at the Judson Student House while attending New York University. ────────

I had come to New York from Franklin, Virginia, to continue my study of business economics. The housing division at NYU suggested Judson House as a convenient place to live.

At Judson House each student had his own room. There were both male and female students. Most were out-of-state and foreign students. Many were doing graduate and postgraduate work and were therefore older than the average undergraduate.

Each student was responsible for his or her own room. In addition, we were required to do general chores, such as doing dishes and cleaning the windows, stairs, and garden. We did most of the work at night and on weekends, as we were all busy during the day.

Hyla Converse was in charge of the Student House, and Betty Murphy was her assistant. Mrs. Converse was a minister and she took her job very seriously. Our initial interview with her was very strict and sober. We sensed that our conduct would be under observation at all times. Betty Murphy, on the other hand, was very relaxed and could be approached on any issue. We were all very fond of her.

Our only obligation, other than house cleaning, consisted in attending a Sunday evening social gathering, often with guest speakers. We were not required to attend church, although many did. I joined the Judson choir and sang in it long after I was a student. I remember Ed Brewer, the choir director, Dora Schively, and Al Carmines well. Through its eclectic environment, Judson House had a great influence on me. I studied cello, piano, and voice.

After I graduated from NYU, I completed a master's in business education at Columbia University. My last postgraduate work was at Harvard, from 1974 to 1977. I worked for the New York City Board of Education and at the State University of New York, teaching business education. For medical reasons, I had to take early retirement.

MCKINLEY BROWN
lives in New York City.

Robert Newman

Robert Newman lived at Judson House as a full-time student from
early 1948 until he graduated in 1951. He wrote the following letter
in October 1976 on the occasion of Howard Moody's twentieth
anniversary as senior minister at Judson Memorial Church. It is one
of several letters exchanged between Robert Newman and Paul
Spike, son of the late Robert Spike, who was Judson's senior
minister from 1948 to 1955. Paul Spike's letter on the same occasion
is included in the section on "The Judson Staff." Both letters are
reprinted here by permission of Robert Newman and Paul Spike. _____

I will try to recall: Veterans were trying to re-adjust. The schools
were full and expanding. College was possible because of government checks. Generations that had never imagined advanced
education enrolled. If there weren't many jobs yet, this was a polite
way to keep it together. "Are you 52–20 or VA?" ($20 a week for
52 weeks or Veteran's Administration scholarship). NYU accepted
everyone, explaining that it would weed out those not meeting its
standards later. Everyone deserved a chance. At the beginning of
1948, still seventeen, I transferred from a lousy small college in
northern New Jersey (disillusioned because I was getting A's with
less work than high school, where my record was undistinguished,
and my effort nonexistent).

Tuition was $13.50 a point; sixteen points was a full schedule. I
was not a veteran, and my father was a clothing salesman finally
climbing out of the depression and paying off a judgment for automobile homicide. A drunk had wandered across the highway as he
was returning from the store at one a.m. after finishing the annual
inventory. We were not insured (couldn't afford it) and the lawsuit
hung over us for years.

I found a job at the NYU library. As a full-time employee of
the university, twelve tuition points were paid for. I was taking
eighteen points, and my salary and some help from my Uncle Willie covered expenses and the other six points. I lived in a furnished room at Tenth Avenue and Eighteenth Street, paying $8 a

week for a couple of months, but it was a bad room, and too far to get to during breaks in a library and class schedule that sometimes began at eight a.m. and lasted until midnight. One of the girls in my shift in the reference room had a friend who lived in a room behind the church just across Washington Square. He could roll out of bed and be in class in ten minutes. It took me almost half an hour. She would tell me when Dominic came into the library next.

Dominic didn't think there were any vacancies, and explained that it was a "student house" with a minister in charge. A chemistry professor [Robert Boyd] and his wife lived there rent-free in return for overseeing the cleaning and kitchen details. Rent was $7 a week if there was a room. The minister's name was Dean Wright. Dean? "That's his first name, here's his phone number. His wife is blond and sings at Radio City Music Hall."

MOVING INTO JUDSON HOUSE

The minister was six or seven years older than I was. I said I was Jewish, but didn't observe anything. He said it didn't matter, but from what I had said, it didn't look like I had enough free time to contribute to the "program." I really needed a room that close to school, I said. He said they would only accept me on the condition that I contribute twelve hours a week to the "program." I said I would try.

The "program" was volleyball on Friday nights, followed by beer at Minetta's until very drunk, and dishwashing and occasional cooking for the group when we ate together, and taking turns cleaning the halls and stairs. There were about a dozen of us in a building that has since fallen down at 81 West 3rd Street, which connected to the top floor of another building on Thompson Street. The lower floors housed the Judson Health Center. All of this was just behind Judson Memorial Church.

I was one of the youngest in the group, which ranged from seventeen to about thirty. Some were vets, there were a couple of students from the Republic of China. Men lived on the top floor, women in "81." They came from the Midwest, the South, were black, white, and Italian, and one girl was Jewish and unattractive.

WRIGHT AND SPIKE

The Wrights had friends they had met while doing student work in Ohio who were coming to live and work at the church while the husband completed his doctorate at Columbia. The Spikes moved in, Bob and Alice and their eighteen-month-old son, Paul. They had lived in the house for about a week before I met Bob Spike. He and Dean were passing the time of day in the office; it was Saturday morning and the house was fairly empty. I was on my way out somewhere. C'mon in and meet each other. They were both very bright. But they weren't Jewish. In 1948, at eighteen, it didn't yet jibe. Also, they read the *New York Post.*

They didn't know me any better than I knew them. I had read a little as a kid as the result of an automobile accident that put me in the hospital for six weeks and with the oral surgeon and orthodontist three or four times a week for years after. My reading was wide but not deep, and kind of spotty. But I had almost a trick memory and could put things together fast.

They were both doctoral candidates at Columbia, had finished college and seminary, knew all of Niebuhr, Tillich and Sartre, talked about Camus. They were both skilled in logic and debate, were charming, witty and sharp, new in New York, and in every sense, very easy to take.

Dean had seen a Bosch print in a Fourth Avenue bookstore. It was of a medieval fair where one of the figures is drawing the crowd into a shell game. Ancient three-card monte. A week before he'd asked the price and was told $8. Now he decided to buy it. The three of us went to the bookstore, and as we were about to enter, I said I would do the talking. Pointing at random to a Rembrandt print, I asked, how much? "Eight dollars." I pointed to another print. "Five dollars." Now I pointed carelessly to the Bosch, as we started to edge out of the store. "Three dollars." OK, we'll take it. Magic. They were that American. We could learn from each other, and did.

A group of us drove to Washington for a couple of days. We did congressional offices, and were excited about the former pharmacist from Minneapolis who showed great promise. We met with his administrative assistant, Max Kempleman, who had been a staff member of the *Manchester Guardian.* We went to the State Department, and tried to psych out the system. Howard Moody was there with some of his students from Ohio State. We had already met on a trip to New Haven, the year before, when Dean's wife, Margaret Wright, opened there in *As You Like It* with Katherine Hepburn. Howard was finishing at Yale Divinity School, and because of Margaret, we knew about Hepburn and Tracy (and her chauffeur looked like Tracy, too).

Spike had raked the backyard one autumn afternoon, and found a couple of used condoms among the leaves. We didn't know whose they were, but the house was a good place to live.

There were hundreds of afternoons at the Cedar bar, nights at the Remo and Minetta's, where the world was explored, settled, and resettled. We cooked sheep liver at 19 cents a pound, and drank Senator beer from the A&P. My mother visited and told either Dean or Spike, or both, that if I ever converted, she'd kill herself. I was a "Student Associate Member—No Creedal Obligation."

John Mitchell was a waiter at the Remo. He later opened the "Fat Black Pussycat" and other bars and coffeehouses, here and abroad. He had run into trouble with one of his marriages, and came to trust and depend on Spike. The church became a place you could get help, whether you were from MacDougal or the Bowery—though we were edgy with those. Max Bodenheim's wife hid out with us when he beat her (she said), and we discovered trunks full of the papers of Earl Browder in the subbasement, stashed there in the thirties.

Paul [Spike] was a terrific kid, and we really took to each other. I was eighteen and he was two. We spent a fair amount of time together. I took him with me to the bar around the corner on Sullivan Street. He put his finger into the head on my beer and announced, "Soap!" By the time he was four or five, he was writing paragraphs on small sheets of paper. Handing them to us, he would ask, "Sign my contract?" His brother John had recently been born, and I remember Alice nursing him during Sunday services, sitting in the back of the church. Paul started school at St. Luke's.

I met my wife in the library. She worked at Stechert-Hafner's on Tenth Street. We married in the last month of my twentieth year (her twenty-second). She had been going with a painter who worked with me. Since that time, twenty-seven years ago, we have all stayed connected, one way or another.

ROBERT NEWMAN
lives in Bay Harbor Islands, Florida.

Tom Roderick

Tom Roderick lived in Judson House as a full-time student from
September 1965 to the summer of 1966.

I can't remember how I heard about Judson or the Student
House. Bill Coffin or Art Brandenburg, chaplains at Yale, may
have mentioned it to me. Howard Moody interviewed me in his
office. I was struck by his blue eyes and his crewcut—not the hair-
cut of choice at that time!

In any case, the Student House suited my needs perfectly. In the
early 1960s, while attending Yale University, I had come down to the
city several times with friends for all-nighters in Greenwich Village.
We would go from coffeehouse to coffeehouse, listening to folk music, talking, and drinking coffee and other concoctions. The Village
had come to symbolize the new sources of excitement and meaning I
was beginning to explore. And now I would be living in the midst of
those coffeehouses, just off Washington Square Park.

I was determined not to repeat the mistakes of my first year out
of college. After graduating in June 1964, I had worked for the
Northern Student Movement in Philadelphia for a year. The experience was a fiasco. Our grandiose scheme was to set up a tutoring
program for children as a base for fomenting revolution in the
North Philadelphia black ghetto. As it turned out, we could not even
organize a competent tutoring program before racial tensions tore
the staff apart. Aside from the terrible work situation, I realized that
I had moved from the sheltered environment of college to a new city
where I knew no one and had undertaken a challenging job, completely unaware of the need to create a network of support for myself outside of work. By June 1965 I knew that I wanted out of Philadelphia and that I would pursue education as my profession. A
friend had enrolled in the one-year master's program at the Bank
Street School of Education, which at that time still was on Bank
Street in the West Village. I decided to follow in his footsteps. Having learned from my experience in Philadelphia, I was happy to be-

come part of the Judson Student House, which promised to ease my transition to life in New York City.

I was not disappointed. Although the living accommodations were cramped and shabby—my room was a tiny cubicle barely large enough for a bed—the people were very special, and it mattered that the Student House was closely connected to the church. We had a cook, Willie Mae Wallace, who prepared our food on an old institutional stove and served us family-style around a big wooden table in the kitchen, which was in the basement just off the corner apartment. I do not remember how many students lived in the house at the time—somewhere between ten and twenty. They included Chris Holt, quiet and intense, who was studying the flute at the Manhattan School of Music; Sandy Padilla, an energetic and outgoing student at New York University, who took part in a number of Al Carmines's productions; and the reserved and beautiful Lurline Purvis, who was studying at the Columbia School of Social Work and with whom I later became romantically involved.

OUR MENTORS

Jack Matlaga and Beverly Waite served as our mentors and lived in the Student House. Jack had recently graduated from Union Theological Seminary. He smoked Gauloises and loved to hang out in bars, practicing the fine art of conversation and making beautiful entries in his diary. Jack later moved to Greece and had an apartment near the Acropolis. I spent two wonderful weeks with him when I traveled around Europe.

Beverly Waite had split up with Ralph by that time and lived in Judson House with her two daughters. We had meetings in Beverly's apartment. I do not remember what the meetings were about, but they probably had to do with issues that arose in our communal life. I recall a visit by Ralph in which he danced beautifully and theatrically with one of their young daughters. The image of father and daughter dancing has stayed in my mind all these years.

Through the Student House I got to know Ed Brewer and Al Carmines, who lived in Judson House as well. Ed was Judson's music director at the time. He played the piano, directed the choir, and brought in his many friends to provide special music. He also built harpsichords and played his harpsichord in church services. He had the corner apartment right off the kitchen, and night and day we could hear him practice his beautiful renditions of Bach and other composers.

Al Carmines introduced me to the Beatles. A classical-music snob, I had actually gotten into folk music and Bob Dylan, but the Beatles seemed to be having so much fun I could not believe they were worthy of my attention. Al pointed out the complexity of their rhythms and arrangements and compared them favorably with Bach in that regard. That was all I needed to give them a serious listen, and they quickly won me over.

I greatly admired Al, of course: his singing and piano playing, his preaching, and his perceptiveness about people. He used to tease me, saying I was "pink and white," referring to the color of my skin, my scrubbed midwestern look, and my naiveté.

While I was at the Student House, the church sponsored an activity for college students called the Urban Life Project. Howard Moody and Ron Bailey ran it. It consisted of a series of seminars and meetings in which the students from Judson House discussed various social and political issues affecting the city. I do not remember much about these sessions except that some of them took place at the house of Ron and Sue Bailey in the East Village, not far from Tompkins Square Park. Howard loved the city and communicated his enthusiasm well.

A PARENTS' VISIT

During my year at the Student House, Yoko Ono and Anthony Cox, her husband at the time, did an art project at Judson, which they called *The Stone*. This was before she and John Lennon got together. They had a young child—three or four years old—who wandered around Judson House completely unsupervised while Yoko and her husband were absorbed in their work. The art project involved taking off your clothes and crawling into a big black cloth bag. You could see out but people could not see you inside the bag. I do not remember any great insights I gained from the activity. However, when my parents came to New York city from Cuyahoga Falls, Ohio, to see how I was getting along, they experienced Yoko's art. They received a special dispensation: they did not have to take off their clothes, only their shoes, before crawling into the bag. Far from being scandalized by the experience, they loved it and talked about it for years afterward.

Through the Student House I formed lifelong friendships, met musicians and artists who enriched my life, and began an association with Judson Memorial Church that continues to this day. I am deeply grateful for the experience at the Student House and for Judson's commitment to reaching out to young people.

TOM RODERICK,
his wife, Maxine Phillips, and their two daughters live in New York
City. Tom still teaches school.

Christopher Holt

Chris Holt was a full-time student living at Judson House in the mid-1960s.

What was it? It was Honeymoon Hotel (with a liberal pinch of Nightmare Alley).

The nuns across Thompson Street wagged their index fingers at us. We were rutting in febrile nuptial fervor. There was no window curtain; there was no shame.

Who were we? We were a pair of shit-soled country boys fresh off the trolley from Hooterville in 1965. Judson Church on Washington Square was a doorway to a larger and more luminous life than we had ever dreamed of in our philosophies, and we were very hungry to start living.

I had come to New York as a seventeen-year-old starting my freshman year at the Manhattan School of Music to study the flute. Not long after I had moved into Judson House I met Donald Gallagher, another freshman at the Manhattan School. He came to visit me at Judson House and spent the night—and ended up staying two years. This happened not without some grumbling. Beverly Waite, our housemother, was wonderful in leaving us alone, but the year before there had been several rowdy incidents at Judson House. Jackie Curtis, who was to become a famous drag queen, lived there, as did several other wild people. The church did not want the house to become unmanageable, and the Judson Board was afraid that two guys living together might set a bad precedent. However, Howard Moody saw no reason not to allow Donald and me to live together, and that was that.

During our first year, most of the other residents were foreign students attending the New York University School of Law. In 1966 the church decided to make space in Judson House available for an artists-in-residence program. Most of the new residents were students at Cooper Union. These students were under great pressure to perform, and a few had nervous breakdowns.

A building stores the lives of its people—the "if these walls could talk" thing. Singular people made Judson House a good home, not just a dingy dorm. There were Miss Willie Mae Wallace, the Reverend Jack Matlaga, fabuluscious Sandy Padilla, elegant Damaris Low, lovely Paul Richter, foxy Beverly Waite, glamorous Jimmy Goodson, so serious Bena Shalit, exemplary Tom Roderick, and dear and glorious Al the singing clergyman to come home to after school. Favorite people—how lucky we were!

Will the walls come tumbling down? No doubt. Will they be forgotten? Nope.

CHRIS HOLT
and Donald Gallagher live in Jersey City, New Jersey. Chris works at the Parsons School of Design in New York City; Donald has his own company of decorative painting.

Sandy Padilla

Sandy Padilla lived at Judson House as a full-time student from 1965 to 1967.

It was late August of 1965. I had just turned nineteen. A friend, Margot Lewitin, knew a student house near New York University, where I was going to school. Margot worked with me at my summer job, was involved in Off-Off-Broadway Theater, and knew someone named Al Carmines. She helped get me into Judson Student House, which would be my home for the next two years and would change my life forever.

I drove up to 237 Thompson Street in my dad's huge Buick Riviera, far too large for the small streets in the Greenwich Village, and took in this old red-brick building, sagging in places. As the door opened, I saw steps with dingy linoleum, high ceilings, and walls heavily coated with years of paint. Someone let me in and led me to the second floor to meet the house manager, Beverly Waite. Her apartment was large and warm. She lived there with her two children, Kathleen and Suzanne. She showed me around the house and then led me to my room on the first floor.

A NAKED MAN ON THE WALL

When Beverly opened the door to my room, I saw a huge figure of a man painted in black on the wall. The walls were about 13 feet high, and so was the naked man. A capped pipe, which the artist had chosen to make part of his privates, was sticking out prominently. I was speechless. The room was about 9 by 12 feet and had a huge window about 9 or 10 feet tall that faced Thompson Street. It had two shelves and a single bed and nothing else—no dresser, no chair, no table.

In a corner of the hallway on the first floor was the only coin telephone in the house. Next to it was the doorway to the apartment where Al Carmines lived. On the other side of the stairs, left of the entrance, was a long hallway with three doorways on the left leading to the only three student rooms on the floor. The middle door led to my room. At the end was another apartment, which housed Ro Lee, the church secretary at the time.

Down the right side of the hallway was a small bathroom with a shower for use by the three students. Two windows beyond the bathroom door faced out to the garden on the ground floor below. The bathroom was dark and dingy. I looked inside the shower and wondered how I would step into it every day. But it was home and I was always the optimist, so I knew I would be fine.

THE OTHER RESIDENTS

I soon met Ro Lee, who lived with her black cat Mister. He roamed freely about the house and considered it his territory, often marking it by spraying freely. Next to me, on my right, lived Bena Shalit, a student. On my left lived another student, Lurline Purvis.

The kitchen, which was in the basement, had four doors. The entry was on its north wall. The west door led to the back yard, a place that no one ever ventured into because of its delapidated condition. On the east wall a door led to Thompson Street. The door on the south wall near the corner led to Ed Brewer's apartment. Ed Brewer was the church music director with a fascination for harpsichords. In fact, he later built a harpsichord from a kit. The final product was spectacular, and he gave a concert on it at the church.

The first year I lived at Judson, there was a meal plan and we had access to the food in the pantry and use of the large kitchen. The kitchen had several long tables and chairs, a large industrial stove, extra large refrigerator, huge sinks, and surface areas and large cookware. Next to the kitchen was the pantry. The shelves were filled with lots of large, institutional red-and-white cans of Sexton foods. The cans included tomato sauce, tuna fish, juice, and more. As residents we could cook food on the large stove. Of course, we were supposed to clean up afterward.

That first year the kitchen was maintained by Willie Mae Wallace, a black woman who did not live in the house. She also cleaned Al Carmines's apartment. It was clear to everyone who was in charge of the kitchen, and she told us so regularly in her large, booming voice, complaining about the students and the conditions of the common areas we lounged in.

On the other side of the stairwell in the basement was a door to the communal living room. This large room had a sofa and lots of chairs. There were small end tables at various places with table lamps on it. Next to the large sofa was a coffee table, and against the right-hand wall was an old upright piano. In the northwest corner of the room was a doorway that led through what we thought of as mysterious passages to the church.

The first thing I did was paint my room and get a 9 by 12 carpet to cover the floor. I didn't know anything about primer, and each time I painted over the large black figure, he would start seeping through the layers of paint again after a few months. Eventually I was able to cover it up.

I met others in the house, including Jon Hendricks. He was a conscientious objector who had been assigned to work at Judson Church in those years of the Vietnam War. I also met Christopher Holt. Chris (or Eugene, as his mother called him when she telephoned and asked for him) was studying flute at the Manhattan School of Music. Chris and I became close friends. We decided to work on the Mozart flute sonatas and spent hours practicing. Later, Chris and I played at the wedding of Larry Kornfeld and Margaret Zipse at the house.

As I talked to other students, I learned they studied everywhere: Cooper Union, Bank Street School of Education, the New School of Social Research, Pratt Institute, and Fashion Institute of Technology. I believe I was the only one studying at NYU that year.

Over the next two years, I would become friends with other students: Carole Petersen, Tom Roderick, Lurline Purvis, Ann Weingarten, Hank Darrah, John Anderson, a girl named Sam, and many others. In the summer we had students from medical schools stay at the house. Their idea of partying was to bring in pure alcohol and mix it with the Sexton cans of juice.

Carole Petersen and I couldn't stand our bathroom, and we persuaded Beverly to provide us with paint and supplies to fix it up. She gave us money to buy mosaic tile and floor covering, and Carole and I went to Pintchiks supply store and bought yellow paint and yellow-and-white mosaic tile. After a few weeks we completed the bathroom and finished it off with curtains.

Living on the first floor, a few feet from the entrance, I heard people coming in and out of the house. I soon met Al Carmines, who initially held no interest for me. I always heard his booming voice and the slam of his apartment door. Every once in a while, he would come down to the kitchen and spend time with some of the people. He was larger than life, warm and friendly, and he always walked quickly. He had a huge laugh. Sometimes a tiny bit of a Southern drawl would come out. People in the kitchen told me he was a composer and did shows that played at the church. How curious, I thought, shows at a church—nothing like the churches I had attended.

AL'S ORATORIOS

One day, I was playing classical music on the piano in the living room and Al came downstairs to hear who was playing. He was surprised and learned that I had studied piano at the Juilliard Prep Division. We talked briefly and I stopped playing. I preferred to play when alone and I didn't care for an audience.

That fall, I went to see a play at the church. It was OK, but I fell in love with the music Al had composed for it. The name of the play escapes me, but I found myself going over to the church just about the time the songs I liked started and then I would leave. That was my first exposure to the Judson Poets Theater.

One day Al asked me if I would be in a show he was directing. I said no. He was surprised that I wasn't interested. Over the next weeks, I heard people going in an out of his apartment to audition. I certainly was not going to be one of them. Chris came to talk to me about this show Al was doing and that Al wanted me in it. I still said no. I wanted to be left alone.

Chris persisted, and so did Al. I learned that Al had written the music for plays such as *Home Movies,* for which he won the Obie award in 1963, and for a play by Maria Irene Fornes, which was being performed just as I came to the Judson. Al told me the new show was called *Pomegrenada,* by Harry Koutoukas, and he wanted me to be a singing flower. It sounded absolutely absurd. I finally figured, oh well, no one I know will see me, and after much effort on their part I finally relented. It was the winter of 1966.

We had the initial smaller rehearsals in Al's apartment at the Student House. There, Al would meet with Julie Kurnitz, Meredith Monk, and me. Other times, we would walk over to the church for

larger rehearsals. I met other members of the cast, including Margaret Wright and David Vaughan. Al directed the show. The set was a
fantasy with makeup by Remy Charlip and lighting by Johnny
Dodd. Harry Koutoukas would swirl into Judson House to visit Al
in his black cape and leave a lasting impression of his artistry wherever he went.

The show opened in March 1966 to great reviews in the *Village
Voice*. Edith Oliver also reviewed it in the *New Yorker*. We "flowers" received favorable reviews as well. I was hooked! We would often have rehearsals Saturday mornings. Since I stayed up all hours
on Friday nights, Al would come and wake me. He would stand in
the doorway of my room singing: "It's morning now, the sun is up,
the moon is down, its really morning now!" These were the first
lines of the flower song in *Pomegranada* and the first lines for the
opening scene of the show. He would boom, "time to get up dar-
ling," and he would not leave until he was sure I was getting up.

BUILT-IN CABINETS

Lee Guilliatt was stage manager for one of the shows. I was amazed
at her capacity for building sets. Lee became a mainstay at the theater, and over the years she moved from stage manager to star performer. She had a unique voice and on occasion would pull out her
guitar and sing ballads. Some she wrote herself, and each was
unique because of the quality of her voice.

I asked Lee if she could build cabinets for my room at Judson,
since I lacked storage space and I wanted things to be organized. She
built me two large bookcases, which I stained and used to store my
books and stereo on the top shelves and sweaters and other clothing
on the lower shelves. My room at Judson House was the only one
with wall-to-wall carpeting, custom bookcases, and curtains. I also
had the only television. On weekends and late evenings, students
would hang out in my room into the wee hours of the morning. Carole Petersen loved to watch the Johnny Carson show. Often, I fell
asleep and they just stayed and chatted and hung out.

In my next year, the plays continued and I would hear music and
singing flowing out of Al's apartment as he created songs and rehearsed with cast members for new productions. One of my favor-

ites was his creation of *In Circles,* a play in which he put Gertrude Stein's words to music. A huge success, it won many awards, including another Obie and the Vernon Rice Award. The director for this was Larry Kornfeld.

AL'S PARTIES

On opening nights of shows or during the holidays, Al often had parties at his place. The apartment was crowded with people who flocked to him because of his immense charisma. During opening nights, the parties didn't begin until 11 p.m. The overflow generally streamed into the house entryway and sometimes down to the kitchen and living room. Booze flowed freely and people got incredibly drunk. Al's favorite was gin. The moment many waited for usually came about 1 a.m., when Al would slip onto the piano bench and start singing the blues. Everyone's favorite was "Beale Street Blues." People lived for this moment.

Also during my second year in the house, I bought a Lambretta scooter, which I kept in back of Judson House. I remember an incident involving that scooter. As I was coming around the corner of Washington Square South onto Thompson Street, Jimmy Waring stepped into the street without looking. I turned wide to avoid him and my scooter went over. I hit my head on the street. I also hit Jimmy Waring's pinky finger, and he went back into the church and passed out from fear. Jimmy Waring was a dancer and choreographer well known in the avant-garde dancing world. It turned out I had a concussion and was sent back to my room to rest. When I laid on my bed, the ceiling above the bed collapsed and pounds of heavy plaster (not plaster board!) fell directly on my head. Plaster dust filled the rooms and hallway. Students came from throughout the house to see what the huge bang had been. No one was seriously hurt, but it was a memorable event to laugh about for years.

The Student House also had its share of artists. The Judson Gallery was part of the house. You could get to the gallery through the living room in the basement level. I remember the gallery getting a lot of publicity during the "Happenings" that took place there in 1967 and 1968.

BABYSITTING FOR KYOKO

I was involved with one artist couple. Their names were Anthony Cox and Yoko Ono, and their little girl was Kyoko. She was three or four at the time. Kyoko would often be barefoot and wander around as children do at that age. I asked Yoko if I could take Kyoko to my room where I could watch her and where I had a wall-to-wall carpet. Often, when I came back from school I would pick up Kyoko and she would stay in my room.

The kitchen was a community place for many of us to hang out at and laugh for hours. Julie Kurnitz would come often at night and sometimes bring her guitar. Several of us including Al would sit around the table. We had a great and sometimes raucous time as Julie and Al, with their incredible wit, would pepper the conversation with humor and dishing.

Jack Matlaga came in 1966 to be resident manager for the students. He was also a minister. He lived on the third floor in one of the smaller rooms. He had a love of Greece and had traveled there and seemed to know everything about Greek culture and food. Jack was delightful and he soon became fast friends with Julie Kurnitz. The kitchen table got larger with fun, talk, and entertainment. Reathel Bean came to live in the house as a CO. He, too, joined the circle of friends and became a part of the theater.

The summer I turned twenty-one, 1967, was the last time I lived at Judson. However, it was just the beginning of what would be years of activity with the church and the theater. Over the next ten years, there would be many visits to Judson House and Al's apartment. The garden behind the house was fixed up and eventually we even had garden shows there. We also had the famous Judson street bazaars as fundraisers, which were always considered great events. In 1977 I left New York City, and my association with Judson faded. My friendship with Al never did, and twenty-eight years after I met him, he was the minister who performed the service at my wedding. He also performed for the guests, many of whom had seen his shows over the years. It made the day extra special and filled it with wonderful memories.

Judson House will influence my life forever. I met extraordinary people through Judson Memorial Church and the Judson Poets Theater, its two forward-thinking ministers, and its small dynamic community. My life has been richer and happier because of the day I walked up to that sagging old building when I was nineteen years old.

SANDY PADILLA
lives near Albany, New York.

Lurline Purvis

Lurline Purvis lived at Judson House as a full-time student from September 1965 to June 1966.

How I managed to complete my second year of graduate work at Columbia University while living at Judson House will always be a mystery to me. This was the year I became a student of life rather than a student of social work. I did not miss a play, a concert, a dance recital, a church service, or a lecture, all at Judson Church. I ushered, I painted sets, I sewed costumes. Just when I thought I could get some time in to study, Julie Kurnitz would show up in the kitchen with her guitar. Her impromptu performances were not to be missed!

The one night that stands out from all others is the blackout of November 1965. The most amazing thing was to be able to look up from Washington Square and actually see the stars. It was magical! The blackout was also an excuse for a candlelit banquet at which we ate what the cook had prepared for us and as much as we could of the refrigerated leftovers. I was glad I did not have to clean up the next morning.

That night Al Carmines came by and visited me. On this rare occasion he sat on the floor with his back to the window on Thompson Street sipping wine and smoking. Like travelers meeting by chance, we shared our truths. And when the evening was over we were off again to our different destinations.

I remember many of the artists who showed at the Judson Gallery (there was a door that opened between the Student House and the Gallery.) Sometimes the artists were hungry and our food would disappear. I was utterly charmed by Yoko Ono's barefoot daughter, three years old as I recall, when Yoko showed and, I believe, slept in the gallery. When Yoko asked for a loan, I was unable to refuse.

Jon Hendricks's room had poetry and sketches on the walls and door. I was often tempted to decorate in the same fashion, but my concern about the paint always stopped me.

It was difficult to sleep on weekend nights. The traffic in the Village was bumper to bumper from early evening until the wee hours of the morning. For a while, an a cappella doo wop group would give a concert at 2:30 a.m. on Sunday morning on the corner of Thompson and Third, mostly singing off key. Only heavy rain or frigid cold would keep them away.

GRIMY BATHROOM—YECH!

I will never forget the unspeakably grimy bathroom. The shower was so mildewed that I became an expert at sponge-bathing in the sink in my room and finding excuses to bathe in other people's homes.

Behind all the events were the relationships in the house. Tom Roderick was a wonderful friend who could be coaxed from his books to take a long walk night or day. Jack Matlaga always had a kind and encouraging word. I learned every beat and lyric of the Beatles' "Rubber Soul" through the wall of my next-door neighbor Sandy Padilla. Other events that stand out are Ed Brewer's lectures on baroque music and Jon Hendricks's on contemporary art.

No living experience of mine has ever been as rich or as stimulating. One might say that for a while I was a "culture junkie." I would never have imagined that I could survive and even enjoy the quiet life I now lead on the Gulf Coast of Florida. However, all things have their time and place. And for the time and place in the Village I will always be grateful. Here's to the spirit of the Judson Student House!

LURLINE PURVIS ASLANIAN
lives in Florida.

THE JUDSON GALLERY

In the late 1950s and early 1960s Judson House was the incubator for radically new art forms. At the Judson Gallery, housed in a small basement room, artists such as Claes Oldenburg, Jim Dine, Marc Ratliff, Allan Kaprow, and Tom Wesselmann held early shows of their works. For many, it was their first show ever. The artists had complete freedom to exhibit what they wanted to exhibit. No gallery director acted as judge.

Bud Scott, an associate minister at Judson Church from 1957 to 1960, was actively seeking out artists in the Village who were looking for space to work and to exhibit. At the time, Marc Ratliff was living at Judson House as a student attending Cooper Union. When Jim Dine, like Marc from Cincinnati, came to New York, he looked up Ratliff and the two started hanging out together. Another Cooper Union student from Cincinnati, Tom Wesselmann, joined them, and the three young artists, along with Bud Scott, hit on the idea of opening a gallery in Judson House.

For the first show, they invited Claes Oldenburg, who was working at Cooper Union, to exhibit a set of figurative drawings they had seen at the Cooper Union library. However, when Oldenburg began to work on the exhibit, he changed his mind about hanging his drawings and instead produced much more radical three-dimensional works that incorporated scraps and objects found on the streets of New York.

This show was followed by an exhibit of works by Oldenburg and Jim Dine, who also created three-dimensional works. Later in the season—this was 1959–1960—a larger group show included works by Kaprow, Ratliff, Wesselmann, and others. "Happenings" became an art form promoted especially by Allan Kaprow.

After a year, Oldenburg and Dine moved to different galleries. They had been the primary movers in the Judson Gallery, which lasted another two years and then closed. Bud Scott had also left in 1960, and the interest in Judson Church moved from the visual to the performing arts. Al Carmines had joined the church staff in 1961, fresh out of seminary, as assistant minister. He soon became involved in the Judson Poets Theater, along with Larry Kornfeld. He began composing music, at first as incidental pieces for some of the plays and then entire oratorios. Out of the Judson Poets Theater grew the Judson Dance Theater, which for eight or ten years presented avant-garde performances that changed the history of dance.

It was not until 1967 that the Judson Gallery was revived by Jon Hendricks, a conscientious objector who had come to Judson in 1965 to fulfill his alternative service. An artist himself, Hendricks was interested in art activism and in artists creating works as a group. After working for a while with runaway kids in a storefront run by Judson Church, Hendricks organized an event in the fall of 1967 called "The Twelve Evenings of Manipulation." Each evening a different artist created a happening. Many of these protested the Vietnam War raging at the time. Some of the artists participating in this show were Allan Kaprow, Kate Millett, and Charlotte Moorman.

In the spring of 1968 the gallery organized Destruction in Art events. In the chapters that follow, Jon Hendricks and others tell of the climate at the time—the senseless killings in Vietnam and the riots at home—that caused many artists to question the value of traditional art. The Destruction in Art performances had an influence far beyond Judson and the Village.

As with other programs begun at Judson at a time when no one else was doing them, the church's involvement in the visual arts stopped when other venues became available. The avant-garde scene moved to the East Village, and Judson withdrew from the visual arts—not as a conscious policy but in an organic development.

Judson's great contribution to the arts was the absolute freedom it granted to the artists. The art, and especially the happenings, took many bizarre forms, but short of using fire and water—which might damage the buildings—the artists were free to express themselves in whatever medium and whatever subject they saw fit.

Bernard (Bud) Scott

Bud Scott was an associate minister of Judson Memorial Church from 1957 to 1960.

I came to Judson in the fall of 1954, barely a week after commencing my student days at Union Theological Seminary, looking for a part-time job. In those days, all first-year seminary students had to take a part-time ministerial assignment of some kind as part of their training, and among other places I was sent to Judson for an interview. Judson was looking for someone to work a few evenings each week contacting students at New York University who had indicated a Baptist or Congregationalist affiliation. This job was the beginning of a fascinating, six-year association that coincided with the last years of Bob Spike's tenure as senior minister and the beginning of Howard Moody's.

I was a native New Yorker and had done graduate work at the New School for Social Research on Twelfth Street, so I knew the Village somewhat. Also, I had just returned from Asia, concluding a four-year stint in Air Force Intelligence. Somehow, all this must have helped qualify me, and before long I was spending several nights a week calling on NYU students. I do not think many of those I visited ever became connected with Judson, but I did manage to involve some in a discussion group I started in the basement of Judson House.

MINISTER TO ARTISTS

That effort led to my being hired, in my second year at Union, to work as a missionary to the artistic community about the church. The idea was that if the natives would not come to church, the church would go to them. I was to hang out and be the church in their midst. It was to be a *travail de présence,* an expression popular with French priests right after World War II. I was not sure what it meant exactly, but I soon began spending time in the streets, cafés, galleries, and bars of the Village. The Beat Generation was in its embryonic, formative stage, and spontaneous poetry readings in the local cafés were starting to spring up.

This assignment eventually grew, after my three years of seminary were completed, into a full-time position at Judson as associate minister with dual responsibility as director of the Student House and as missionary to the local community. It was the latter assignment that captured most of my attention. The Student House and student involvement gradually became a secondary focus, not only for me but also for Judson Church generally.

I took the missionary assignment most seriously. Given the inclinations of my nature, I soon became a native Villager myself, a true bohemian—something of a convert in reverse. I grew a beard and spoke the white Negro jargon of the jazz scene, where money was "bread," things were "cool, man," and anyone who lived north of Fourteenth Street was "out of it."

LIVING ON THOMPSON STREET

My wife, Gisela, our daughter, Erica, and I lived in Judson House in the main street-level apartment. Our large living room with its tall ceiling became a salon of sorts for gatherings of artists, poets, and musicians. I recall one such occasion when a gifted friend of ours was playing the upright piano in our living room. An incident occurred that more or less characterized our life in those days. It was an unusually warm day in late March, and the floor-to-ceiling windows were wide open. From where I sat I could see that several black men had stopped on the sidewalk outside and were listening to the piano. I recognized one of them, a local drug dealer who had been a hip jazz musician at one point in his life. The other two looked to be junkies already a little stoned. The dealer caught my eye and broke into a big smile. *All right,* he said, his whole body suddenly become alive. *I like that. Who's making that sound? A friend of mine,* I shouted back through the window. *He's alll rrright. Hey man, can I come in? Let me come in. I got to catch this man.* By this time, my pianist friend had turned around and was looking at the small mottled audience outside our window. *Hey, just me, man,* the dealer called through the window. *Just for a minute. I got to catch this. I ain't gonna cause no problem.* A moment later I found myself opening the door to this junkie, who took a seat without a word as my friend resumed his playing, this time as if especially for him. The man first sat rather tentatively on a straight-back chair, but he soon got up and stood over the piano, his streetwise face lit up with pleasure. He did not stay long, but the encounter left a sweet taste in everyone's mouth.

That's the way life was living on the ground floor on Thompson Street in the 1950s, right in the midst of Greenwich Village life, with all its complexities and contradictions, its art and poetry, its music, its problems, and, yes, its decadence (there were three strip joints on the corner of Thompson and Third, grinding away every night until three in the morning, one of them being Ernie's of *Catcher in the Rye* fame).

So many different people came through our Student House doors in the late 1950s—Jack Kerouac (he took a bath in our apartment), Paddy Chayevsky, Norman Mailer, Martin Luther King, Jr., scholars and commentators like Harvey Cox and Peter Berger, the legendary poet/artist DeHirsch Margules (known in his day as the unofficial mayor of Greenwich Village), and indeed many others, particularly in the world of art.

THE BEGINNING OF THE JUDSON GALLERY

Around 1958, as part of my so-called missionary activities, I started an art gallery in a suite of rooms in the basement of Judson House, directly beneath our apartment. One of the student artists living at the house, Marc Ratliff, helped me get it get started.

The Judson Gallery had a walk-down entrance off the street outside our windows and almost immediately became a center of activity. I developed a friendship with two painters in particular who would go on to become famous artists: Claes Oldenburg and Jim Dine. Claes and I got to be good friends, and for a while we saw each other a lot. Some of the very first "happenings" ever, involving Allan Kaprow, the inventor of that unusual art form, were put on by this little gallery. Tom Wesselmann, who later also became a well-known artist, became one of our early exhibitors. For some of these artists, the Judson Gallery gave them their first New York show, and Claes and Jim Dine were intimately involved in making the gallery a happening in its own right. In fact, the Pop Art movement of the 1960s, famous for its turning away from abstract expressionism back to rep-

The Judson Gallery on Thompson Street, 1959. Photo by Grace Goodman. Reprinted by permission.

resentational, albeit often Dadaist, images, can be said to have had one of its roots in the Judson Gallery. This is how it happened.

Claes Oldenburg, Jim Dine, Marc Ratliff, and I were in the gallery late one Saturday afternoon. We had just closed Jim Dine's one-man show and were sitting on the floor with our backs against the wall beneath Jim's paintings. We were wondering what to do next when I suddenly had a thought. Let's have a group show, I said, and suggested some ideas for it. For the next hours we let our imaginations go free. The notion that I was working with was that of the interpenetration of art and reality. I suggested to Jim Dine that he create a painting that you could walk inside of. It was a long, spontaneous but somehow reflective meeting during which something seemed to gel.

RADICAL ART

One thing led to another, and before long we opened a show called *Ray Gun Specs*. It had a painting by Jim Dine that was literally a room you entered. On the outside, it looked like a small square hut that some homeless person might have put together under the Brooklyn Bridge. Inside, the three-dimensional space was packed densely with a plethora of painted objects—some found, some made, but all essentially just junk—hanging from the ceiling, projecting from the walls and floor, and blended with special lighting. A tape recorder emitted a flow of spontaneous sounds and meaningless utterances, including some by our own voices. The whole thing was not very memorable—just old stuff like boots and such, arranged and painted to take on the properties of art. Claes's work in the exhibit was a scene of lifesize paper maché figures and objects (a "paperbag bum," a fire hydrant, street litter) plus his wife (in the flesh) done up in painted burlap bags stooping among the litter. It was all done in flowing ribbons and patches of gray and white paint bathed in an eerie light.

This notion of a painting that was "entered" gave Jim Dine another idea. In conjunction with the *Ray Gun Specs* exhibit, Allan Kaprow organized an evening of so-called happenings or "performances" to be put on by this little band of artists. It was held in the Long Room of the church, which had its own entrance on Thompson Street. It was in fact a little theater. Jim's area for his own performance was to come on like a painter, dressed in beret and smock, and go up to this huge canvas and start to paint humming some zany song. As he worked, his motions would become more agitated until he flipped out and began tossing pots of paint first onto the canvas and then over himself. Finally he leapt forward and dove into the canvas. Jim did it twice in one evening, and the small crowd that took in his performances that night went wild. (I chanced to hear Jim Dine describe this scene, with something of his original gusto, during an interview on NPR in 1999.)

The confusion of art and reality that underlay the *Ray Gun Specs* exhibit, and that Jim Dine parodied in his performance, seems rather amusing in retrospect. But the notion touched a genuine impulse in these painters. Some time after I became a Catholic and left Judson, Allan Kaprow was invited by Judson to continue the gallery. A painting, he told the Judson representatives, was "not something you look at but something you enter." I am not sure that he or any one of us at the time could have explained to onlookers what that notion really meant. It was just the way it was in Greenwich Village and other such places in those days—artists and poets with their coteries looking for meaning in the most unlikely places, as in a pair of boots, seeking to uncover mystery in a consumer world that looked to them as if it had stamped mystery out, and finding hints of mystery in its refuse, like crumbs from a table of a time long ago when everything was colored with wonder.

LITERARY INITIATIVE

Around this time I also started an avant-garde literary quarterly called *Exodus*. There were only three issues, but the publication surprisingly made an immediate impression and today is a collector's item. (I am told it was included in a 1999 exhibition of Pop Art at the Whitney Museum, mounted in a glass case.) I had picked the name *Exodus* because it was to be a magazine looking for a way out. There was nothing overtly religious about it, despite its title and the fact that its editor was an unordained Protestant minister. Indeed, there were pieces that could be considered scandalous to conventional mentality, but the magazine nevertheless had a religious preoccupation that was hardly concealed. Today it would be surprising for a so-called little magazine to have spiritual undertones, but in those days it seemed to fit in easily with the soul-searching tenor of things in places like Greenwich Village. The magazine attracted a fair amount of attention in its brief life; in one newspaper editorial it was described as "not *beat* but definitely far out," meaning that the magazine was not seen as part of the Beat movement but that it took its own stance on the fringes, so to speak.

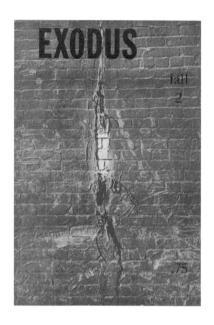

Covers of the three issues of Exodus.

Unfortunately, almost simultaneously with the appearance of our first issue, Leon Uris's novel by the same name hit the bookstores and became an instant best seller. This upset us at first, but the respective readerships were so different that no one seemed to notice. Conceivably, the name even helped us. *Exodus* was great fun and the quality of writing, poetry, and art was actually quite good. Daniel Wolf was co-editor, Howard Hart poetry editor, and Marc Ratliff art editor. Dan was the founder and editor of the *Village Voice;* Howard Hart was a poet of considerable skill and sensitivity (Jacques Maritain called him the "best Catholic poet writing in English today"); Marc was a gifted young artist who afterward made it big as a designer in the New York commercial art world; he finally also gained recognition as a serious artist.

Money for *Exodus* came from Whitey Lutz, who was married to the heiress of the Lilly pharmaceutical fortune and who took an interest in the Village culture. They kept an apartment on Twelfth Street. I went there one day, through the agency of Dan Wolf, and told them what I had in mind. Not long after, I received a generous check that got us started.

Launching a little magazine had its unexpected obstacles, chief of which was the difficulty in getting it circulated. Circulation is usually so small that distributors do not want to bother, especially with unknown startups operating on a shoestring, as ours obviously was. Financially, such magazines are almost always losing propositions. There was one lone distributor in the East, out of New Jersey, who handled "little magazines."

One day at my request he came by in a stationwagon filled with bundles of every variety of little magazine imaginable, some recognizable, like *Partisan Review,* most unheard-of. It was clear that he worked hard for a living. He explained that he was already overcommitted and could not take on any more business. After some persuading, he agreed to take three hundred copies on a one-shot basis. Hoping for more success than that, I printed fifteen hundred copies of our first issue. It was not long before this distributor came back asking for additional copies, first a few hundred more, then another five hundred. Finally, he wanted five thousand more. More people than we had dare dream were picking *Exodus* off the literary-magazine racks in cubbyhole bookstores all over the country.

Unfortunately for us, we could not supply the demand: The typographer's lead had been melted down right after the first printing. No matter, it cost us more to produce the magazine that we could sell it for. *Exodus* could not last very long on that basis and it did not, although the immediate cause for the quarterly's demise was not finances but my sudden departure from Judson in the spring of 1960.

My years at Judson were a vivid, fascinating time, and to this day they are never far from my consciousness. The friends I had then, both in Judson and in the surrounding community, continue to mean a great deal to me. I am very grateful for the experience.

BUD SCOTT
lives in Florida.

Allan Kaprow

Allan Kaprow was part of the Judson Gallery in the early 1960s. —

Bud Scott, den-father of Judson House and assistant minister of Judson Church in 1959, was a serious poet. Not an academic, he appeared to me the archetypal "beatified" artist popularized by Jack Kerouac's twist on the Beat Generation: not beaten down but inspired visionary.

Judson House, next to the church, was home then to a small group of likeminded poets and students. It radiated with street-smart hipness, and around Bud Scott there formed the promise of a renewed religious experience not to be found in Scripture alone.

You might have found it in the bars and in the gutters and trash baskets outside the church. Or you might have found it in the tiny basement room that Bud started as an art gallery. Jim Dine and Claes Oldenburg were already active there, and they introduced me to Bud. It was through Bud that I met Howard Moody, Judson's senior minister.

Howard Moody, in contrast to Bud Scott, was the only "man of the cloth" I'd ever come across who did not cloak himself with pietisms of goodness. It wasn't that Bud was falsely "spiritual." Bud was more possessed, more fired up. He was a perfect magnet for the turned-on hippie. Howard's feet were on the ground. His speech was plain but strongly principled, and he attracted a following of artistically and socially committed liberals. The two men seemed to me an ideal match.

In 1960 Bud was planning to move on to a monastic retreat and I was asked to help continue the gallery program. A slot in the calendar was open and I set to work filling the little basement room with an environmental maze of chicken wire, colored lights, bunched-up newspaper, straw, cloth, fake and real apples, and much litter (Apple Shrine).

The show was an obvious firetrap but Howard never lifted a finger. One Sunday morning when I was working, he stopped by to invite me to hear a sermon he and Bud had planned for that day's service. The talk was unusual. Its central theme was the role of the arts in everyday life. I do not recall which of the two was speaking, but the gist was, "In the past the artist went to the Church for spiritual instruction. Now the Church must go to the artist."

Very flattering, I thought. But I could not imagine why anyone would want to be instructed by the experimental art I and my friends were making. In retrospect, the sticky word was *spiritual*. What did (does) it mean?

Today, I suspect that the word *art* is just as problematical. We have inherited a notion that art itself is spiritual, and that it can make life better, or clearer, just as religion and church can do. Art (or spirit) comes packaged in poems, sonatas, plays, paintings, church buildings, and ceremonies. If these are better, or clearer, than life and its difficulties, why aren't they gobbled up like drugs and money?

Maybe the problem with religion and its relative, art, is that we are terribly unhappy unless we create problems we cannot solve with words. And here I am using words to say so.

This latest problem I attribute to that Sunday sermon.

ALLAN KAPROW
lives in California. He was curator of the 1999 show "No Limits" at
Judson Memorial Church, which celebrated Judson's
involvement in the arts in the 1950s and 1960s.

Phyllis Yampolsky

Phyllis Yampolsky was active at Judson Church and at the Judson Gallery in the late 1950s and early 1960s.

How Bud Scott came to my loft at Little West 12th Street to look at my paintings, I don't remember, and neither does he. What I do remember is that I was a two-year-old transplant from Philadelphia having just completed a few semesters at Hans Hofmann's Eighth Street Atelier. Since I had been recognized as an artist from the time I was old enough to hold a pencil—in a family and an environment that had never seen an artist and few paintings—I figured that the next sequence in my life would be as an exhibiting artist.

Accordingly, I went up to the galleries whose exhibits appealed to me and asked them to come see my work. I should probably have brought slides, but I may not have known that. I don't remember the style of the rejections except the one from Andre Emmerich, the owner of the gallery who exhibited Hofmann. Perhaps he was amazed at my innocence; perhaps he took my request to be amazing chutzpah. In either case, he came to my studio. He looked, smiled gently, and said: "In a few years, come again." I never went back.

But Bud Scott looked and said simply, "OK." I became one of the six members of the first group of Judson Gallery artists. The others were Jim Dine, Claes Oldenburg, Marc Ratliff, Dick Tyler, and Tom Wesselmann. During my association with the Judson Gallery I had two one-man shows of my paintings. They were called "one-man" shows at the time. I didn't mind, and I don't mind now. "Man" was short for "mankind," and I have always felt pinched at being identified with one half of the world's population.

The first show, in 1960, was called "Inside Out." It was the culmination of all I had learned at Hofmann's—the transformation of a flat surface into volume in which each stroke is a directional signal thrust into space, reverberating its energy into, out from, and about the environment, interweaving with the dynamics of all the other form/color energies until all of them together click into a balance, seizing the space into a unit of stillness.

By the second show, held in 1962, the struggle to achieve this balance had found resolution. There emerged a series of very simple paintings: a horizon line, a green field pushing up against it, a gray field pushing down on it from above. These became landscapes to me. The green field then gave birth to a very small, hesitant creature. In the dicta of abstract expressionism it felt like heresy and it was frightening. The creature persisted, however. It grew and eventually burst through the horizon as a woman. Though none of my works has ever been guided by literal intentions if any, in recalling this time I realize that the series was developed during the years of two pregnancies. This second show was called "Adam and Eve in the Garden of Eden and Other Short Stories." The primitive green/gray landscape had become inhabited with men and women, often making love.

Eight of the pictures in the show were bold brush drawings on brown wrapping paper, each of a man and a woman in the act of making love. They were called "Embrace #1," "Embrace #2," and so forth, to "Embrace #8." One day a man phoned, wanting to buy "The Embrace." "Which one," I asked, "there are eight of them." "You know," he answered, "the one of two people fucking." He was from Westchester and wanted to buy it to hang in a bar. At that time, I suffered a big disconnect between internal and external realities. His calling what the two people were doing "fucking" and his wanting to put the painting in a bar incensed and embarrassed me. My trigger response was an outlandish price. I can't remember whether it was to make sure he recognized this was "art" or to make sure he did not buy the picture. He chose not to buy it. I still have not learned not to give trigger responses.

The Judson Gallery was in the basement of Judson House. The door had a window in it to welcome passers-by with a view of the exhibits. The idea of barring or blocking the windows did not exist. One of the paintings in the second show hung on the wall opposite the window. One day someone aimed a rock at it and blew it apart. I don't think it was the man from Westchester. It was probably yet another person moved to respond. I guess the show was a success.

Since the 1960s, **PHYLLIS YAMPOLSKY** has concentrated on participatory arts. Driven by a "burdensome missionary consciousness," she continues to be engaged in community projects in New York City.

Marcus Ratliff

Marc Ratliff was involved in the Judson Gallery in the late 1950s.

I found out about Judson House from the office of student housing at Cooper Union. It was just good luck that a room was available. Norman Keim, the associate minister for students at Judson Church, was kind enough to help me move my stuff with his own car from a shared Upper West Side apartment I was desperate to get out of. This was the winter of 1955–1956. Toward the end of that school year I became friendly with Eva Hesse and told her about Judson. She could not wait to move in. I took the next year off to travel to Europe and came back to Judson House in the fall of 1957.

Sometime in the next year, probably the fall of 1958, Bud Scott moved up to Norman Keim's apartment, and that seemed to correspond to the changing times. Soon after, I wanted to use the storage room, just off the lounge, as a studio. However, Bud Scott preferred to make a space to show a collection of Rouault prints and to make the room into a "gallery."

Unofficially, that space began to be called the Judson Gallery. As I recall it, no one was really in charge of planning future events. Before too long, I invited Claes Oldenburg to show his drawings and paintings. I knew Claes through Cooper Union, where he worked in the library. Another Cooper Union student, Tom Wesselmann, who lived in Brooklyn at the time, joined the small group of artists that began using the gallery, as did Jim Dine. Jim was living and teaching in Patchogue, Long Island. He was an old friend of mine from high school in Cincinnati. Then there were others, including Dick Tyler, Bob Thompson, Red Grooms, Jay Milder, and Phyllis Yampolsky.

After I graduated from Cooper Union in 1959 and no longer lived at Judson House, I was involved with shows and happenings for another year or so. The magazine *Exodus* was in its third (and last) issue. Slowly, the center of gravity for the original group shifted to the Reuben Gallery and then to the big time uptown. I was not happy with my life as a painter, so I began to learn about printing and book design. Judson was still cooking long after my time there, but I had moved into a new career.

MARCUS RATLIFF
lives and works in New York City.

Claes Oldenburg

Claes Oldenburg was associated with the Judson Gallery in 1959 and 1960.

I came to New York in 1956 from Chicago and started working at Cooper Union. It was a very nice job. I had to spend four hours a day in the library, but I could choose my time. If I did not feel like working in the morning, I would come in in the afternoon. I worked there for a long time.

In 1959 I had an exhibition of drawings in the art school library, which had been arranged by the head of the library. These drawings were figure sketches of Patty, who was not yet my wife. Patty was a figure model, and I was living with her.

One of the students at the school at that time was Tom Wesselmann. Tom had come out from Cincinnati, as had Marc Ratliff and Jim Dine. They had come to New York about the same time. Tom Wesselmann, who was very much attracted to figurative subjects, especially female, liked the drawings very much. He said, "I think it would be wonderful if you could join us. We are going to start a gallery in the Village, in the Judson House." I said, "Fine, that sounds great." I had not had a show anywhere at that point, so this was really my first one-man show. I got to know Tom and also Marc, who was then living at Judson House, and I got to know Dine and his wife Nancy. And, of course, I got to know Bud Scott, who was there. I don't really remember all the chronological details of all this, but in May 1959 I was scheduled to do a show.

FIRST SHOW AT JUDSON

I had intended to do a show with figurative subjects, having started with those that attracted Tom's attention. I was painting a great deal at the time, painting figures. As the spring wore on, I changed my mind, and eventually the show that was put on at Judson was much more radical, consisting of constructions—three-dimensional objects made out of scraps and street stuff. It had quite a different

Claes Oldenburg outside Judson Gallery, 1960. Copyright © 1966
by Allan Kaprow. Reprinted by permission.

character than a figurative art show. It was really the difference between reality and illusion—the thing that you could hold in your
hand versus the painted image. This was all part of the attitude at
the time.

I had always done work in three dimensions, but I had focused
on painting. At the time there was a kind of figurative movement
that I identified with, and I had been going in that direction, but
then I realized that it was not radical enough to have a strong show.
So I changed my course, and I fell back on the other things I had
been doing at that time. There was a small catalog published for that
show, with a poem; I still have a copy of it. There was one review of
the show, by Hillary Dunstable in the *Village Voice*. It was a friendly
review, and that was my first experience with Judson.

Then the summer came along, and we all scattered but resolved
to meet again in the fall. I went to Lenox, Massachusetts; I don't
know where Jim was. There were some other characters on the

Jim Dine outside Judson Gallery, 1960. Copyright © 1966 by Allan
Kaprow. Reprinted by permission.

scene, Peter Farakis and Phyllis Yampolsky, his wife. We scheduled a
show for Tom and perhaps for Marc, I can't remember. We also
scheduled a two-man show with Jim Dine and myself, where I did
show some figurative paintings. There are posters and documents of
all these things. The poster is quite descriptive. By then I was doing
figurative work, but I was doing it in a sort of primitive style that I
derived from graffiti. I was also influenced by the work of Jean Du-
buffet and by *art brut,* mainly because I was becoming inspired by
my surroundings. I lived on the Lower East Side and walked every
day to my work at Cooper Union.

TWO-MAN SHOWS AND GROUP SHOWS

The new season began after the summer with the two-man show.
Then at Christmas, we had an invitational group show. I don't quite
remember who all was in it.

Everything was given a poster but not catalogs. There were also
announcements. For our show Jim Dine and I covered the front of
the gallery with monoprints. To create a monoprint you draw some-

thing on glass, say, and you press it onto absorbent paper. We made all these monoprints and not only plastered the gallery with them but also hung them up on the street surrounding the gallery.

In those days New York was very different in appearance. There was hardly any street advertising and there were hardly any graffiti. When you put up something, it was very visible. The monoprints were in the style of graffiti. You saw some graffiti in the subways then but not above ground. Our graffiti were intended to be a means of expressing ourselves by scrawling and writing. It was more like that than gangs and individuals advertising themselves. These posters made a big impression. They were up there for months and no one defaced them or tore them off. I have one that I peeled off the wall three months later, and it was intact. They were all original drawings; that was kind of amusing. The posters stayed on for the whole season. They were actually hard to get off the walls because of the glue.

The season in 1959 had been relatively conventional in that the gallery had one show after another—Jim and I, Tom Wesselmann, and maybe Phyllis Yampolsky. We decided to become more unconventional when 1960 began. By "we" I mean Jim and myself, Tom Wesselmann, Bud Scott, and Marc Ratliff, the ones that formed the nucleus of the gallery. I think that Tom Wesselmann would have preferred to go on with a more conventional schedule, where he would make paintings and hang them, and Ratliff was not so much of an artist as a designer, and he went on to develop in that direction. Ratliff wanted a show, but that would also have been in a more conventional way. I suppose that it was Jim and I who pressed for more radical art. At that point Allan Kaprow came into the picture, and also Red Grooms. It is a very complicated moment.

In December 1959, the artists at the Judson Gallery held a panel discussion on "New Uses of the Human Image in Painting." There were Jim and I, and we invited Allan Kaprow and Lester Johnson, another painter. We all sat around and discussed figuration. That was the issue: abstraction or figuration, metaphysics versus realism. The discussion was very well attended. We were still a little bit into the human image thing, which was hanging on. Soon after that it ceased to be painted images. It became real images—facsimiles of reality rather than illusions. The figurative vanished.

Four drawings by Claes Oldenburg, 1960. They were originally published in the third issue of Exodus, a magazine edited by Bernard Scott and Daniel Wolf. Copyright © 1960 by Bernard Scott. Reprinted by permission.

HAPPENINGS

Kaprow had done a performance at the Reuben Gallery, which is a gallery that he had started in late 1959. Red Grooms had also started his own gallery and called it the Delancey Street Museum. He was doing performances there. Grooms was doing performances and Kaprow was doing them, and this was a direction Jim and I wanted to join, I especially. Jim was more drawn into it, let's say. I formulated the concept of a month in which there would be environments by Jim and myself. There would be a period in which we would not only do performances ourselves but would invite others to do performances, such as Red Grooms and Al Hansen and Bob Whitman and Dick Higgins and people that we began now to reach out to.

Jim's work was, and is, extremely autobiographical. To a certain extent, mine is, too. At that time, Jim was very much a product of his experience. It was also one of my principles that art should come out of experience, so that everything I did at the time came out of my experience. Some of my experiences came out of my contact with my surroundings in New York. This even took the form of playing the roles that I had seen, for example, a beggar or a house painter, and so on. It was an attempt to put art and reality together. This was seen as an antithesis to the attitude of the abstract painters, who tried to remove art from reality. Of course, they did not completely succeed. Art is always in some way related to reality.

When I say realistic images, you need to understand that they were transformed by the medium. It was not like the Ashcan School. The images went through a metamorphic process, it was surreal. No one was doing realistic art, though many artists were using real people, such as Al Hansen. When we did later happenings, people were used as objects in a composition. So it is a very complicated aesthetic that was being developed here.

RAY GUN SPECS

We were defining the avant-garde at that moment. Every time we found someone that was interesting we proposed this collective idea of Jim and me, Bud Scott, and whoever else hung out at the gallery, including poets. It was a very nice meeting place. We decided to pull these people together if possible.

Jim Dine and I built environments in January 1960. The name given to the performances was *Ray Gun Specs*. People have often wondered what the name means. Robert Hayward, a critic, points out that it contains sex and it also contains spectacles. Actually, "specs" is a Swedish term for spectacles. I was born in Sweden, and a lot of Swedish language still circulates around my head. It has also got a suggestion of spectacles as a visual thing—it has all kinds of suggestions. It seemed like a good name. Ray Gun was an invented figure at that time.

In the middle of the month of performances there was a kind of pause, and everyone gathered in the gymnasium at the church, where we auctioned off some of the junk we had gathered on the street. We had printed something called Ray Gun money and given everyone who came a million dollars. They could spend that money on the junk.

RICHARD O. TYLER

At that time, another person was involved in the gallery who does not get enough credit, and that is Dick Tyler. Dick Tyler is the wood-cutter who made the woodcuts that are printed in *Exodus* #2. Dick was a very unusual person, someone I knew in Chicago. He was a woodcutter extraordinaire, but he was more than that. He was also trying to develop art based upon all sorts of abnormal sources, let's say, psychotic sources and drug-induced states and hallucinations. He was a precursor of the 1960s. He had a lot of insight into what was to come.

Dick was the janitor of my building on the Lower East Side. He had come to New York a little bit earlier than I and had taken an apartment in the basement, where he had set up a studio of print-making. When I was looking for an apartment, he said, "Why don't you come to my place? I think there is an apartment available." So we started to live in the same building. Mine was on the top floor and his was on the bottom floor. He had a great deal of influence on my thinking. When I got involved with Judson in 1959, Dick also became involved. It seemed as if he fit in perfectly with—this is very hard to define exactly—the mystical atmosphere that some people connected with this project had created. One has to think a bit about this. From the Judson side there was a desire to establish

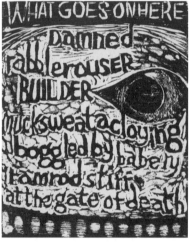

Three woodcuts by Richard O. Tyler originally published in Exodus, Vol. 2. Copyright © 1960 by Bernard Scott. Reprinted by permission.

some kind of religious feeling in the secular surroundings, as expressed by Bud Scott. On the other hand, there was in the secular a kind of reaching out for the transcendent, which dominated in the 1960s. Dick was one of the people who was most tuned into that. He was perfect for the gallery in that sense. He stayed with the gallery for many years. He had a pushcart from which he sold books and tracts that he printed—a very interesting artist who has received absolutely no attention.

Dick did not participate in the performances, but you could say that Dick's entire life was a performance. Everything about him was a performance. He was a very theatrical person. He lived a fantasy life. He is always left out of accounts of avant-garde art in the 1960s because he was too strange and too individual. However, he fit into Judson and fit in with the poets.

THE MOVE UPTOWN

The Ray Gun Specs show was the culmination of that particular period. Then the action moved elsewhere, although it later returned to Judson. But our activities after that first season moved to the Reuben Gallery, which Allan Kaprow had set up. The Reuben Gallery had a number of interesting artists—Lucas Samaras, Bob Whitman, Al Hansen, Dick Higgins. It was the leading avant-garde gallery downtown, and Allan was the first one who showed his performances. That was followed by a group show called Below Zero, which took place in the beginning of the sixties. There was Red Grooms with his Delancey Street Gallery, there was the Judson, and there was the Reuben, all three running together. We all met with Allan Kaprow and the people at the Reuben, and we decided to do an entire season of performances. The Reuben was relocated to a larger space off Second Avenue where we could do performances. The Gallery was totally independent. It functioned like a co-op, and we all contributed to it.

As the action shifted away from Judson, I lost track of the gallery. Bud Scott left, and that may have had something to do with it. So I only had one season with the Judson, from 1959 to 1960. I had a show at the Reuben Gallery in the spring of 1960 and used some of the materials from the performances at the Judson. I stayed with the Reuben Gallery for two seasons, and again there was a splitting up. Jim Dine went to the Martha Jackson Gallery uptown, and I went to the Green Gallery on 57th Street, an interesting downtown gallery uptown.

Judson became involved with dance and music and theater through Al Carmines, and that was a different period entirely. We were there in the very early, primitive period, the time of the beat poets, and it had a kind of dark character. The Judson Gallery was dormant from about 1962 to 1965, and then reopened under Jon Hendricks. There was Yoko Ono, and Allan Kaprow became involved again.

IMPACT OF JUDSON GALLERY

The Judson Gallery was an absolutely unique experience. We had total independence and freedom, but we also had the feeling of being part of a community. We had theoretical discussions, but I can hardly remember any of them. We all drank a lot of beer at the time, that's why I can't remember much. There was a lot of talk about what art should be—whether it should be part of life, whether it should be outside of life, whether it should be somehow part of the soul or the spirit. Basically, it was still a church, and the church was trying to get in touch with artists.

People came down from uptown. In those days, uptown and downtown were strictly divided and uptown people rarely ventured downtown. And then it was discovered that things were happening downtown. Of course, they had spies to come down to check you out. We were lucky. In New York, no matter how talented you are, success is always a matter of being there at the right moment. The early sixties were a moment of great change in America. The pent-up energies of the fifties were finally turned loose. It was a very important moment in art history, and it took place at Judson House, the beginning anyway.

I do appreciate what Judson did. It is an absolutely unique institution. We were breaking new ground at a time in New York that had a lot more values and principles than now. It is good to recall it.

CLAES OLDENBURG
and his second wife, Coosje van Bruggen, who is also an artist, create large-scale projects commissioned by cities and private individuals throughout the world.

Tom Wesselmann

Tom Wesselmann was involved in the Judson Gallery in the late 1950s and early 1960s.

I never lived in the Judson Student House; I lived with my wife in Brooklyn. My best friend at the time, Marc Ratliff, did live at the house.

I was an art student at Cooper Union, along with Marc. Bud Scott and Marc hatched the idea, or one of them did—I was not privy to that but that is how it was presented to me—to start an art gallery in the space downstairs at Judson House. It sounded like a good idea. Jimmy Dine and Marc and I are all from Cincinnati. I did not know them there, but they knew each other. So when Jimmy came to New York City directly from Ohio University, he took up with Marc, and I fell into that relationship also. So the gallery was started by Bud Scott, Marc Ratliff, myself, and Jim Dine. I don't think that I had any powerful role in it. It was really Bud Scott who was organizing the stuff. We decided to open a gallery. We had liked the figurative drawings we had seen at Cooper Union by Claes Oldenburg, at the library. We did not know him because he was not Claes Oldenburg yet! We offered him the first show, a show of his drawings. It was a nice show.

Claes got involved in the gallery and started using it as a springboard for some more exciting things he was just beginning to get interested in, getting away from regular, representational paintings and drawings, which he had been doing. He and Jimmy Dine seemed to catch fire, and this was their outlet. There were a lot of advanced ideas coming together. For me, it was just a place to show or not to show. Marc Ratliff and I had a two-man show there well before I was ready to have a show. I was still a student at Cooper Union, not even a third-year student. Marc may still have a copy of the little announcement we did. I was just beginning to get involved in art because I was from another background—I was interested in humor, cartoons. I got that from the army. I hated the army so much I had to make fun of it. The trouble was I could not draw, so I went to

Cooper Union on the G.I. bill to stall for time and to teach myself to draw.

CARTOONS AND COLLAGES

I came to Cooper Union at the urging of my drawing teacher in Cincinnati. I had started taking some courses at the art academy in Cincinnati. Cooper Union was free, it was in New York, and New York was the cartoon market. I used to come to New York from time to time to visit the editors to take my cartoons around. So that seemed to make sense.

I was still early in that process of learning to draw when we had that show. It was strictly student work. Marc was precociously talented in art school and he was well advanced. I don't know the date of that show but it would have been either 1957 or 1958 because we graduated in 1959. Marc and I later had another two-man show at the Judson Gallery of a more serious sort. In this show I exhibited early portrait collages I was just beginning to do. This must have been in 1959 because we had just graduated from Cooper Union, and I began doing these collages after graduation. These were collages mostly of people's faces with the general subject matter of a Hans Memling, who was my inspiration at that point: a seated figure inside of a window next to the face, mostly women. This was when I got my first critical review. A woman from *Art News,* I think, said: "Wesselmann shows weird collages of women." I was pleased to get some kind of mention.

I could have had a one-man show and maybe would have, but I lacked the confidence. I did not really feel I was an artist or could be an artist, so I took the easy way out and had a two-man show. My works were all very small, because my studio was small. I had just separated from my wife and I was living in a tiny place on Bleecker Street in a studio of about 10 feet square. Everything I did was little at that point. I felt I always had to work that way. I could not accept the fact that there were people out there who might buy my work, so I gave away half of the show to friends, even to people I was not very friendly with. And indeed, nobody bought anything. Consequently, I still have a nice collection of those early works and have since bought back and reacquired some works as they have come up at auction. I want to keep them together as a group. It was a very interesting, successful first attempt to be an artist.

At Judson, I was impressed with Jim Dine and his ferocious energy. He was spewing things out. Dick Tyler seemed crazy but he was an interesting guy. I would chat with him about his anarchist book cart. He was always outside the gallery, especially on Sundays. Claes Oldenburg was interesting. I remember his show at the gallery, although I don't remember what his drawings looked like. Phyllis Yampolsky, another artist hanging around Judson, was a very pretty woman. I found her very attractive.

I WANTED TO PAINT LIKE DE KOONING

There was a group show at the gallery that I thought was important. It was a rather large group. We invited all kinds of artists. That was the first time I ever ran into Red Grooms; he was in it. He had a very amusing piece. He stretched a blue work shirt on a stretcher; it had a tobacco label on the pocket. Jay Milder was in that show and others, whose names I had not heard of before. It was a very lively show, and it was the first time I had the feeling there was something bigger going on in the art world. A lot of people were beginning to loosen up a great deal. I did not feel a part of it because I was going in the opposite direction. I was doing this little tiny work. I so idolized Willem De Kooning, and I wanted to paint like De Kooning, but I could not do it because he was already doing it, so I moved in the exact opposite direction in every respect. Instead of abstract, I did representational; instead of big, I did small; instead of loose, my work was tight. I felt isolated from everybody else.

I remember little about the group show, which was called *Ray Gun Specs,* but I do remember the impact it had. It was extremely interesting, to say the least, Oldenburg's work especially. Dine was more performance oriented. Those two guys were on fire. The Judson Gallery, in a sense, became theirs.

HAPPENINGS

The Judson Gallery, under Allan Kaprow and Jim Dine, started the "happenings." They were a key ingredient in the incredible energy in New York City. Looking back, one realizes that the amount of energy in the city at that time, in the early 1960s, was phenomenal. The Judson Gallery, one could almost say, was the first public manifestation of this energy; it seemed to precede everything. The gallery played a very important role.

My relationship with the Judson Gallery lasted just about as long as the gallery lasted. When the gallery closed, I moved on to the Greene Gallery uptown.

At Judson Church, support for the gallery was superseded by that for the Judson Dance Theater. That became much more exciting than the gallery. The gallery peaked in the early 1960s. The Dance Theater remained active for eight or ten years. We used to relish going there to see that stuff.

TOM WESSELMANN
works as an artist in New York City.

Jon Hendricks

Jon Hendricks reopened the Judson Gallery in 1967. ————————————————

Icame to Judson as a conscientious objector from Vermont in 1965. The Vietnam War was heating up, so I applied for CO status with my local board. I thought I would like to work in a museum, but they had only jobs for guards. The Museum of Modern Art was not very sympathetic to conscientious objectors. They asked me what I would do if there was a rowdy crowd. They asked: "Are you such a pacifist that you would leave them alone?"

My brother Geoffrey knew about Judson Church because he had worked with Al Carmines teaching students who came to New York from midwestern colleges such as Earlham, so I applied to be placed there because Judson was an approved site. Judson had had one earlier CO. Little did the draft board know that the government was letting me enter a subversive role of resistance. Judson had no money to pay me but they agreed to give me room and board. I had a room on the second floor with the students. Beverly Waite also lived there. Downstairs, below Beverly's room, was Al Carmines's apartment, and to the left at the end of the hall was Ro Lee's. She was the church secretary at the time. Below Ro's apartment was Ed Brewer's. He was the church organist. There was a cook who provided meals, so I had food and a place to live. But I had no spending money. I would do odd painting jobs, and at Christmas the church gave me $50.

NO JOB DESCRIPTION

I worked for the church full-time but there was no job description, so what I did was things like setting up chairs for the theater and moving the platform in the meeting room, because we had theater on Saturday night and church services on Sunday morning.

Howard was very interested in the idea of finding some alternatives to drug use. This was a time of heroin. This was before methadone. So he asked me to look into LSD. Was this an alternative? Was this a possibility? This led to discussions of mind expansion, psychedelic experiences, away into some other state of being. We then began discussions about creating an environment for artists where one could experience something other than drugs. At the time, I was also very interested in groups and group activities. I wanted to find out what happens when a group of individuals gets together and something forms that is outside of the self.

The gallery was located in the student house under Al's apartment. It had not been used much since 1961 when Allan Kaprow, Jim Dine, and Claes Oldenburg exhibited there. These artists had been brought in by Bud Scott. Bud would go to the cafés and talk to the artists to see if there was a need for space to exhibit. The artists showed some very radical art in the gallery and began to have happenings there.

From the gallery you could get into the Garden Room (called Long Room at the time) and from there into the gymnasium. Some of the happenings of 1960 took place in the Long Room and the gymnasium but also in the gallery. But certainly by 1962 the gallery was closed, and it was just empty space.

THE GALLERY REOPENS

I was aware of this very important early history of the gallery. So I asked Howard if I could reopen the gallery, and he said yes. I began to talk to artists about this idea of creating an environment that would be sustaining over a period of time, that would change our state of being. We came up with the idea of something called *The Stone,* by Anthony Cox. It was really written by a group of us: Michael Mason, who created repeated loop sounds; and Yoko Ono, who had done eye bags and questionnaires. You would come down into the gallery and fill out a questionnaire, then you would be given a bag, take your shoes off, and then you would be in this room. The gallery was small and the room was smaller. Jeff Perkins did film messages, which were looped films that repeated. This became a famous event in art history.

We had a budget of $50 a show, $300 a year, money that the church gave us. We also had free use of the mineograph machine. Yoko Ono and Tony printed *The Stone* and I helped. They wanted to charge $1 for it, but I felt it had to be free. We did a lot of things in the gallery that were different from the things that were done at the church. The gallery was more independent.

My work with the church was primarily with the arts program. And slowly Judson House became a place for artists rather than for students. The Judson Board decided that it would be more meaningful to provide living space for artists. At that time there was a very active program at the church in theater, dance, music, as well as the gallery.

ARTISTS AND RUNAWAYS

In 1967 I was asked to devise a program for artists in residence. Beverly Waite was the manager of the Student House. Beverly was a wonderful person. She was already at the house when I came. The idea was to create some kind of community, to make sure that the artists felt part of a community.

Then there was a program started in a building on Third Street with runaway kids, where people from the arts worked with teenage runaways. I did a program with Elaine Summers one or two days a week. Larry Kornfeld did something on theater. So we had this storefront, and each day kids would come in and freely hang out and use the materials. Some of the kids also lived in the Judson House. There was a feeling at the church that this might be a better use of the space. Giving the space to performers was very necessary, but here we had a crisis on runaway kids without a place to live. At that time there were a lot of runaways in the Village.

MANIPULATIONS

In 1967 the Vietnam War was in full swing and I wanted my own art activities to be more engaged in protesting the war. I had been a painter but had moved away into critical art activism. This was a transitional time when painting seemed to be a pretty poor way of addressing the war. Painting is a very removed form. You paint a painting, then you have to find a place to show it, maybe someone will buy it, and then you won't see it anymore, and here were these traumatic images on television of Americans murdering Vietnamese. So we were looking for other forms, other ways of expression. Certainly, the idea of art as performance and happenings was not new, but still we felt we could do something within the gallery space or within the church.

I had invited a wonderful artist, Carolee Schneemann, to do an installation, but she was not able to get together what she wanted to do, and I was a little down. And then I had the idea to do a series of events over a period of three weeks, where each artist would be given one day and in that day they could do anything they wanted but they had to deal with destruction. So I started talking to people about this idea, and we came up with the title of *Manipulations,* and it would be held in the gallery space. I had organized several shows before, such as Kate Millett's furniture, but this was to be a major show.

The show took place in October 1967. The official title was *The Twelve Evenings of Manipulation.* Lil Picard had a piece called Construction-Destruction-Construction. That winter Andy Warhol asked Lil if she had something for a movie he was making. We went over and recreated Construction-Destruction-Construction in Andy's loft, and after we did our thing Andy and his friends started to do their thing, which was actually later.

Manipulations took place before DIAS, the Destruction in Art Symposium, that was held at Judson in March 1968. The Destruction in Art movement had begun in London in 1966, but I did not know about it, although subliminally I might have. It is not hard to jump to the idea of destruction with a war raging on. In the spring of 1968 we organized a DIAS-USA 68 and invited a bunch of artists to come. We canceled the show when Martin Luther King was killed. We then did another series of events where each artist was invited to say something about destruction. This was another very important event in the gallery. For all these events I acted as coordinator.

The artists involved in *Manipulations* were:

Ralph Ortiz, a Puerto Rican who now is a professor at Rutgers University.
Bici Hendricks (now Nye Ffarrabas), who did a wonderful piece.
Jean Toche; we formed a group called the Guerrilla Art Action, which produced very provocative art actions. They were really theater pieces but we moved into an area that we considered art. They were provocative, direct, confrontational

art actions. Jean and I worked very closely for a number of years, and still do.

Allan Kaprow, who had run the Judson Gallery in the early years.

Al Hansen

Geoffrey Hendricks

Malcolm Goldstein, a composer who had worked with Elaine Summers on a piece for the Judson Dance Theater. For this show he did a wonderful piece where he took a tape with President Johnson's State of the Union address and invited people who came in to cut up the tape and resplice it and then play it. He had several tape recorders sitting around.

Steve Rose—I don't know where he came from. He came and set up a division in the gallery. He had a dog or maybe it was Beverly's dog. Anyway, the dog came in through the window.

Carolee Schneemann, a great early-happenings artist.

Lil Picard, a critic and artist, and a refugee from Nazi Germany.

Kate Millett, who later wrote *Sexual Politics*.

Jud Yalkut, a film artist.

Nam June Paik, one of the original video artists.

Charlotte Moorman, who was famous as the topless cellist but also was an interpreter of Paik and other avant-gardists.

All during the winter of 1967–1968 we had events having to do with destruction. In March 1968 we invited artists from all over the world to participate in our DIAS preview. Kurt Cren was there and other artists. One of the pieces by Ortiz was Henny Penny Up in the Tree. We bought two chickens, a white chicken and a black chicken, and we would climb up the tree and yell insults at each other and throw blood at each other and fight with the chickens, killing the chickens in a race war. Before we could start, Michael Kirby and one of the Motherfuckers, an anarchist group, grabbed the chickens and threw them over the fence. So here we were, stuck without the chickens to do our Henny Penny. Ralph said, Do you have any saws? And I said yes, and we climbed up the tree and we did this very silently. It was actually quite beautiful. We each sawed a branch of the tree and poured blood into the cut of the tree branch. We then climbed down and put the American flags into a pool of blood. It was actually a better piece.

CHARLOTTE MOORMAN PERFORMS

Then we went inside and we were going to have a symposium. Charlotte Moorman was to have performed but she had not shown up. She was notoriously late. We started without her, and then she walked in, upset that we had begun without her performance. We explained to her that we had done our performances and were now at the symposium part of the program. "No, no, no, I have to do my performance," she cried. We gave in but warned her not to take a long time. Her piece was called *One for Violin,* by Nam June Paik. Charlotte raised the violin slowly above her head with the idea to bring it down fast and smash it on the table. Someone in the audience yelled not to smash the violin, a kid on the Lower East Side could use it to make music. Charlotte answered: "It is my violin. I am going to make my kind of music." No, someone else yelled, you can't smash that violin. This gave rise to a big argument back and forth about the idea of material versus art—whose was the material? Is it better to do this? What about the kid on the Lower East Side?

Finally Saul Gottlieb came from the back of the room and sat on the table facing the audience, and Charlotte started doing a very abbreviated, quick version of her violin piece and hit Saul on the head with the violin. Well, that was the end of that symposium on destruction and all hell broke loose. Jill Johnston wrote a piece about the event in *The Village Voice* (March 28, 1968), in which she described the chicken rescue and violin performance as "the most unusual manifestation of a performer-audience situation I have witnessed in a decade of attending a theatre in which the performer-audience relationship has been pushed in every conceivable direction. Unusual is a mild word for it."

I left Judson House in June of 1968. Even after I was gone, I did three more shows, including the flag show in 1969. I also did a couple of benefits for Judson.

The artists-in-residence program was probably a failure. Some of the other things we did were probably failures. But what was important to me was that anyone living in the Judson House at that time would have been exposed to and taken part in the different productions—theater and dance and so on. And they would have been enriched by what they experienced.

NO LIMITS

The gallery was not programmatic, it was not planned. Maybe that was the failure of our thinking, that we could have programmed or planned something. But anybody who was there, and you would have to have been pretty dumb not to trip over it, would know that something was going on: artists going in and out, events going on, and so on.

Howard had a great deal of trust in what we did in the gallery. Once a decision had been made about the gallery, Howard defended the arts. There was never any interference. The church had made a decision to have an arts program in the gallery and I was to run it. There was actually one time when Beverly got very upset because her kids saw a dead lamb being smashed around in a piece by Hermann Nitsch, and there was kind of a division within the church. People were outraged at this destruction stuff and had very strong feelings about what we were doing.

Howard got up there and was so strong about free speech. There was never any wavering. He said, We may not like this but we have to be able to allow it. I have such a respect for the man, for sticking up for us. It was not a question of whether he liked it or not. It was not a question of whether it was good or bad. It was a legitimate artistic expression, and the church was not going to interfere with that. That was always the feeling at Judson. Once a decision was made there were no limits. The only limits were on fire and water. Fire could destroy the building and water would ruin the floor. Anything with fire and water had to be done in the garden. When we burned the flag we did it in the garden. But language or nudity were OK, even simulated sex acts. It was all part of that wonderful support of free expression that Howard especially was strong in.

I don't regret for a minute my time at Judson. The last year I was there the church gave me a little money. To be able to be free to do these things was great. Judson changed my life, but at the gallery we also did things that changed other people's lives. We weren't just spectators. What we did with destruction art changed art history.

JON HENDRICKS
lives in New York City.

Geoffrey Hendricks

Geoffrey Hendricks was involved in the Judson Gallery in 1967 and 1968.

In the 1960s, Judson Memorial Church, and especially the Judson Gallery in the basement of Judson House, became an important part of my life. That space at 239 Thompson Street was modest but versatile. Throughout the decade I witnessed many transformations of it as friends and artists, including myself, created work there.

The gallery's small size and roughness were perhaps assets. One could work freely and make it into what it had to be. It was a container for each person's ideas, dreams, images, actions. Three people in particular formed links for me to the space: Allan Kaprow, Al Carmines, and my brother, Jon Hendricks.

It must have been through Allan Kaprow that I first got to know about the Judson Gallery. When I began teaching at Rutgers University (called Douglass College at the time) in 1956, Allan and I became colleagues, and I went to the Judson Gallery to view his *Apple Shrine* (November 30-December 24, 1960). In that environment one moved through a maze of walls of crumpled newspaper supported on chicken wire and arrived at a square, flat tray that was suspended in the middle and had apples on it. With counterpoints of city and country, it was dense and messy but had an underlying formal structure. His work of the previous few years had had a tremendous impact on me: his *18 Happenings in 6 Parts,* at the Reuben Gallery (October 1959), his earlier installation accompanied with a text entitled *Notes on the Creation of a Total Art* at the Hansa Gallery (February 1958), and his first happening in Voorhees Chapel at Douglass College (April 1958). From that time I also remember environments by Claes Oldenburg and Jim Dine, who transformed the Judson Gallery with reworked material brought in from the street. In December 1963 Al Hansen took over the space for a 3rd Rail Viking Dada extravaganza *Oogadooga.*

Throughout the early 1960s, my wife, Bici (Nye Ffarrabas), and I were often at Judson for a whole range of events, including many dance and theater performances. As we went on to create pieces in the space, bringing our children with us as we worked, Judson Gallery became like a second home.

In 1964 my college art teacher, Bill Darr, asked if I would be interested in helping to create a New York winter term in music, art, and drama for Earlham College, where he was then teaching. Bill also asked about my thoughts of someone for theater, and I suggested Al Carmines. Together with Al and a music professor from Earlham, Larry Apgar, we created something that turned out to be considerably more radical than what Earlham originally had in mind.

Al took the students into the world of Off-Off Broadway theater, the theater at Judson, and Café Cino. I took them to the world of Happenings, Fluxus, and Pop Art. We had gatherings in Al's apartment at Judson House and at our apartment. We staged events in different parts of the church. Each winter from 1965 to 1969 I worked with a group of about twenty students, taking them to meet artists such as Al Hansen, Roy Lichtenstein, Claes Oldenburg, Hui Ka Kwong, Bob Watts, Bob Morris, Yvonne Rainer, Carolee Schneemann, George Segal, Arakawa, and Jean Toche. We also went to galleries and museums, discussed what we saw, and created new work together. For the drama portion Al Carmines organized comparable events. During the first program in 1965 Bici and I did a reading, *Selections from the Friday Book of White Noise* (our collaborative journal) at the Café au GoGo (part of the Watts & Brecht *Monday Night Letter)*. As part of the same series I did Happening *Weather* there, in which the Earlham students participated and which we did again at Judson in the back area of the Meeting Room.

In late 1964, while Al Carmines, Larry Apgar, and I were in the midst of planning the Music Art Drama (MAD) Winter Term for Earlham students, my brother Jon was called up by his draft board. As a conscientious objector he needed to find a place where he could carry out his alternative service. I put Jon in touch with Al. Jon met Al and Howard Moody, and his draft board approved Judson as an alternative site.

Soon after arriving at Judson, Jon began to reactivate the gallery, which had been closed for several years. He organized a piece by

Yoko Ono and Anthony Cox called *The Stone* and an exhibition with Bici Hendricks. Jon was showing women at a time when the art world was dominated by men. Bici's show had a vanity table where you could shed your ego and balance an egg; an array of ice cubes with the American flag, called *Defrost the American Flag;* a neon sign flashing "Über alleS"; *Word Work,* consisting of horizontal boxes with a moving text on a perforated tape lighted from behind; among other things.

Together with others, Jon conceived of a group of events in the Judson Gallery in which each person had that basement room for just one day. The morning was spent setting up; the exhibit or activity took place in late afternoon and evening; and the space had to be cleared that night for the next person. The *Twelve Evenings of Manipulation* was planned to run from Thursday, October 5, to Sunday, October 22, 1967, and turned into a dense three weeks. Exhibit goers wanted to get to every event, and with four events a week, time needed to be planned carefully. I have memories of rushing from teaching at Rutgers back to Judson. Three-year-old Tyche and eight-month-old Bracken called for further planning by Bici and me. Our children became part of this whole mix of art and life. The participating artists were Ralph (Raphael) Ortiz, Bici Forbes (Nye Ffarrabas), Jean Toche, Allan Kaprow, Al Hansen, Malcolm Goldstein, Steve Rose, Carolee Schneemann, Lil Picard, Jud Yalkut, Ken Jacobs, Kate Millett, Nam June Paik, Charlotte Moorman, Takahiki Iimura, and myself.

MANIPULATIONS

My evening was an environmental performance titled *Sky/Change* on October 13. I began with 100 cardboard boxes in flat bundles that I assembled and painted white. The only light came from changing projected slides of sky that became visible as the boxes became white. As the stacked boxes filled the room, shadows were cast. Some of my sky laundry was hung in the space—two sheets on which I had painted sky on both sides. These I also painted over white, so that the projected sky, first in interplay with the image of the sky on the sheets, then became the image. On a red table I had a bouquet of orange and yellow flowers that I covered first with shaving cream and then with a sheet of plastic. The event lasted three hours.

For her evening, Bici had a large cake of ice to chip and melt, with her event scores and word pieces projected on the wall and on the ice. Were burning candles floating in water? Memories of other pieces include Ralph Ortiz destroying furniture and objects; Jean Toche filling the space with blinding light and sound; Malcolm Goldstein taking a tape of President Johnson's State of the Union address and splicing and resplicing it into garbled incoherence; Steve Rose caging himself; Lil Picard in a performance focused on the Vietnam War, spraying perfume and burning objects in a frying pan; Kate Millett building a large cage of vertical dowels that filled the space, which she packed with the audience and then left them to their own devices; Charlotte Moorman playing the cello lying on her back while Nam June Paik cut a fine line on his arm with a razor blade bringing forth beads of blood. Was this Nam June atoning for Charlotte's arrest while performing his *Opera Sextronique?* (The latter event had taken place on February 9, 1967, the day our son Bracken was born. Bici and I missed that performance.) These events changed the basement room every day, each time giving it very different energy. Sometimes it was a focused performance, sometimes a total environment, and sometimes it moved into the garden behind Judson House. They were three great weeks of sharing.

DESTRUCTION IN ART

Then there were the DIAS (Destruction in Art Symposium) previews that took place in the Garden Room (Long Room), the Gallery, and the Garden. In September 1966 there had been a big *Destruction in Art Symposium* in London, and the plan was to have another one in New York. The previews in March 1968 were in preparation for the big event, which was later canceled because of the assassinations of Martin Luther King and Robert Kennedy.

At the inaugural gathering, speakers and performers sat behind a long table alongside the wall, with the audience filling the rest of the room seated on folding chairs and the overflow crowd standing behind them. The most vivid moment of the evening came when Charlotte Moorman set out to perform Nam June Paik's *One for Violin.* The piece consists of holding the violin by the neck, very slowly raising it over one's head, and then rapidly, like a Zen slap, bringing it down to smash on the surface below.

Everyone in the audience knew the piece, but with each performance there was new suspense and anticipation. This one was unique. Saul Gottlieb, a political activist in the East Village and organizer of alternative programming, felt that Charlotte should not destroy the violin. From the back of the room, he got into a dialogue with Charlotte, explaining how the violin should be given to some poor child on the Lower East Side who wanted to play the violin—it could be the beginning of a great career.

Charlotte said yes, things like that should be done, but this was music by a great composer and should be performed. Charlotte was determined to continue and complete the piece. The suspense was great. Slowly she raised the violin high over her head. At that point Saul pushed his way through the crowd, slid over the long table, and stood in front of Charlotte just as she brought the violin down, smashing it on Saul's head.

Everyone was stunned.

I was sitting in the front row and retrieved the neck of the violin. Later, I painted a bank of cumulus clouds on the fingerboard. I saw the piece as a collaborative work between Nam June, Charlotte, and myself. I titled it *In Memoriam: Saul Gottlieb,* for within the year Saul was dead of cancer.

During another exciting DIAS preview someone freed two chickens that Ralph Ortiz had planned to kill.

As to the Judson House building itself, I am drawn to nineteenth-century Federal architecture. I like the scale, the simplicity, the dimension of the spaces, the character of the windows, the relation of the Judson House to the houses that used to line all of Washington Square. It is unfortunate that the building is slated to be torn down.

GEOFFREY HENDRICKS
lives in New York City.

Kate Millett

Kate Millett was active in the Judson Gallery in 1967–1968. ———————

Like a number of more distinguished artists, I had my first show at Judson—my first show in New York, my first show in America. It had been damn hard to get and a very long time in coming. When it happened, in 1967, I had been back from Japan for four years, hoping for a break.

The two years in Japan had been a series of miraculous breaks and opportunities: introductions to a few friends who found me a studio, fed me when I was out of pocket, showed me the town, even distinguished artists who cheered me on. A wonderful dealer gave me a show in the same gallery where Jean Tinguely and Jasper Johns had just exhibited. I was not only lucky but also a rarity, a "geigin no onna," or white female, a thing hardly ever experienced by the Japanese and a relief from the American GI male. I was courted and photographed and published in a way my Japanese women artist friends were not. I realized the spurious character of this attention but could not fail to enjoy it.

Back in my own country in 1963, I seemed to be getting no-where. There were no opportunities to exhibit. It was hard even to earn a living. In America, my Oxford First Class Honours degree qualified me only for a job as temporary file clerk since I did not type sixty words a minute—the only job open to women generally. Of course, I became a feminist, but this hardly advanced my art career.

Then came the Vietnam War and the Angry Artists Against the War, and suddenly there was opportunity to meet other artists and to exhibit without a jury or pull or connections. At New York University in 1966, I showed an installation with a plastic human head lit from behind by an electric bulb. However, the boss of the event was a fellow who disliked this piece a great deal and continuously unplugged it, rendering it pointless.

Jon Hendricks, who was fulfilling his conscientious objector duties by running the Judson Gallery at the time, noticed my dismay. He intervened on my behalf a few times, was generally sympathetic, and turned out to be immune to the usual male chauvinism of the art world then. Jon was the first person to visit my studio and see the four years of sculpture I had produced since my return. He offered me a show. I was thrilled.

Judson was Mecca to us then, a haven for artists. I would show in the same venue as Jim Dine and Claes Oldenburg. I have always been grateful to Judson and to Jon Hendricks.

In October 1967 I was part of a group show called *Manipulations*. Over a period of three weekends, each of a group of artists took over the gallery space for one day. I called my piece "No." The performance happened to fall on the day of a demonstration against the Pentagon. The event consisted of ushering the audience down the stairs of the gallery in the dark and closing them into a big cage. When the lights went on, the people in the cage at first were amused but then became restive. They finally realized that they would have to find their own way out. They did, in various ways.

In early 1967 I had a solo show at the gallery, which was called *Furniture*, consisting of a suite of fantasy furniture. A television station interviewed me for it.

I have loved and admired Judson for some thirty years now and I hate to see the place that was such a unique exhibition space destroyed. May it live forever as an idea.

KATE MILLETT,
author of *Sexual Politics* and other works, lives in New York City.

Nye Ffarrabas (formerly Bici Forbes Hendricks)

As Bici Hendricks, Nye Ffarrabas participated in Judson Gallery shows in 1966, 1967, and 1968.

I t began for me one evening late in the fall of 1966, when Jon Hendricks was over to dinner. I showed him some of my work, and he asked me point blank if I would like to have a show at the Judson Gallery. I said I would, and asked when. December, he told me. Wow, just like that. For a few minutes I experienced sheer, unadulterated thrill. Then, reflecting that almost my entire oeuvre consisted of a series of notebooks, much of it in the form of events and abstruse conceptual whatnots, that I had a scant three weeks to prepare, and that I had a two-and-a-half-year-old daughter and was entering my third trimester with child number two and had never had a show before, I had a pretty good case of panic.

WORD WORK

The panic passed, and I settled down to work, creating tangible realizations of the scribbled notations in my journals. Since I am a poet, and the pieces had their genesis in words on a page, we called the show "Word Work." Pretty quickly, with a lot of infrastructure support from Geoff, logistical assistance from Jon, and encouragement from both, it came together.

I remember the black, wrought-iron railing with sections missing, smeared with many coats of shiny black paint ... the clanging metal stairs down to that mysterious, dingy—almost clandestine—space that was a tabula rasa, all mine to transform and adorn the way I liked. I remember the clink of the latch on the heavy iron gate and the way the gate rang when it slammed. I remember trudging up and down those steps—the baby out to *here*—carrying crates of objects, lumber, and furniture past the black-and-white sign Jon had painted to announce the show. I was so proud of that sign; it stood for my first solo show. I meant I was an artist and part of a community of art and mystery and celebration. I was wonderstruck.

The show opened on December 2. There were found objects: a flag misprinted with all the stars pointing down; everyday materials transformed in various ways: a small restaurant sign with letters pressed into the slots spelling DAILY SPECIAL: bread; a pair of found deco chairs I had painted, one black, one white—my "Separate But Equal Chairs"; four birdseye diapers pinned to a clothesline, one dyed pale blue and painted with the emblem of the United Nation flag.

There were Word Boxes (moving message displays) bearing communications such as MEMENTO MORI; ingen plant, ingen retur ("no deposit, no return" from a Norwegian beer bottle); and, given the season and my opinions about the Vietnam War, PEACE ON EARTH, GOODWILL TO MEN — NAPALM VILLAGES FOR FUN AND PROFIT. I also found that haiku fit very comfortably in that format as did, with a little squeezing, quatrains.

We built two booths. The first one was painted black, with a black burlap curtain across the front, and a blackboard inside with an eraser and a black chalk. To make sure the booth was dark enough, I painted the ceiling black. On top of the booth sat a slide projector that played a continuous series of typed "Events" on a nearby wall: instructions such as "Go for a mushroom walk (a) in the Metropolitan Museum, (b) on the Staten Island Ferry," or "Imagine that today's newspaper is a book of mythology." (Doesn't that last one resonate, after the Monica Lewinsky soap opera? Maybe today, that would need to be changed to "Imagine that today's newspaper is an episode from a Stephen King novel.")

Opposite the black booth was its counterpart in white: white walls, white burlap, bright white overhead light, and inside a white vanity table with round mirror and a white chair to sit on. On the glass surface were two white saucers with dymo label instructions. One held a needle and white thread (THREAD A NEEDLE), the other a white egg (BALANCE AN EGG).

People reported that they enjoyed going into these mini meditation spaces and making little performances for themselves with the materials provided. The black booth, especially, evoked thoughts of confessionals, voting booths, and dark corners where you could write any messages or draw graffiti with absolute privacy and freedom.

There were tables displaying my unbound book *Language Box, Punctuation Poems,* and *Egg Time Events,* and there were several ice pieces: *Ice Jigsaw Puzzle, Ice Candles,* and an ice disk with a crumpled American flag embedded in it, lying on a bed of beach pebbles (*Defrost the American Flag*), all of which had to be made anew and toted down from 104th Street every Friday, Saturday, and Sunday for the show's six-week run. I had difficulty unmolding the jigsaw pieces at the opening, and one of the knobs broke off. Dick Higgins popped it in his wine glass. "I've never had sculpture in my drink before," he chuckled, and proceeded to put the puzzle together.

There was a bright-red, slat-back rocking chair with a square blue cushion with white stars sewn on it. When the chair was placed against a white wall, the ensemble instantly turned into a flag (*American Rock #1*). I had made several calligraphies with stencilled letters on rice paper. Examples are:

C
ALL
IGRA
PH
Y

and this prayer:

O
HOLY
MAD RAY
MOTHER OF MAGIC
PRAY
FOR
US
NOW
&
AT THE
A & P
ROACH
OF
DEATH

Lee Guilliatt reads a Language Box card in Bici Hendricks's Word Works installation, January 1, 1967. Copyright © 1967 by Peter Moore. Reprinted by permission of Barbara Moore.

Two major pieces—both as to size and as to complexity (and as to future notoriety)—were *Dinner Service,* a table set with a rainbow cloth with Ford hubcaps as plates; empty Coca-Cola bottles for glassware; a windshield-wiping paper towel and a hammer, screwdriver, and pliers to complete each place setting; and a neon sign that flashed, in steady yellow capitals, "U S," and, in rapid blue flashes, an umlaut over the U and the letters "ber alle" between the U and the S, so that the total effect was

U   S
ÜBER ALLES

At the Happening and Fluxus Retrospective in Cologne, in 1971, the table was spread with a 5 × 8 foot American flag instead of the rainbow cloth. The letters "US"—instead of "Deutschland," as in the German anthem—were disturbing to Germans and older Americans alike, though most younger viewers needed historical fill-in.

This flag imagery, which may have been one of the precursors of the Judson Flag Show (1969), was born in the contemporaneous context of U.S. aggression in Vietnam, just as the black and white chairs were conceived against the backdrop of our national struggle toward racial equality and justice.

Several encounters I had at the show were especially memorable. One was with the photographer Diane Arbus, who liked the work a lot. Another was with art critic John Gruen, whose book *The New Bohemia* had just been published; he came up and asked me if I was in the book!

All of this work, however iconoclastic or playful some of it was, had a devotional quality that was intensified by the rough, underground character of the space itself. It proceeded from a love of the natural and the ordinary, delight at the surprise of discovery, and outrage at atrocious events and attitudes. In this respect, my work was a form of moral statement, abstracted and torqued and right at home in a church whose ministers authored cutting-edge, innovative social programs and wild, high-camp operatic extravaganzas and whose front entrance carried a sign tallying the weekly body count on both sides as the Vietnam War raged on.

The ice pieces, to my mind, were accelerated examples of the ephemeral nature of all persons, works, and materials. The Sphynx abraded by the desert sands and the sulfurous atmosphere of Florence eroding Michelangelo's *David* so badly that it had to be moved to an indoor location are only two versions of the same phenomenon.

The show closed in January 1967, a month before my son was born (on February 9, the night of Charlotte Moorman's arrest at her Town Hall concert for playing the cello barebreasted). The show was revived on February 24 as an intermission and post-show diversion for Judson Poets Theater goers attending a performance of the Gertrude Stein/Al Carmines amazing *What Happened* and song-and-dance pieces by several other artists.

MANIPULATIONS

In October 1967 Judson Gallery was also the scene of *Twelve Evenings of Manipulations*. On the second evening, I presented some large ice works in the gallery, with more candles and projected word pieces, in a piece called "Deteriorations: Bici Hendricks on Ice." I had been asked to provide icepicks to hasten the melting process, in consequence of another installation, at Trude Heller's *Trik* discotheque, where this had been requested—rather against my better judgment—for the enhanced entertainment value of viewer participation.

With a three-year-old and a baby, I did not make it to most of these events. I did, however, get to Kate Millett's installation, a wooden cage of heavy dowels set in two-by-fours, top and bottom; it made a very sturdy enclosure perhaps 8 x 8 feet and 7 or 8 feet high. The audience was courteously escorted to a gap in the bars and asked to go inside, which we all did. There was quite a crowd of us, maybe fifteen or twenty. Suddenly, we became aware that the remaining dowel had been snapped into place, and there we were, *in jail.* I don't recall if Kate remained outside the enclosure or whether she and her helpers left the gallery altogether. I rather think she was somewhere where she could see our reactions. These were quite varied, and some were intense: claustrophobia, depression, embarrassment, outrage, bravado, ennui. I do not recall any amusement. One woman who had an appointment uptown she "really *had* to get to" became extremely self-righteous. After ten or twenty minutes of listening to her kvetching and moaning, a couple of us flexed the bars and let her slip out, to Kate's apparent annoyance (we weren't playing by the rules).

I have no idea how long this event went on, but at some point I was seized by an urge to revolt *within* the context of the piece. The top two-by-four was within six or seven inches of the ceiling. I eyed it, took a deep breath, and began to climb. Somehow, I shinnied up the bars, probably with the help of many hands, though all I remember is the seizure of will that carried me up and through the right squeeze at the top, over, and down. I experienced an incredible exhilaration, a triumphal "No" to our unceremonious caging. I don't remember whether the others stayed inside or whether I just left. It was a powerful event.

This was the first occasion at Judson at which I felt seized by the energy of the matter at hand, and it took me very much by surprise.

ORDEALS

About this time, the Judson arts program was getting a good deal of publicity, which resulted in the creation of several "catered" productions. One was *Conjunctions,* the afore-mentioned event at Trude Heller's *Trik,* in which Larry Kornfeld, Geoff, and I participated along with Roland Turner, Arlene Rothlein, and Florence Tarlow, among others.

Another event, staged all over the premises at Judson, was *Ordeals* (August 1967), a production mounted expressly for the International Congress on Religion, Architecture, and Visual Arts. It was contrived as a fantastic evocation of many of the real-life horrific and humiliating situations visited upon persons and populations all over the world by individuals and groups vested with authority and power.

The masterminds of this enormous undertaking were Al Carmines and Larry Kornfeld, aided and abetted by Carolee Schneemann and myself. Both of us created environment/happenings that augmented the other goings-on. Jon Hendricks was the herculean stage manager, assisted by a cast of dozens, both illustrious and obscure.

The general flow of events was as follows. People entered through the front door of the church, where they were subjected to bureaucratic processing with much shuffling and signing of papers. Then they went up the stairs, where each participant was kissed by a black woman and had a hangman's noose placed over his or her head ("courtesy of Black Power") by a silken-voiced black man. Everyone was given a paper cup of blood-colored mashed potatoes to eat. From there, by twelves, the curious and eager priests and nuns, architects, teachers, artists, and scholars were led through a nightmarish sequence that included an intimidating police line-up with bright lights, crawling through a dim passageway, and being photographed on a large, rough wooden cross while being verbally harassed. Immediately thereafter, they passed by a placard carrying a long, nonsensical passage from *Through the Looking Glass* and one of my Word Work boxes under a strobe light. "PAY ATTENTION," the message warned, "YOU WILL BE TESTED ON THIS MATERIAL. PAY ATTENTION. YOU WILL BE HELD RESPONSIBLE." This was followed by a kindergarten version of a song teaching the children to adore "the one true leader." Then came nap time on cushions on the floor while listening to a humorous horror tale.

From this point, the participants were led down the stairs in back of the church, where the walls were plastered with lewd and explicit magazine photos, past an open door where a man was

Bici and Geoffrey Hendricks grade "exams" during the Ordeals show, August 29, 1967.
Copyright © 1967 by Peter Moore. Reprinted by permission of Barbara Moore.

seated on a toilet, trousers down around his ankles, and out to the Garden, with music and dim lights, where each participant was escorted to a dancing partner of his or her own sex.

Entering the Garden Room, the participants had to pass a man in black wearing a clerical collar who was hacking meat on a butcher block with a huge cleaver. This was the beginning of my environment, *Final Exam*. The participants were shown to seats at long tables with bluebooks and pencils and were peremptorily told to keep silent. The exam had ten multiple-choice questions, ending with "What makes you think there ought to be ten questions: (a) There should be but there aren't; (b) Ten is arbitrary; nine is just as good; (c) This is a question; (d) This is not a question, it is a philosophical statement on the nature of expectation." There was also an essay, "This I believe ..." to be completed in twenty-five words or less, while the exam proctors insulted and harried their charges. As they left, each participant was given a report card stamped "Fail," with predetermined "reasons" for said failure. They were also thumbprinted and received a rubber-stamped "Fail" on the back of their hands.

Then came the enforced flagellation of a nude female mannikin in bondage and a disconcerting journey through Carolee's smothering, pink foam "burial" environment on the way to the "nurse's station," where participants were subjected to pointless "physicals" and humiliating questioning. Abruptly, they were escorted to the side door, which was thrown open as they were told, "Get Out!" The next moment, the heavy wooden door slammed behind them and they were standing on the Thompson Street sidewalk facing bright lights, a TV news camera, and a crowd of onlookers. The feedback that we received from those who wrote to us afterward was that *Ordeals* caused in many of them an awakening to the daily realities of millions of people throughout the world. It had been a profound and sobering experience that many of them would never forget.

If I have concentrated on my own part in this and other events, it is because, typically, Judson at that time was a place of rich simultaneities. I could be in only one place at a time, and I have more complete and reliable documentation for the work I was involved in. In describing *Ordeals,* I have relied on remembered descriptions by other people and on a detailed, well-illustrated, unsigned account in the *Boston Sunday Globe* of November 12, 1967.

DIAS

The Destruction in Art Symposium (DIAS) was a broad-based and truly international venture. A large number of artists participated in the events, which took place at Judson, Finch College Museum, and elsewhere. Its main event at Judson, in the spring of 1968, was a sprawling group exhibition in the gallery and the garden, with the symposium convened in the Garden room after a series of performances outside.

At the far end of the garden, against the brick wall, was my piece, a shrine made out of a monolith of ice and paved with at least twelve dozen large white eggs, with flagstones radiating out to the surrounding space. Candles and mirrors were interspersed among these, and again there were icepicks—an element I considered foreign to my contemplative feeling about the piece, in which the "destruction" would be accomplished without human agency at the natural pace of melting ice. Nevertheless, I capitulated to the action orientation of the day, and I also provided the flagstones as steps by which one might make one's way among the eggs, up to the ice block to chop at it. (Some people also got into smashing the eggs, and the stench in the garden lasted for weeks.)

At the other end of the garden, Ralph Ortiz was preparing to kill two chickens *(The Sad End of Henny Penny,* or something like that). One of the hens was black and one was white. Amidst much squawking and flapping, they were hung by their feet from two tall ailanthus trees and their throats were cut.

There was great commotion about this ritual (?) slaughter, and voices rose to loud, angry, and righteous heights. It was "art," it was "race politics," it was "senseless brutality," it was "freedom of speech," it was "wanton," "sadistic," "over the line," et cetera. My focus was at the other end of the courtyard, and I was glad of the opportunity to refrain from getting involved. Having worked on a farm and plucked chickens many times, I was not horrified by the killing, but there was a jagged and polarized energy to the whole thing that haunted me.

This piece was followed by an action of Hermann Nitsch, involving a sacrificial lamb that had been professionally and humanely killed prior to the event. Nitsch dragged the flayed carcass up and down the yard on a rope. I stood watching, with an icepick in my hand, since nobody was "doing" ice at that point. I found myself seized by pity for the lifeless animal. It was perfectly clear that the body was in no pain, yet there was an aura of implied suffering around it that galvanized me. Stepping forward, I leaned over the carcass and plunged the ice pick into its rib cage several times with all my might as if to still the heart. The moment soon over, I withdrew, shaken.

In the symposium that followed people asked me what the stabbing was all about. I said it was about pity for the lamb and wanting to do the merciful thing and end its misery. This did not make sense to people who wanted my action to have been about rage, vengeance, stompin', stormin' macho stuff: a political statement.

The symposium was filled with controversy, rhetoric, politics, and theatrical grandstanding. There must have been 150 of us crammed into the Garden Room. Charlotte Moorman performed

Nam June Paik's *One for Violin,* raising a violin slowly, slowly, high over her head, and bringing it down with full force to smash on the table. Just as she completed her excruciating five-minute swing, Saul Gottlieb jumped up, shouting that this was shameful and wasteful, depriving some hypothetical kid on the Lower East Side of music lessons, and so on. He charged at Charlotte to grab her arm and prevent the smashing, but she had already reached the apex and was starting the descent like some overcoiled spring. There was no way she could stop as Gottlieb's head was suddenly thrust into the path of the fiddle. Down the violin came, creasing his forehead with a pretty nasty gash before it hit the table and exploded into splinters. People thought that Charlotte had gone for him deliberately, but that was not the case. It certainly fed the chaotic energy in the room, though.

I don't remember much of what was said during the rest of the symposium, but I do remember the passion of the arguments, the sarcasm of the rejoinders. When my turn came, I read my statement. At this distance, it seems thin and inadequate. I was trying to confront the kind of knee-jerk sentimentalism that many rosewater liberals use to object to art works and actions that push boundaries, the very attitude that turns explorations into commodities, discoveries into collector's items (from which the dealers, not the artists, reap the profits), and that inexorably trades in the authentic, radical insight for the comfortable anaesthetic. Today, I would say that in art everything depends on transmutation of the object, the moment, the phrase, *even if infinitessimally slightly,* so that new meaning emerges.

Surprise, double-entendre, even shock, and certainly humor are effective transformative means, but what was manifestly missing in a lot of this very in-your-face work was a basic humanity, or patience, the artistry to take it to the next step. Some of the art, and the criticism that accompanied it, was such shrill, scornful, antisensibility polemical overkill that it tended to preempt attention like a five-year-old's tantrum: interesting, perhaps, but scarcely edifying. Here's a condensed version of what I said at the symposium:

> Although my own work involves *nonviolent* destruction, I'd like to say a few words to answer the objections to these strong methods and materials. Few areas of imagery could

be more appropriate at this moment in history. Art has no obligation to be pretty. It does have an obligation to be relevant in its time. Art is educative in function, but not didactic in method. Art appeals to us through the intellect, but even more through our emotions *[and our senses!]*. Intellect may have carried us nearly to the stars, but emotionally we are still very close to the Aurignacian cave-temples of 20,000 years ago. In a culture so characterized by violence and bloodshed, this imagery *is* legitimate in art. This imagery should be tolerated for the sobering and civilizing insights it can offer.

My participation in Judson Gallery events was part of *living at the edge,* which was clearly happening in my life. Geoff and I were in the thick of a very yeasty soup—the art world in New York at that time. We were both experiencing huge creative upswings. I loved my children dearly and had an intense connection to them, but in this maelstrom I scarcely broke stride for childbirth. I kept going. In addition to the events detailed here, I was involved in perhaps a half dozen other shows and performances that year. I was stretching and growing convulsively, and emotionally I was close to my limit. Much of the real and implied violence and other raw weirdness in other people's work troubled me profoundly. Geoff seemed to get off on it: the edgier, the better. As much as he helped and supported me, he may also have felt competitive and threatened by my new high profile in "his" field. I felt vulnerable and unprotected, especially in my parenting. Eventually, a rift formed and gradually began to widen. I could not continue to nurture my children or myself in the midst of so much "danger music." I felt it as a rising tide in the real world, too: overwhelming, menacing, psychotic. This was no mere projection of my inner state on outward events. It was, I think, a very accurate perception of the world. Remember the year was 1968. My unease was reality-based and prophetic.

TERMINAL READING

There was one further occasion in the gallery, probably in 1969, in which I participated. It was *Terminal Reading,* the first of three readings of an unfinished novel of mine (I had three copies). The second was performed at the Arts Lab in London, in the fall of 1970, and the third was at the Billy Apple Gallery on 23rd Street, in the spring of 1971.

Four performers are seated in the center of the space, like a string quartet with music stands in front of them. (These may be pre-selected readers or they may arise spontaneously from the audience.) On each stand is one-fourth of the manuscript, loose-leaf in black folders. In the middle of the square formed by the music stands is a hibachi or other small, contained fire. The audience sits or stands around the perimeter and may approach, withdraw, circulate, or simply listen.

Performers begin to read, first one at a time, then one voice over another, fast, slowly, loud, soft, repeating passages at will, holding silence, sometimes all four speaking at once, sometimes none. As performers are finished with a page, they may crumple the page and throw it in the fire, or they may pass it on, or another may reach over and start reading it. Thus, all manner of musical structures—theme, counterstatement, development, recapitulation, solo, duet, stretto, fugue, and so forth—are spontaneously produced from the written word on the page.

This process continues until all the pages are read and finally consumed. At Judson Gallery, the performers were Geoffrey Hendricks, Ronald Gross, myself, and one other person whose face and name elude me after thirty years. It was difficult but very cleansing to rid myself in this way of a piece of writing that never would finish itself, and the resulting "piece" was remarkably strong and beautiful, irrespective of the quality of the manuscript and different each time with other readers. This was one of my favorite art works.

THE GALLERY'S LASTING INFLUENCE

I want to emphasize how incredibly steadying, nurturing, and seminal Judson has been to me—and to generations of artists of all kinds. Permitting maximal creative exploration, it provided stability and context when we ventured farther than our own internal gyroscopes could manage, and safety when censorship and other challenges threatened from without. It is hard to imagine now, but in 1970, participating in the Flag show was scary business, borne out by the arrest of Jon Hendricks, Jean Toche, and Faith Ringgold—

the stalwart souls who agreed, at an all-artists' meeting, to stand for the rest of us as the exhibitors if push, or should I say Putsch, came to shove. It did, of course, and the case of the Judson Three went all the way to the U.S. Supreme Court before the ACLU legal team let it slip through the cracks.

My contribution to that show was a documentation of ways in which *Newsweek* and *Art in America* had misrepresented a large barbed-wire-and-ice work, shown at the Finch College Museum as part of DIAS, sensationalizing and totally fabricating a fictitious piece in which "a flag, a wedding dress, and old shoes, melted down into a sodden mess of garbage." I never made such a piece. I would have considered it pointless and aesthetically alien. The caterers, in a statement of their own, threw their detritus onto the remains of my ice piece in the courtyard, after the opening. The critic David L. Shirey, who "reported" the show, only interviewed me on the telephone and, by admission, never saw my piece in the courtyard at all.

When the world became too grievous, there was the comfort at Judson of being reassured that, yes, that was reality, that was how it was. There was ferment and fellowship, and, always, celebration. For me, much of this happened in the gallery and in the garden, and it has traveled outward into the world in widening ripples, with me and with the others, in all our lives ever since.

I'd like to end with an observation I wrote in October 1967 for inclusion in John Cage's *Notations*. It captures the spirit of bold and resolute good humor and support with which Judson took all our reeling and writhing in stride. To have had such a sandbox was good fortune beyond measure for dozens, maybe hundreds, of artists of many stripes and persuasions.

> Creative work defines itself. Therefore confront the work.
> There will always be critics eager to fashion opinions for
> the lazy and incapable ... but what has that to do with
> enchantment?

NYE FFARRABAS
lives in Vermont.

Raphael Montanez Ortiz

Raphael (Ralph) Ortiz was involved in the Judson Gallery
in 1967–1968.

The year was 1967, one year after my participation in the
"Destruction in Art Symposium" in London in 1966. My
Pratt Institute schoolmate, artist colleague, and friend Al
Hansen, who also participated, had informed me of the symposium
and given me the London phone number to call.

It was again Al Hansen, ever helpful to his artist friends, who
spread the word of the performance and installation event that was
being planned at the Judson Gallery. The person to talk to, said Al,
was Jon Hendricks. The event was being called *Manipulations*. I met
with Jon, who was already familiar with my work in destruction-
ritual performance-art. He was enthusiastic about my project, a mixed
media, audience-participation event in which the audience destroyed
objects within an aesthetic appropriation of ancient biblical and in-
digenous culture rites, as in the sacrifice for redemption from sin in the
book of Leviticus or the release from the vanity of possession and
greed of the Potlatch ceremony of the natives of the Northwest.

The title of the ritual installation was "Destruction Room." It
would consist of the fall-out of all sacrificed and destroyed objects,
wherever they fell.

I was assisted in the performance work of "Destruction Room"
by Jean Toche, Lil Picard, and Jon Hendricks. In the large, front gallery room, participants milled around exploding paper bags and tearing up books and furniture, while Jean, Jon, and I stood in the semi-
darkened smaller back room, each with a single-edged razor blade in
one hand and a cup of cow's blood in the other. We poured the blood
into incisions made into and through two hanging screens each consisting of three layers of suspended white, three-by-four-foot sheets of
paper, with nine-inch spacings between them. On each of the screens
was projected a three-foot-wide color slide, one the image of a brain
and the other of a heart. Like master surgeons, we carefully made our
incisions, thereby exposing the projected image into deeper layers of

paper and by illusion deeper layers of the brain and the heart. Throughout the performance a strobe light flashed on a hill of bubbles in continuous overflow from a washing machine. The bubbles formed a mountain next to the screens. Participants were assisting in the surgery while others took cups of powdered soap and threw the contents into the open, top-loading washing machine.

Lil Picard was under a small spotlight at an ironing board in the front room, teaching people how to burn clothing they helped her iron.

Through all this, a Zen incantation at double speed sounded over the loudspeakers, joined by the sound of heavy breathing and a loud heartbeat and the commentary to the world of potential and arriving immigrants on the plaque of the Statue of Liberty: Send me your suffering, your refuse, etc., followed by the racially biased statistics of which people from what race were admitted from where.

In my performances at the Judson Gallery I wanted to make clear the radicalness of the experiment in performance-installation art at the time of the civil rights movement and the Vietnam War protests.

The *Manipulations* event of 1967 inspired Jon, Jean, Al, and me to design and publish the first and only issue of the Judson Church Art Magazine, which we also entitled *Manipulations*. I still have a copy.

Can you imagine any other church on this planet that would open its doors to the Destruction in Art Symposium? It was spring 1968. The event was organized by Jon Hendricks, Al Hansen, and myself. I had proposed the idea to Al Hansen after our participation in the Destruction in Art Symposium held in London in 1966. Al and I then talked to Jon. The idea of a destruction in art symposium at Judson made him blink, but then he said it could probably be done if a lot of details got ironed out. (While we engage in the exercise of remembering Judson House, we must pay special attention to Jon Hendricks, who played an important part in the history of art at Judson.)

The list of artists that shared their obsession at Judson is long and full of Who's Whos in contemporary performance and visual art history. I can only reference a few of the performance artist participants in the Destruction in Art Symposium USA 1968 at Judson.

The list includes Charlotte Moorman, Al Hansen, Lil Picard, Nam June Paik, Hermann Nitsch, Jon Hendricks, Jean Toche, and myself. At the height of the symposium, someone came running into the lecture room and announced that Dr. Martin Luther King had been murdered. Stunned, we stopped everything, bowed our heads in a silent prayer, and canceled the remainder of the symposium.

I do not know how many artists thought of Judson as a church or were even conscious that they were on church grounds. I was, and at first I felt awkward and self-conscious, as if GOD's eyes would be more sharply focused on me. I wondered if my art would be a desecration on church grounds. I was young enough also to imagine, in my naïveté or perhaps wishful understanding of the Bible, that in some way our art would serve a spiritual purpose. My wondering was all resolved when a small voice spoke in the quiet of my mind during a prayer meditation of mine at Judson Church. The message was clear and simple in its compassion: "Welcome, Prodigal Sons and Daughters, Welcome."

In my own interpretation at the time, I imagined myself as an artist practicing some Old Testament ritual, some Levitican redemptive sacrificial rite, a releasing of sin through the sacrifice of mattresses, sofas, pianos, and other objects.

I will admit that I was amazed that a church would so eagerly engage avant-garde art, culture, and politics: civil rights, the Vietnam War, etc., etc. I grew up in an orthodox Catholic church and was an altar boy in the 1940s. Later, I attended a high Episcopal church for several years. Of course, if anyone would open the doors of his house to us crazy experimental artists—some of us doing very weird stuff—it would be Jesus, certainly in the 1960s. To put the radicalness of it in perspective, you have to imagine a Renaissance church opening its door to the heretical Alchemists, during the Inquisition yet. In the infinite compassion and patience it represented, the Judson Gallery was an experience that reawakened in me a long dormant connection with GOD.

Events such as *Manipulations* and the Destruction in Art Symposium were not exceptions in the cultural programming at Judson. By permitting radical art to enter its doors, Judson Church has sponsored, baptized, and blessed as much art that is still relevant today as the churches of the Renaissance.

The last event I attended at Judson was a performance event in 1995 dedicated to the Joyful-Mourning of the Wonderful-Art-Life of Alfred Hansen.

RAPHAEL ORTIZ
teaches art at Rutgers University.

Over His Dead Body

The following article appeared in *The Village Voice* of March 28, 1968.
It was written by Jill Johnston, whose permission to reprint it here
we acknowledge with thanks.

I was privileged to be present Friday night, March 21, at Judson
Church, at the most unusual manifestation of a performer-
audience situation I have witnessed in a decade of attending a
theatre in which the performer-audience relationship has been
pushed in every conceivable direction. Unusual is a mild word for it.
It was a kind of psychological trauma involving two principals and
the rest of us in a spontaneous drama expressing the agony and the
comedy of the condition called human. The occasion was the Destruction in Art Symposium preceded by Destruction events in Judson's back yard.

The atmosphere in the yard was a bit like a bazaar—the spectators milling around passing from one set-up to another: an excerpt
from Hermann Nitsch's Orgy-Mystery theatre; Lil Picard with plastic bags full of feathers set to flaming on a charcoal burner; Steve
Rose standing by a frying pan on a hot plate cooking an orange and
a banana; Bici Hendricks handing out ice picks to anyone wishing to
hack at a large vertical hunk of ice surrounded by raw eggs. Preparation for Ralph Ortiz's chicken-killing event was the first presenti-
ment of a rumble nobody expected. The two live chickens were
strung up from trees several yards apart. John Wilcock calmly cut
the chickens down and, assisted by Michael Kirby, made off with
them to an adjoining yard to release them over a high fence. Ortiz
later said he was delighted the chickens were rescued. He accepted
the frustration of his plans as a worthwhile event in itself and repro-
grammed himself by subsequently attacking the two trees (he
climbed one, Jon Hendricks the other), sawing a limb off each one
after a preparation (pouring) of the cow's blood originally to have
been part of the chicken scene.

The attitude Ortiz assumed about the interference in his thing became relevant to the amazing drama that ensued inside at a scheduled

panel of the artists involved. A soap-box orator from the yard, whose hysterical blather was punctuated by a few brilliant remarks, threatened to dominate proceedings in the lecture-room. Hendricks, Ortiz, and [Al] Hansen accepted him without relinquishing their own purpose and somehow finally integrated him in the total situation.

Hendricks announced a performance by Charlotte Moorman of Nam June Paik's *One for Violin,* a piece dating from 1961. I knew the piece from Paik's performance of it in 1964 at a Fluxus concert. In a rather disorderly atmosphere Miss Moorman assumed the appropriate concentration and a courteous hush fell over the room. The piece entails the destruction of a violin after a long preliminary passage in which the performer raises the instrument in slow motion from a position at right angles to the waist to a position over the head in readiness to smash the thing on impact with a table.

Miss Moorman got maybe one minute into the act when a man from the back tried to stop her. She dispatched him with a push and resumed the performance. Another more determined spectator approached the table and the war was on. Charlotte was angry. She demanded to know who he was (translated: who the hell do you think you are?). He said he didn't want her to break the violin. "By breaking the violin," he said, "you're doing the same thing as killing people." And something about giving it to a poor kid who could use it. Attempting to go with the piece she said, "this is not a vaudeville routine" and "this is not an audience-participation piece." But he persisted and I think Charlotte slapped his face and suddenly there was a tragedy in the making and shock-waves in the air and terrific agitation all around. Someone suggested he give her his coat in exchange for the violin. He removed his coat but she wouldn't have any of it. I was inspired by this suggestion and found myself hollering in the din: GIVE IT TO HIM. Charlotte accused her intruder of being as bad as the New York police. He announced that "we are sitting down and refusing to allow this violin to be broken." He forthwith stretched himself out on his back on the table in front of her. As Ortiz said later—she had to over his dead body. It happened very fast and there are probably as many versions of the climax as the number of people who were there. As I saw it, Charlotte's tormentor sat up and was sitting on the edge of the table and at some moment turned to face her at which point with malice aforethought she bashed him on the head with the violin and the blood was spilled.

Charlotte Moorman, Jon Hendricks (center), and Saul Gottlieb argue during the performance of Nam June Paik's One For Violin. Copyright © 1968 by Fred W. McDarrah. Reprinted by permission.

My description can't do justice to this extraordinary situation. The ramifications are extensive. It wasn't so much who was right or wrong (I thought, if pressed, both were right and wrong), but what might have been done to avert the inevitable. That seems the ultimate political question so brilliantly posed by this little war right in the ranks of those so violently opposed to the war at the top.

The victim introduced himself as Saul Gottlieb. Charlotte was contrite and ministered to his wound. She explained the point of the piece is to show that we think nothing of killing people in Vietnam and we place a higher order on a violin. She said she didn't mean to hit him but he was in her performance area. Speaking of the therapeutic value of such actions Ortiz said Charlotte was trying to displace her hostility onto an inanimate object and Gottlieb wouldn't let her do that. Our soap-box man said that if "we the people want to come into the government" (represented here as artists) "we should be able to." He also told Gottlieb he was sick because he stood there and let her hit him with his back turned. Gottlieb said that Charlotte was determined to break the violin regardless of what happened and was unable to deprogram herself.

The adjustment Ortiz made in his chicken event became instructive. What were Charlotte's alternatives in the face of being robbed of her artist thing? Blowing her cool she was left with a literal destruction. The irony of a symbol converted into a reality. Yet why didn't Gottlieb honor her appeal for attention? "I request the honor of your presence at … ," etc. At what? At the daily level, let's say, how we take turns in a conversation piece.

Many more things were said at the Judson gathering. The last thing I saw was a touching demonstration by Steve Rose of a simple exchange based on respect. He requested the indulgence of his audience in a piece he wished to perform. He said it would begin when he finished talking and it would end when he sat down. He stood as he was and looked round slowly at the people there gathered, with some slight perplexity, I thought. And that was the piece. And the audience expressed their appreciation at a point well taken.

Jean Ovitt

Jean Ovitt's experiences with Judson House fall into two categories: a brief visit in 1958, when she stayed at the house, and a longer commitment, from 1968 to 1974, when she was involved in the arts program.

MARCH 1958

At Ohio State University, both before and after Howard Moody came to New York, Judson Memorial Church was a bit like the Holy Grail. So it was that during spring break in 1958 the Ohio State Glee club was to give a concert at Carnegie Hall and I decided to make my second trip to New York City, the first on my own. Only the young assume their expectations will be fulfilled. I don't remember how I arranged to stay at Judson House.

Driving in New York City can be a little intimidating for the first time at night after a ten- or twelve-hour drive. I had no idea where Thompson Street was, let alone how to get there. I said goodbye to my traveling companion who went off to Long Island, put the car in a garage (I have no idea where), and called up Judson House. A short time later I arrived there in a cab, more than a little befuddled. I was welcomed and led to a room so tiny there was room only for a bed, a chair, and a chest. Men were on one floor, women on the other. A pretty depressing shower room was down the hall. I was too excited to be on my own in New York City to care.

Washington Square and surroundings were very different then. Buses still came through the Arch into the square, where they turned around and went back up Fifth Avenue. Neither the highrises of Washington Square Village nor the other buildings east of Judson existed, but the process of demolition and construction called Urban Renewal had begun.

My stay was brief, less than a week. There was a big kitchen downstairs in the house, and people often gathered around a table to eat and talk. Someone on my floor showed me her room. It seemed that everybody fixed up their own space, so the other rooms seemed at least homey. It would be nice to say that the visit made me want to return. This was not the case. I was fascinated but intimidated and in over my head. Yet who knows? One of the other Ohio State migrants gave me a book, and I spent the last night in New York reading *Catcher in the Rye*.

1968: THE CONGREGATION MOVES IN

I moved to New York in November 1968. Judson House had changed again and was now a runaway house, although not for long. In 1969, after the runaways left, it would never be a residence hall again. I am not sure the building was in much worse shape than when I visited in 1958, but times had changed, and there was no way to renovate the space and make it into an acceptable dormitory.

The staff and the congregation began to use the space in different ways. Staff continued to live at Judson House and, while Grace House was being renovated, so did Howard and Lorry Moody. The congregation began to use the rooms on the ground and first floors more intensively. Many meetings and discussion groups now took place there.

Now that the students and runaways were gone, many of us who were at loose ends or figuring out what to do with our lives just spent time hanging out around the house. Sometimes we just talked, at other times we cooked and ate together. Puppies and kittens were growing up in the garden, including Tony Clark's golden retriever and John Tungate's cat, Toby. After a visit to the Midwest, I returned with armloads of hostas. These and other plants got added to the garden.

There was always some work to do, such as scraping and painting. John Tungate gave classes in home repair. No one was sure what to do with the space, but that did not mean it was not used. There were committee meetings, parties, classes, discussion groups. For those of us who often hung out during those years, it was also a last chance of being able to live cheaply in New York and not have to worry much about whether we were earning enough money. The sixties were over, but it wasn't yet the eighties.

A GALLERY AGAIN?

By late 1969 I began to feel the lack of the visual arts at Judson. Jon Hendricks had left in June of 1968, and with him went the Judson

Art Gallery. The Judson Dance Theater was in its last year. We had theater, and Al Carmines's first oratorio, *Christmas Rappings,* was about to have its premiere. But I missed the visual element. I looked around to see if others felt the same way.

A small group of people got together to see if there was still a need for a gallery. We thought that if we could provide a space and the interest, people would come. It was not so easy to agree on what kinds of shows we would have or want to have at Judson. This was the period of concern over "participatory democracy." Building consensus was the theme of the day. We did agree to two shows: a photography exhibit by Theresa Wright and a painting show "About Purple" by Sharon Gold.

The committee disbanded after about a year. The committee approach was not considered successful and the Judson Board wanted the gallery space for other uses. There were a few other shows in the gallery space, but these shows were individual and not part of the little committee's efforts. I know of shows by Lee Guilliatt and Lyn Miller. There were other shows at Judson during the 1970s, but these, like the Flag Show of 1969, related to political and social issues.

As for the need I felt for a dialogue with visual artists, such was not to be. The timing was wrong. It was a period when many maintained that painting was dead, and multimedia was the art of the day. Also, what painting there was in the 1970s was monumental in size and often took over entire rooms and buildings. Judson's little gallery had become irrelevant. A new community of artists, young and daring, did not appear for another decade, and their center was the East Village.

JEAN OVITT
lives in New York City.

THE RUNAWAY
HOUSE

rom June 1968 to the fall of 1969 Judson House was the site of a program that reached out to the many runaways in Greenwich Village at that time. It was a place where teen-agers could get off the street and stay for a few days while the staff helped them make up their minds about going back home or not.

A small group of boys and girls ended up staying more than a few days and became official residents. They went to school or work, and their parents knew where they were. A staff of five or six acted as counselors and house parents. Arthur Levin was the director of the program.

Aaron Crespi recalls his experiences as one of the resident runaways, and the article from *The Village Voice* describes the program against the background of the Village at the end of the 1960s. Further details can be found in the chapter by John Tungate, in the section on "The Building"; and Arthur Levin gives his perspective in the section on "The Judson Staff."

Aaron Crespi

Aaron Crespi lived in Judson House as a resident runaway. ————————

I ran away from home when I was thirteen. It was 1968. Junior High School in Queens. Pissed off father ready to go over the edge with my act, get me out!

Stuffed some clothes in an army surplus knapsack and just left. I wasn't alone. Thousands of people were on the streets in 1968. Saint Mark's Place, Washington Square, Tomkins Square Park swarmed with people twenty-four hours a day.

My father's little sister was living in the Village. She was always on my side, guess she knew her brother's monsters. Man, was she cool! She had a little apartment on Prince Street with a musician boyfriend. Aunt Lee wore black skirts and sweaters and tall boots, long jet black hair under a beret, Rob in navy bell bottoms and a peacoat. We walked arm in arm downtown to parties, or dinners with their friends. Lee was in the theater then, she sang in plays by Al Carmines at the theater at Judson Memorial Church.

I guess I slept on Lee's couch for a week or two and then she sent me over to Judson House, at that time a runaway house. I don't know much about the start of the house. When I arrived, it was run by Arthur Levin (who's never left) with a "staff" of a couple of conscientious objectors. I guess the idea was to get some of the thousands of kids off the street for a few days or weeks and then contact their parents in Iowa or Wisconsin or Queens, and do what then I don't know, send them home, I suppose. It was going to take more than a little talk over coffee to get me back, and some of the kids really had nowhere to go back to.

Robbie was a tall, skinny gay kid from South Carolina, home was not an option. One black kid, I think from Harlem, I don't remember his name, would show up after electroshock "therapy," shaking and weak, stunned out of his senses. We would bring him upstairs, sit with him on his bed, man, what are they trying to burn out of you? Don't go back, stay here.

Judson House is a three-story red brick building on Thompson Street attached to Judson Church. Three steps up to a black steel door, ring the bell, wait for the buzzer, step into another world, our place, off the street. First floor to the left was Art's office. There was an alcove with a bed, though I don't think he ever stayed there. Art came and went. When he was there, we liked being with him. I remember half a dozen of us sprawled out around his office, on the floor, couch, bed, telling him stories about whatever wildness we got into the night before on the street or in the house. He was supposed to be responsible for us, I don't think he wanted to know too much.

Lots of kids came and went, but there was a core of us, a gang, who took up semipermanent residence. We had the third floor, maybe a dozen rooms painted black or purple, posters and candles and mattresses, books, incense, hash pipes, drawing books, poetry painted on the walls.

"Home is where I hang my soul" in Jimmy Jones's room. Jimmy was my soul brother, dark in skin and spirit, brooding, devilish smile, kinky, bushy black hair, and a walk, I mean, cool. I never knew where Jimmy was from or what he was running from. Whatever it was seemed more fearful than my life. I heard he joined the merchant marine, a dream we shared, and sailed the world for many years.

When I took up residence there were no rooms left upstairs, but I wasn't going to go downstairs! So I took a hall closet about five feet square, painted it up and hung my soul. My art, candle, books. When I slept there I left the door open and my feet stuck out into the hallway. That was the first of my offbeat living quarters. I've since lived in a construction shack with a potbelly stove and lived a year in a treehouse thirty feet off the ground, now a bamboo cabin in the Jamaican mountains.

Other upstairs people I remember: Claudia "Jesse" Gray from Madison, Wisconsin. She might as well have been from another country. Strawberry hair, white skin, blue denim work shirt and jeans, boy, I dug Jesse. Michael Hurst, whose mantra when stoned was "Nothing Matters." Tina, Samantha.

Arthur Levin was the adult of the house, but Michael Parker was the spiritual center. Parker was a CO doing alternative service at Judson House. Parker *was* Judson House. I remember his face perfectly, a tall, skinny guy with a straggly goatee, shoulder-length frizzy brown hair, pock-marked face. He could not have been over twenty-four, though I think of him as a sage. The Judson House Gang spun around Parker. A bunch of ragamuffin, freaky teenagers all sleeping with each other, running around the city, hash, grass, acid. Parker turned us on to our spirit guides, Herman Hesse, D. T. Suzuki, Gary Snyder, poetry, painting. He saw the cream of the crop, wild, free, dangerous, rebellious, misfits for all the right reasons. We would hang with Parker and talk for hours, late into the morning. Parker accepted us, encouraged us, lauged at us, and I imagine loved us. My mother and sister met him and liked and trusted him. What a wise young man he was. I do wonder about him.

There was another CO there, Bob, a vegetarian hippie from Vermont. Bob was mellow, but I think we freaked him out. He and Parker had some differences about our "upbringing."

There was a kitchen and hangout in the lower level of the building, right on Thompson Street. And the streets were alive! We'd hang out listening to music, smoking dope if there was any. When we ran out, everyone would gather up all the pipes and we'd scrape them for resin. We'd also wait and see who came in off the street that day, new freaks, drugs, or girls. The short-stay kids always spiced things up. The regular gang was always coming and going through the day, but touching base at night before hitting the street again or doing whatever we came up with.

Someone, maybe Parker or Beverly [Waite], came up with the idea to have a little store in a room that opened onto Thompson. We made beads and woven god's-eyes and paintings. I don't remember much about that except the name: On-The-Lamb (Lam?).

All this was a long time ago, thirty-two years. The chronology of my wanderings is a mess. I came and went, between Judson and Lee's, between home and the juvy joint, up to Woodstock, hitchhiking across the country, county jail in Kansas. Lots of faces come to mind of Judson kids and adults, but it's all disorder.

Judson House is an important and pivotal place/space/time in my life and consciousness. I thank everyone who was involved and had anything to do with creating and supporting Judson House. I submit only my story/view. I have always hoped to meet or hear from anyone else who was there.

AARON CRESPI
lives in northern California and designs and builds custom furniture. He sometimes hangs out in a bamboo shack in Jamaica.

The Judson House Gang: Runaways Cum Laude

The following article, written by Steve Lerner, appeared in the December 5, 1968, issue of *The Village Voice*. It is reprinted here by permission of *The Village Voice*.

It's too early to forget that a runaway is a child who leaves home—everything that is known and familiar—to live in the liberated streets of Berkeley and the East Village. In the aftermath of the hippie flower power fad, shock waves are still being felt around the peripheries of the cultural vanguard. Although everyone in the East Village knows that hippie is long since deceased, the word has not yet spread to the sticks.

So fifteen-year-old kids from the South, Midwest, New Jersey, or even an uptown tenement are just getting hip to long hair and beads. They are just beginning to split from their homes and schools to be free—to be hippies. The trouble is that when they arrive they find themselves at least a year too late. The scene has changed; the mood has shifted. They are part of a time lag, a kind of distorted tape loop, because our culture has moved more rapidly than our communications.

Stranded, having cut themselves off from whatever kind of home situation they escaped, they have to face the grim prospect of hustling a living in lower Manhattan. For a minor (boys under 16, girls under 18) this can be a formidable project. To begin with, they can be busted by the police at any moment, detained, and sent home to their parents special delivery. Often they are returned to what have euphemistically been labeled "broken homes"; many face another euphemism, institutionalizing—junior grade concentration camps—for having committed minor drug offenses or simply because they are chronic runaways.

But even if the runaways manage to avoid the police, they will still have a hard time: too young to work legally ("you oughta be in

Graffiti by the runaways, still visible in 1999. Photo by Alice Garrard.

school, kid"), they face the choice of being exploited by employers who know they won't complain, or they can panhandle.

Finding a place to live is another hassle. Most of the famous crash pads have crumbled—Linda and Groovy blew that—and a runaway is, by definition, too young to sign a lease. So they either sleep in the street, in abandoned buildings, float from one friend's apartment to the next, or take up with someone who wants something from them.

Arriving in the city confused and scared, they start to rethink their decision about leaving home: maybe home isn't so bad compared with what you have to go through to make it as a minor in New York, maybe they can wait another year until they've finished high school and can get a job, maybe dodging the police every minute isn't the freedom they've been dreaming of.

Last summer when the number of runaways in the East Village reached crisis proportions, the Free Store—now defunct—was funded by the city to provide minimal facilities and act as a communications center for stranded minors. In addition, a pamphlet entitled "Fuck the System" appeared with instructions on how to survive in the dirty streets of the big city.

Teen runaways in the basement of Judson House. Copyright © 1968 by Fred W. McDarrah. Reprinted by permission.

In June, Judson House—attached to Judson Memorial Church—initiated a crisis referral program and a runaway residence at 237 Thompson Street, near Washington Square. During the first two months it offered sixty to eighty runaways sanctuary for a few nights—"a place to get their heads together"—while they were deciding if they were going to stick it out in New York or go back home. According to Arthur Levin, director of the program, almost 90 percent of the minors who came to him eventually went home. Often, it would take days before the runaways would trust him enough to give him their last name or telephone number.

When a runaway came to Judson House—having heard about it by word of mouth—he was told that he had four or five days to decide if he wanted to go back home or not. Levin would only make the first call to his parents with the kid's permission. Then he would try to talk with the parents about why their child had run away, try to make them understand what was happening in the child's head, and often offer them the services of a consulting family therapist. "If a boy finally decided to go home," Levin said, "he usually had a lot more communication at his disposal than he did before he ran away. The kid always knows that if things start getting rough again at home he can call us—that's a safety valve he didn't have before."

While Judson House continues its crisis referral program, it has added a kind of small community of permanent runaways who live—with parental permission—at the four-story brick structure on Thompson Street. Fourteen of them are living there. The average age is fifteen, and each is a special case chosen from among those who stayed at the residence last summer—where it was decided that it would be better for them if they didn't have to return home immediately. One of them, a black girl who has been in and out of Youth House and other city agencies for years, has no real home to go back to. For her, as for another young boy who had spent a good deal of his time sleeping in abandoned houses, Judson House is the first stable community she has lived in. With three full-time staff workers, part-time helpers, a house manager, and a cook, the runaways have some choice of older people to talk with. "They aren't just confronted with a new mommy or daddy they have to get along with," Levin says, "they can choose among a number of older people with different kinds of background and experience."

The permanent runaways are fed, clothed, and housed by Judson House. All of them are either going to school or working. In addition they have become involved in an informal reaching program, "Demian" and Jung, which one of the staff members described as comparable to college courses he has taken. They hold group discussions about drugs, sex, politics, school, or anything that interests them. There are also art supplies—one of the girls turned out to be a good painter—instruments for a rock band, movies, and free tickets to the Fillmore.

From a group of fourteen isolated runaways coming from vastly different backgrounds, a remarkable community has emerged, probably unlike any other in New York. Sitting around together they discussed their former problems with candor. One girl talked about the three months she had spent on the street before coming to Judson House: "I had VD and lice when I arrived, but that's what you get for living on the street." A number of them agreed that they found it easier to talk with their parents since they had been at Judson House. A boy from the South whose father was a career officer in the military said that now he had a perspective on his home situation that he hadn't had before: "When I left home I thought that my problems were the worst in the world. But when I came here I saw other people who had it worse than I did. Now at least I can talk with my parents and try to communicate." Most of them go home from time to time to see their parents: "Last time I went home," one of the girls said, "all my parents would talk about was whether or not I was going to come back and live with them. It wasn't until the end that we really started talking about what was going on here."

A small redheaded fifteen-year-old who had run away from his home in Brooklyn explained that he had left because he couldn't get along with his mother. The first time he ran away was in the middle of July. He arrived in New York not knowing his way around, with no friends, an extra pair of pants, a raincoat, and $20 he had made from selling his guitar. Not willing to trust anyone who offered him a place to sleep in their apartment, he spent a month and a half sleeping outside—usually on the roof of a building in the East Village. Three times during the summer he was picked up by the police, and twice sent home, only to run away again. Now he is one of the permanent members of the Judson House community.

While I was there, a young girl came in who had just left home. Gnawing at the end of her plastic comb, she announced that she had just run away: "Everything started closing in on me—my problems with my mother, things going wrong in school—and then we busted up my mother's house. I just had to leave. I am not going back." One of the counselors tried to convince her that a call should be made to her mother so that a warrant wouldn't be issued for an arrest: "In three days they will be after you for running away and truancy."

The atmosphere in Judson House seemed permissive but far from wild. One of the kids was walking around in bare feet, another returned from school with a headband, and a fourteen-year-old lit up a Winston when he wasn't blowing on a whistle. All of them had long hair but they looked as if they cared about their appearance. Each had his own room and was allowed to decorate it and use it as he pleased. The refrigerator in the kitchen had been painted, and the whole house looked as if it were lived in by a community of people with a particular style.

"The kids help each other here," one of the staffers commented, "they talk to each other about their problems and if someone new comes in they try to make them feel at home." When one of the youngest boys refused to go to bed before four in the morning, others talked with him about it and he started to reform. The same boy, who has had a problem with reading, is now in the process of teaching himself by copying columns of newspaper type on a typewriter.

Money is a problem for Judson House. Although they managed to scrape up enough to get started, they don't have enough to continue much longer.

PEOPLE WHO DON'T FIT INTO ANY OF THE PREVIOUS CATEGORIES

From time to time people came to Judson House who were neither students, Urban Institute participants, staff, program directors, volunteers, nor teenage runaways. They ended up staying several weeks or several years. Still others never officially lived at Judson House but hung out there often enough to be considered residents of sorts. Their stories follow here.

Mei-Mei Hull

Mei-Mei Hull did not spend much time at Judson House when she lived there and did when she didn't. ───────────────────────

It was Memorial Day weekend of 1962. I dumped my bag of clothes and guitar in my new room on the first floor of the Judson Student House. The room was hot; the window stretched from floor to ceiling about the width of the narrow room. I had no time to unpack because I had to rush to my first meeting with George Younger, the minister of Mariner's Temple Baptist Church, where I would be spending my intern year of seminary. I hiked in my Indian sandals down through the Bowery, past little Italy and Chinatown, until I reached Chatham Square. I was to spend the next twelve months learning how to be a minister in a church modeled on the style of the East Harlem Protestant Parish.

When I arrived at the "Temple," Margaret Zipse, the director of children's programs, and Leonard Chapman, the new assistant minister, were already waiting for me. I was breathless and excited. I had just come from the quiet, neat campus of Yale Divinity School, and this was the first year of my life that I would not be going to school!

As soon as the meeting was over, I took a more leisurely walk through Chinatown and the Village back to 237 Thompson Street. The Village Outdoor Art Show was being mounted on the fence just below my bedroom window. It was noisy and the air was swelteringly hot. I was thrilled. I loved being in my room with the bottom of my window opening virtually at eye level to the passers-by. I could see the backs of the paintings through the mesh screen protecting my room from invasion by robbers and other evil-doers.

I was living in the Student House as part of an arrangement between Mariner's Temple and the Baptist City Society, which was the confederation of Baptist churches in New York City, Long Island, and Westchester County. I say I was living there, but that first summer I really only slept there. I spent every waking hour working in the day camp with fourth graders, teaching Sunday School to eighth graders, and running activities with teenage girls in the evenings.

The majority of the kids lived in the Smith Housing Project and were poor, black or Puerto Rican. There was a middle class apartment building on the block next to the Temple. One of my first duties was to survey every apartment to find out who lived there and to inform them of our wonderful Temple. This was an attempt to serve a more representative population of the community. We were also trying to assess the needs of the residents. What programs could we offer that were lacking in their lives?

Mariner's Temple was truly a wonderful church. Although the building was in need of refurbishing, the members and the staff were eager and vibrant. We all met weekly and planned our strategies for outreach. We felt we could solve some of the problems of our area of the Lower East Side.

Two people I met at the Temple made a strong impression on me. I idolized George Younger and was amazed at his dedication. He could have entered any professional arena but chose to give his life working in an almost defunct church. Margaret "Zip" Zipse was the hardest working staff member. Margaret knew everyone, knew where everything was kept, and handled all the crises. She was close to everyone: staff, church members, and neighborhood professionals. She made all of us recently transplanted staff feel welcome and essential.

Then there was the Student House. Although initially I was hardly there, I did attend Howard Moody's orientation meeting. Howard warned us about city living. The summer residents were largely from the Midwest and were very naive about the city. Howard told us never to look strangers in the eye: "Sitting in the sun in Washington Square Park reading a book isn't just enjoying the air. To New Yorkers, it's an invitation." I nodded and couldn't wait to saunter out and discover what kind of invitation I would find.

When fall came, the children of the Temple were in school. Now I had a chance to snooze all morning, scrounge up my breakfast in the kitchen, and smoke a few dozen cigarettes in the lounge. The lounge! That was where I met the most interesting people. And those interesting people met each other. There were at least a few marriages and dozens of friendships, and perhaps a few feuds, all begun in the lounge. I met many musicians there, some in person and some on records.

The lounge had a piano and a record player. Everyone played their favorite albums. Al Carmines lived in the room next to mine. He would sit in the lounge playing Bessie Smith on the record player while smoking his Gauloises. He usually did not show up until the afternoon but he could be found there any hour of the night. I was intimidated by his intelligence and all his accomplishments. Usually, we nodded and puffed up a smokescreen between us, listening to Bessie or Billie Holiday. Sometimes Al would give me a benevolent, distracted smile. Once in a great while he would sit down and play some of his own songs on the upright in the corner. When there was a party, everyone would beg him to play and sing, and sometimes he would.

I also met Larry Kornfeld in the lounge. You could find him reading or fixing a snack in the kitchen. He and Al were collaborating on the Judson Poets Theater productions. I admired their work. Larry chose plays that were unusual and opened up the world of theater to many of us in the Student House and the church.

That's how he met my supervisor, "Zip," whom he later married. Larry used to say that I was the only person who lived with both him and Margaret before they got together. It was true. I nominally lived at the Student House, but I spent most of my waking hours with Margaret at the Temple. It was only after their marriage that we stopped calling Margaret "Zip." She was a director of Christian Education; he was a director of Theater. Everyone who knew them was astounded that they got together, but then began to understand what a creative marriage it was. When their daughter, Sarah, was born, I was lucky to be her first babysitter. When Sarah was eight years old, she used to come over to play with my infant daughter Melanie.

In the lounge I also met the amazing Carman Moore. Carman introduced me to John Lee Hooker and "Big black snake suckin' my rider's tongue..." (whatever that meant). Carman was very easy to talk to. He had grown up in Lorraine, Ohio, and was familiar with my alma mater, Oberlin. We knew people in common. He was writing a choral piece, and I felt honored when he asked me to sing in the choir performance. It was difficult but beautiful music. He moved out of the Student House soon after that and married Susan Stern, another Judson House resident.

Susan Stern had moved into the house from an NYU student dorm, a victim of the dreaded curfew, administered so harshly until the early 1960s. Judson had no curfew. Ergo, Susan applied. That was lucky for me, since it was the beginning of a very close friendship. I considered Susan and Carman's son Martin my "first baby." I loved to play with him. Carman called me "Martin's only living aunt." Living close by, that is. Martin had aunts aplenty in Ohio and upstate New York. Martin later babysat with Melanie.

Lou Marsh was another face that could on occasion be seen in the lounge. He had moved out of the Student House to Macdougal Street before I got there. He worked with a gang of Puerto Rican boys in an attempt to stop the violent "rumbles," as gang fights were called then. He was killed by some of the boys he was working with. I went with Howard Moody and others who knew Lou well to the funeral in Philadelphia, where his family lived. It was one of the first times I heard Howard preach. One of the members of the little Baptist church in North Philadelphia was incensed at the boys who killed Lou. Howard struck a plea for mercy for these boys and powerfully turned the mood of the service toward sorrow servicing love instead of revenge. I grieved a great deal for Lou Marsh. A few years before I had briefly been very smitten by him. Lou was the first person I really knew who had died in such an abrupt and tragic way.

The following summer I met Reathel Bean in the lounge. He was raving about this new singer, Bob Dylan. I professed not to care for him. But soon I was teaching "Blowin' in the Wind" to my day camp group. Reathel let me know that Bob Dylan was great and that he would be playing with Pete Seeger at the new Loeb Student Center at NYU. When Pete Seeger introduced Bob Dylan to the audience, Dylan was wearing his harmonica on his shoulder stand. I was won over, like the rest of the audience and the generation. I became involved in folk music myself and began playing in the lounge for the first time.

One other interesting thing happened in my family about that time. My father, Angus Hull, who was a minister and for eight years had been the executive secretary of the Cleveland Baptist City Society, was being considered for the same position in the New York City Society. He landed the job! This was thrilling to me, since I knew it had been a job he had always hoped to have. Now my parents were moving to the city that I had decided to live in. And I got there first! He became the administrator who oversaw Mariner's Temple, Judson Memorial Church, and Judson Student House.

In the summer of 1963, my internship at the Temple was over and I had to move out of the Student House. Marjorie Saunders, a fellow resident, also had to move on. We got an apartment together—an illegal sublet ("People do this all the time!"). The apartment was on Bleecker Street between Sullivan and Macdougal. I felt amazed at my good luck. A real apartment of my own ... finally! And in the heart of Greenwich Village!

The day after we moved in, Marjorie and I came home to find a padlock on our door. We were horrified. I had never been locked out of my home before. We called the lessee. He was nowhere to be found. I called my father. He was in Europe. I called a lawyer who was on the board of the Baptist City Society. Everyone said the landlord had the "law on his side." The lawyer helped us get our stuff out of the apartment. We had no money and no place to go. But we did have the Student House lounge. I don't remember if Marjorie slept there, but I spent the rest of the summer on one of those short hard sofas in the student lounge. It was ironic that I spent more time in the Student House after I no longer officially lived there.

Living in the lounge, I got to see everyone who came and went. I don't think I slept very much. I was content, though, and stayed until I went back to Yale Divinity School in the fall for my last year toward a bachelor of divinity degree.

Judson made New York my new home. I moved back as soon as I got my degree in 1964. The Judson Student House had been a stepping stone for me. I met many people who became lifelong friends, people who introduced me to theater and new genres of music. Judson has continued to acquaint me with some of the most creative religious and artistic people in New York City. Under Peter Laarman's leadership Judson remains in the forefront of changing social issues.

MEI-MEI HULL HAMMER,
a psychotherapist, lives in New York City.

Julie Kurnitz

Julie never lived in Judson House but during the 1960s she hung out there a lot.

On the evening of November 9, 1965, as I was browsing in the Sheridan Square Bookstore, the lights went out and did not come back on. It wasn't just the bookstore lights that had gone out, I realized, stepping outside into a strange, dark village with no street lights, no traffic lights, no glowing store or apartment windows. It quickly became clear it was not just the Village either. There was no lit Empire State Building! New York was dark! It was the first of the big blackouts. This was an amazing event, and I was part of it. What should I do? Where should I go? The answer came immediately: Judson House, of course.

Walking east on West Fourth Street in a New York City without lights was like a dream—a place I had been hundreds of time, still the same but completely different. Above me in the night sky you could see the stars. At the Student House, lit by candles and flashlights, there were people to share this magical night with me.

I had discovered the Student House in the summer of 1964. A friend from the University of Wisconsin was a resident for the summer, and from the first time I visited the Student House, it became my second home. I had just moved to the Village, to a little apartment on Grove Street—my first time living alone. I was loving it, but I had no community. The Student House became my community.

I was not quite twenty-three that summer. Many of the residents were younger than I was, fresh-faced infants from the Midwest. Many others were "grownups." Not that they necessarily acted like any grownups I had ever met, but hey, they were in their thirties. The infants and the grownups came from everywhere—any number of states and several countries. I remember that Canada, Israel, India, and Pakistan were represented.

Some of the friends I made are still in my life today. I made discoveries that shaped my life and my future. Hearing me sing and play the guitar in the kitchen late one night, Al Carmines asked if I would like to be in a show at the Judson Poets Theater. More than thirty years later I am still singing in shows.

Beverly Waite, a wonderful, strong woman who ran the Student House, became a good friend. She offered me another career path. Willie Mae Wallace, the cook and also a wonderful, strong woman, had either quit or been fired under circumstances I no longer remember. "Why don't I hire you as the cook," Beverly said to me, "you are here all the time anyway." True enough.

My cooking skills were, and are, minimal. My stove often was, and is, dusty from disuse. But as usual I was game for just about anything. So I said OK.

My time as cook was short and disastrous. I have blocked most of it, but I do remember the scalloped potatoes. First came the fun part. I would get whoever was passing through the kitchen to help peel and slice the potatoes while we talked and laughed. Then came the cooking part. I swear I followed Beverly's recipe exactly, but somehow the potatoes managed to be burned and raw at the same time, swimming in an unattractive liquid that never quite turned into the promised creamy sauce.

Willie Mae was quickly reinstated as cook, and I went back to hanging around the kitchen singing and screaming with laughter. Late at night we would talk about our dreams, our passions, and the meaning of life.

Inevitably, in a house in Greenwich Village with lots of young people and lots of bedrooms, early in that brief magical time after the pill and before AIDS, when promiscuity carried no retribution, there were constant and endless romantic and sexual encounters. The morning after one wild party, I remember waking up early in someone's room and, through some trick of the light and the Venetian blind, seeing the cars passing on Thompson Street refracted or reflected onto the strip of ceiling over the window. Later, having breakfast in the kitchen, I told someone about this strange phenomenon of physics, not realizing I was also giving away what I had been doing, where, and with whom. Julie, can't you ever keep your mouth shut?

Oh, those parties! They were everywhere—in the kitchen, in people's rooms, in the garden. I remember dancing madly, in the lounge that looked onto the garden, with Robert E. Lee Smith, to Peggy Lee singing "Fever," the room packed with gyrating bodies.

But the real parties were at Al Carmines's place. Who could forget the deadly punch, the crowded room, the laughter, the fights, the wonderful singing around Al's pitifully mistreated piano, the glory of Al singing the blues, the strange bedfellows, the resulting hangover, remorse, and gossip?

Judson House opened doors that led me to a career in the theater, to new ideas, to dear friends—some now lost, some dead, some still close and constant. For a few wonderful years it was my playground, my school, my family. When the lights go out in Judson House for the last time, they will continue to shine in my memory and in my life.

JULIE KURNITZ
lives in Greenwich Village.

Ed Lazansky

Judson House was a temporary refuge for Ed Lazansky. _____

In the summer of 1967 I desperately needed a place to stay in New York City on arriving from New Bedford, Massachusetts, where I had lived for two years as a teacher of art. My wife and I had separated there, and she had returned to New York earlier. When I returned to New York and found our relationship to be untenable, I called my old friend Larry Kornfeld, who suggested I try and stay at the Judson House, as a temporary room was available.

After a fitful night at the notorious Albert Hotel (now a condo, I believe), I fled to Judson the next day into the welcoming embrace of Beverly Waite, famous housemother, who situated me into a tiny room on the southeast corner of the building. My quarters, modestly appointed, had a certain existential gloom about them, an air of Parisian *chambre de bonne* or a window overlooking Sherwood Anderson's Winesburg, Ohio, or a room inhabited by Jack Kerouac.

As I sat on my bed staring out of the window at the passing throng coming off Washington Square Park, I felt myself to be on another planet. The quiet of New Bedford and my depression yielded to the brash, noisy city outside. Motorcycles turned the corner, fire engines tore out of the firehouse with bells ringing, kids screamed. My end of the building seemed perfectly projected into the melee. It took me a while to relax, and at night only with the help of earplugs.

I spent time at Judson mostly at night, while I went apartment hunting during the day. I recall evenings at Beverly's place, chatting with her friends and a few housemates. I remember especially Chuck Gordone—a fine playwright who went on to win a Pulitzer Prize—and Jon Hendricks, who was involved with the Judson Gallery.

My daughter, Nadja, who was six at the time, would come and stay with me on weekends. I rigged up a modest cot for her from one of the vacant rooms. Not so long ago, she surprised me with a rather Proustian recollection of the place. We were together somewhere, and all of a sudden she announced, "Daddy, that smell! Does that odor remind you of something?" "That smell, yes," I said, "what is it?" Suddenly, the déjà vu revealed itself: the antiseptic used in the washroom at Judson! She recalled something I had not thought of for years, but the memory came flooding back. For my daughter, it brought back feelings and moments of her stay at Judson when she was a little girl and of her somewhat depressed absentee daddy.

My sojourn at Judson was short, no more than a month. I found an apartment on the East Side and returned to Judson only to visit Beverly and a few others. Ten years later, Judson figured in my life again when I designed a few sets for the Gertrude Stein productions by Al Carmines and Larry Kornfeld, the result of a long relationship in the theater with Larry that began at the Living Theater and ended with the Theater for a New City.

Judson was an important catalyst in my life. I shall always cherish my memories of the place, as will Nadja, who helped out behind the scenes.

ED LAZANSKY
lives in Woodstock, New York.

Carman Moore

Carman Moore needed a place to stay, rang the doorbell at Judson House, and moved in. _____

My first encounter with the Judson Student House was on the sunny fall afternoon of my first encounter with Judson Church. It was 1961 or so. I had just blown in from Ohio, a graduate of Ohio State University, where a few years before Howard Moody had been pastor to students. I did not meet Howard there, but Mary-Ellen Pracht, a mate from the OSU Music School, swore by him and advised me to get to know Judson.

Actually, I was stuck in the Bronx without a piano on which to compose and, desperate, came to beg Assistant Pastor Bud Scott to let me use the church's instrument. Bud lived in this strange red-brick construction abutting the yellowish brick of the church. I rang the bell and Bud stuck his head out of the wooden door. I began to beg and offer a deal that would involve my singing in the choir, mopping up after services, anything. Bud, in a hurry, shushed me and handed me a key to the church. Wow, just like back in Ohio, I thought, what a kind dude, or maybe he is a New York weirdo, or maybe he reads auras and catches my basic, honest naïveté.

As my daily gig was at the New York Public Library on 42nd Street, I soon realized that the Bronx was nowhere for a self-respecting, Manhattan party-appreciating, deep-concentrating student composer to seriously reside. Sleeping through my station at White Plains Road at 2 a.m. was devastating and was becoming a habit. So I cleared out, and for about a year I shared an Alphabet City apartment with a fellow Judson choir mate, Steve Andry, until the experience of returning from work to find we'd been burglarized again began to get old. Back I went to Judson, this time to beg for living quarters behind that wooden door. I got in.

The Village was pulsating ... it was probably the heat center of the world. Washington Square Park was like a big, cultural laboratory working on some juxtapositions, mixes, quirks, and behavior patterns that would not reach the rest of America for another five or six years, if then. Hair of all nations flew. Shirts were doffed. Music never ended.

The Student House itself was in part an international living space based on one bedroom per person, a group kitchen, and a downstairs living room with a recordplayer and beat-up furniture. But mainly, the house was a haven in the storm of sixties living. This was especially true for those of us from the hinterlands: Margaret Underwood and Bob Sargeant from North Carolina, Juell Krauter from Texas, Beverly Bach from Alabama, Reathel Bean from Missouri, Anne French from Massachusetts, Susan Stern from Queens, and others I can't remember from Illinois, California, and Michigan, not to mention Hyun Duck Shin and Grace Liu from South Korea, Masayoshi Katsuta from Japan, and Kala Pant and Vir P. Daka from India. We learned so much from being together that the training from whatever schools we were attending paled by comparison—we all basically stopped inquiring about each other's studies.

Among my best teachers were our house parents, Beverly and Ralph Waite and their three daughters, Sharon, Kathleen, and Suzanne. Bud Scott was no longer there. He had "run off and joined the Catholic church," as it was explained to me. On the fall afternoon of my moving in I went to Beverly to request my linens, wherupon she gave me a pile consisting of about ten pillowcases but no sheets, towels, or blankets. Fearing I had encountered rampant amateurism portending a hopeless future at the place, I returned to find that Bev did know how to make a bed but was not so accomplished in running complex operations. It all worked out in time.

I came to spend many evenings with the Waites, typically watching the girls' costumed theatrical improvisations amid torrential giggling (by them—I was just being polite—and, of course, I adored them). At some point during my two-year stay at the house Sharon, the oldest, developed leukemia. Watching her very young beauty fade and sharing the ups and downs of Bev, Ralph, and the girls even from a respectful distance was one of the major lessons in human relations I had experienced up to that time.

The other major training ground at the Student House was the living room. I don't remember if we called it the living room or the parlor ... we certainly were too cool to call it the rec room. If memory serves me, not one cool or hip person lived in the Student House in my two years there. Many a hip person visited, though: Chuck

Gordone, the stage director and future Pulitzer Prize-winning playwright; Richard Tyler, the merry, mustachioed ex-jazz drummer who manned a cart selling Gnostic tracts and calendars for pennies; the almost starving pop artists Jim Dine and Claes Oldenberg; various misunderstood Judson Dance Theater pioneers; and the occasional East Villager who somehow got past the door masquerading as some resident's friend. Mainly the place was just for residents and close friends, with the lights always low (I don't remember anyone spending much time there during the day).

I played records there—jazz items by Sonny Rollins, Horace Silver (one featuring "Señor Blues," "Song for My Father," and "Filthy McNasty"), and the all-powerful, mega-important, and now-forgotten Mississippi blues album featuring John Lee Hooker singing "Wednesday Evening Blues" and "The Flood at Tupelo," self-accompanied on folk guitar (not the electric one that made him famous)—and wore them totally out. I probably wore out my house mates, too, although no one ever complained. Maybe all those blues depressed them so that they could only climb up to their bedrooms and cry themselves to sleep—or maybe some of them actually cracked a book or prepared a paper.

Of course, the main function of the living room was to hold the Friday night parties. Constructed around gallon jugs of red wine that cost maybe $2.50 (beer was for Middle American frats, and the grass was between weak and oregano at the time), these gatherings sometimes had lots of people and sometimes just a few. I do not recall invitations, only expectations. I do remember long hours of experimental dancing to basically unremembered music. Juell Krauter was my sturdiest and best dance partner, one who had great rhythm and a great laugh and one who did not mind pirouetting across rickety furniture. While I mostly don't remember the music (maybe Ray Charles), I do recall around midnight feeling the floor reel and undulate like some pirates' caravelle out on the bounding main (had to have been Ray Charles).

The most startling moment of Judson House dance history has to be the night when two unknowns showed up with music by someone called Chubby Checker and started moving to something they called The Twist. The event occupies a special niche in my memory. The two dancers were both white and cool- to poker-faced. He was tall and thin; she was short, well-dressed with heels, and gorgeous.

They were totally absorbed in the music, paying no attention to us or each other. Without any sweating they floated glamorously on this fabulous new rhythm and clear tenor vocalizing to the gasping delight of all—or was I the only one impressed? Was I the only other person there? Time past can make you stupid. Anyway, it did happen.

PARTIES, PARTIES, PARTIES

Another characteristic of the parties was their shapelessness. Larry Kornfeld might be in a heated discussion with Al Carmines, Mei-Mei Hull (always wearing black before it became hip), or Chuck Eaton. The main public interest of these talks might be discussion as a form, it seemed to me, not content. This notion was confirmed by the fact that they always ended in gales of laughter. I might have stopped dancing to join in, but that would have been too great a price.

Of course, the parties were also the occasion for a certain amount of wooing appropriate to the sixties (supposedly the Age of the Pill, but all I ever saw were diaphragms). And yet my memory of Student House romance was at best a within-the-family kind of curiosity fulfillment and a feeling that basically this feels like incest, so let's do our serious hunting outside these walls. Maybe I should reconsider this last sentence since...well, among other things, I ended up married to a Student House girl and had some long and sweet relationships with several extremely fine female housemates. We're just airing some perceptions here, so I'll leave the topic.

Occasionally, one of these parties just stopped and somebody just started performing. Usually it was late, people were full of bad wine, and Chuck Gordone (who did not live there but did not miss many parties) would borrow someone's guitar—say, Reathel's—and cover some Harry Belafonte tune, usually a croonable ballad to heat up the ladies. He was worth stopping a party for. Most memorable to me was the night when Mr. Shin, as I called him, went up to his room and reappeared with his flute. Hyun Duck Shin was an ex-Korean War fighter pilot and martial arts expert who, though slight of build, was known to be able to bust the heads of any three thugs at a time. Charming, he was a great conversationalist, but I did not expect the flute. But when he floated and moaned his way through the

"Intermezzo" from *Cavalleria Rusticana,* I was bowled over, partly from the playing and partly from the realization that the intensity of feeling probably also derived from horrors of war I could hardly imagine.

CIVIL RIGHTS

Raging in America at large at the time was the civil rights movement and the whole question of race. Typically, the Student House and the Judson community in general had their own special style around the issues, one that allowed important learning to proceed in relative psychic safety. Basically, we were all pretty intent on healing the nation's madness. Most of us, black and white alike, did freedom marches, demonstrations, and even some jail time for the cause. Reathel Bean came to Judson as a conscientious objector, already having protested virtually alone in his Iowa college town square, probably in danger but too young to fear it.

Susan Stern and others went off to the March on Washington. A bunch of us went on a bus down somewhere dangerous in Maryland to integrate an amusement park (how appropriate for Judson) and ended up getting booked at the jailhouse. It was fun for a while. In the Judson community there seemed to be an unusual number of whites from the South, but the ones I knew seemed ready and even eager to experience real equality. And while one white house mate tearfully admitted to me one day that her southern upbringing was giving her a terrible time with the notion of blacks being equal to whites, she did say it to my face and truly seemed to try and rise to something more human.

Black/white/Asian dating was regular and pretty casual, as I remember it. There was a wonderfully light, almost Shakespeareanly breezy romance between a while southern woman and a Nigerian man, both of them charming and bouncy characters. There was a very proper Hindu woman, vocally very critical of all the sexual revolution stuff going on in the house, whose diaphragm and supporting paraphernalia fell out of her bag in the crowded kitchen one evening. There was the planned marriage of Peggy Eaton from Cleveland, Ohio, to the lively Trinidadian Roy Watts, for which I composed a wedding cantata. (I suspect they never heard it because they could never decide when to get married until we were all long gone from Judson.) In the Judson community at large, there was the wedding of Isa Hermann, born in Germany, and Howard Irving, my soul brother and extremely popular director of the Judson gym youth program for teens from Little Italy. There was Chuck Gordone and Jeanne Warner. And certainly not least, there was black, nominally Christian Ohioan me marrying Susan Stern from Whitestone, Queens, and spawning two fabulous boys. The inspired Master Cook and Philosopher General of the Judson House kitchen, Willie Mae, contributed an enormous carrot cake that she mixed literally by hand—no spoon big enough—in a scrubbed (she said) garbage can. Today I am happily not married, but I also was happy for much of the time that I was.

These are some of the things I remember about Judson House, at least what I feel comfortable divulging. After all, I am a Grandpa now. The true Judson story is that it was one of the most successful human relations environments I have ever experienced, and I'd give plenty to re-experience one party night with the best of the gang that I remember there. In lieu of that, I do appreciate having made this mental excursion, flawed and inaccurate as it probably is. I am a creative artist, after all, and old habits die hard. But the spirit of it is right on.

Those red bricks may be on their way toward the great melting pot of Landfill, Detritus, and Effluvia, where they will languish at the bottom of some pile along the Hudson or off in Tidewater Virginia. However, they will never be forgotten by this old Judsonian. What those bricks have seen and what they held inside was some of the best music, dance, and real-life theater anybody has ever known, and I for one will always honor and gladly salute them for it.

CARMAN MOORE,
a composer, lives in New York City.

Paul Richter

Paul Richter spent time at Judson House in the mid-1960s.

The 1960s are a blur to me. I can't remember how I found Judson House, although it was probably because I had seen some of Al Carmines's productions. I seem to have materialized there in December 1964. I do know that I spent the entire summer of 1965 and parts of the summers of 1966 and 1967 at the student house. During the summer of 1965, a contingent of foreign students, mostly from Israel, were staying there. They were a friendly, lively group, and I remember having good times and good parties. I have forgotten a lot, but I can still hear Willie Mae's voice ringing through the house.

I have one clear recollection. I took a group of these students to Shea Stadium for a baseball game, using discount coupons from milk cartons. It was a bad year for the Mets, and the game was a tight pitcher's battle. None of the students understood the game. Given that nothing *seemed* to be happening and yet the fans were going wild, they concluded that Americans were even nuttier than they had imagined.

My closest friend in the house was Beverly Waite and I hung out with her most of the time.

I remember going to an agape service at Judson and hearing music played by the guitarist boyfriend of Davida, a Judson House resident, who played the solo guitar in the production of *Man of La Mancha,* which was then playing in the Village.

The Judson community was a mixed bag of hippie artists, scruffy students, antiwar and pro-choice activists (Howard was very much in the forefront here), and admirable missionary ladies. It was one of the more interesting places on the planet, and the summer of 1965 was the happiest one of my life.

PAUL RICHTER
lives in Vancouver, British Columbia.

Index

A

Adams, Charlie 150, 158
Agenoux, Søren 151
AICP *See* Association for Improving
    the Condition of the Poor
Alden, Renato 20
Amster, J. Lewis, M.D. 61
Anderson, A.A., 79, 93, 94
Anderson, Elizabeth Milbank 65, 93,
    95
Anderson, Jeremiah Milbank 95
"Annex, The" 7–10
Apter, Jeffrey 152
Artists *See* Judson Gallery; *see also* un-
    der specific names
Ashforth, H. Adams 84, 98
Aslanian, Lurline Purvis *See* Purvis,
    Lurline
Association for Improving the Con-
    dition of the Poor (AICP) 59,
    62, 75, 93
Aziza 51–52

B

Bach, Beverly *See* Cassell, Beverly
    Bach
Barth, Marcus 207, 209–210
Bean, Reathel 26, 186, 236–239, 270,
    364, 372
Beat generation 277, 286
Berger, Peter 143, 236
Bertolotti Family 19
Birt, Donald H. 147, 216–218
Black, Ellen, R.N. 90–91

Blackout of 1965 137, 160, 272, 366
Bland, Virginia 160
Borchers, Gail 229, 231
Bosco, Pearl 226, 229
Bowling Green Neighborhood Associ-
    ation 62, 77–78
Boyd, Robert 111–113, 116
Brewer, Ed 138, 156–161, 252, 259,
    265, 307
Broughton, Philip S. 81
Brown, McKinley 252

C

Campbell, Eleanor A. 59, 62–65, 68,
    70, 76, 79, 89, 93–99,
    100–105, 114
Cantrell, Shirley 151, 218
Carlson, Mary Margaret 230
Carmen, Arlene 32, 177–180, 185,
    187, 201, 204
Carmines, Al 22, 25, 30–31,
    147–155, 162, 185, 212,
    242, 260, 266–267, 272,
    307, 315, 327, 363
    aneurism 155
    cast parties *See under* Cast par-
        ties
    renovation of apartment 44–45,
        154, 193–194
Cassell, Beverly Bach 149, 213, 218,
    219–221, 372
Cast parties 45, 152–153, 172–173,
    269, 368
Cavalieri, Mrs. 113, 114

Center for Medical Consumers 23,
170–171
Champagne and Carmines at Christmas 185–186
Chapman, Paul 197–199
Church in Urban Life Program 117,
139, 205–243
Civil rights movement 144, 210–211,
375–376
Conscientious objectors 169, 237,
307, 350
Converse, Hyla 252
Copeland, Royal S., M.D. 61
Cox, Anthony 260, 270, 308
Cox, Harvey 143, 236
Crespi, Aaron 349–351
Crespi, Lee 349
Curtis, Jackie 262

D

Deering Center, New Hampshire 98
Department of Health (New York) 61,
69, 75, 81
Destruction art 237
Destruction in Art Symposium 310,
317, 329–332, 336–337,
339
Dine, Jim 145, 147, 279–282, 290,
292, 294–295, 303, 373
Drugs 182, 218, 307–308
Duffey, Joseph 236

E

Eaton, Chuck and Ann 149, 157, 374
81 West Third 13–15, 88, 107, 111,
116
collapse of 21–22, 108, 117
83 West Third 19
Emerson, Haven, M.D. 61
Employment Project 197–199
Exodus magazine 145, 282–284

F

Father Divine 117, 143, 213, 214,
234

Federal Emergency Relief Administration 74
Ferrell, Donald R. 222–223, 224, 225
Ffarrabas, Nye 310, 315, 316,
321–334
Fornes, Irene 151
Franklin, Jennie 137
Frantz, Andrew 200–204
Freer, Marcia 224

G

Gallagher, Donald 262–263
Garden 23, 29, 48, 51–56, 165, 200,
242
worship services 52–54, 203
Givens, Cornbread 175
Goldstein, Malcolm 311
Goldwater, Sigismund S., M.D. 61
Goodman, Paul 162, 164, 236, 241
Gordone, Charles 137, 220–221, 369,
373
Gottlieb, Saul 312, 318, 331, 341
Greenwich House 75
Greenwich Village 1, 60–61
Grooms, Red 290, 298
Guilliatt, Lee 138, 163, 268, 324
Guttu, Lyle 147

H

Hacker, Alan 247–249
Hacker, Seymour 247–249
Hammer, Mei-Mei Hull See Hull, Mei-
Mei
Hancock, Lee 187–190, 191
Hansen, Al 298, 301, 311, 335–337
Happenings 220, 281, 305–306
Hays, Lee 249
Hazzard, Stanley B. 89
Health education 81–82, 83
Henderson, Verne 120–121
Hendricks, Bici See Ffarrabas, Nye
Hendricks, Geoffrey 307, 311,
314–318
Hendricks, Jon 46–47, 138, 165,
237–238, 241, 272,

307–313, 319, 321, 335,
336, 339, 344
Hennessy, Amon 143
Hesse, Eva 127, 290
Higgins, Dick 298, 301, 323
Holt, Christopher 259, 262–263, 266
Hosie, Laurence T. 18, 248
Hull, Mei-Mei 361–365, 374
Hyun Duck Shin 374

I

In Circles 154, 172
Infant mortality 61, 76

J

Jacobsen, Kathy 151
Johnson, Michael 240–243
Jones, Mr. 174
Jordan, Clarence 133–134
Judson, Edward 6, 7, 11–13
Judson Council 107, 111, 114, 115,
118
Judson Dance Theater 153, 168
Judson Gallery 22, 28, 45–46, 145,
164, 275–345
1959–1962 277–306
1967–1968 307–342
1969 343–345
Judson Health Center 57–105
establishment 15–17, 59–65
funding 63, 65, 68–69, 79,
83–84, 86
home visits 66, 82
move to Judson House 64
move to Spring Street 90–91
postwar expansion 86–88
programs 66–67, 83
school programs 69–70
staffing 63
statistics 72, 73–74, 79
Judson Hotel 10, 18
Judson House
as Student House 20–21
physical description 25–50
as property 7–24

purchase of buildings 7, 13–14
Judson House plot, early history of
3–6
Judson Memorial Church 20, 87, 140,
156, 261
Judson Neighborhood House 15, 62
Judson Poets Theater 153, 172, 267,
367
Judson staff 107–204
See also under specific names

K

Kaprow, Allan 147, 220, 281, 282,
286–287, 295, 301, 311,
314, 316
Katchel, Nancy 138, 169
Keeter, Larry G. 218, 225–231
Keim, Norman O. 127–129, 290
Kennedy, John F. 136, 229–230
Kerze, Therese 81, 83
Kilpatrick, Thom and Joan 159, 160
Koinonia Farm 133–135
Kornfeld, Larry 150, 162–165, 242,
309, 327, 363, 369
Koutoukas, Harry 138, 152, 267, 268
Krauter, Juell 149, 151, 212–213,
220, 372
Ku Klux Klan 133–135
Kurnitz, Julie 137, 164, 267, 270,
366–368

L

Laarman, Peter 24, 197, 365
Lamberton, Bob 138, 238, 351
Lazansky, Ed 369–370
Lee, Ro 157, 159, 166–167, 265, 307
Lemley, Bernice 207–211
Lenapes 1
Levin, Arthur A 51–52, 138,
168–171, 186, 187, 238,
350, 354
Living Theater, The 138, 162, 370
Lounge, The 35, 189, 198, 363
Lower West Side Health District
76–79

M

Maige, John 138
Mailman, Bruce 154
Malcomson, Bill and Laurie 24,
    195–196
Manipulations 309–311, 316–317,
    320, 325–326, 335–336
Mariner's Temple 361–363
Marsh, Lou 364
Mason, Michael 308
Matlaga, Jack 137, 164, 259, 270,
    273
Mayes, Bernard D. 130–136
McCarthy era 123, 145
McClain, Les and Ellen 241
McKim, Mead & White 8
Mead, Margaret 215, 236
Milbank, Dunlevy 68
Milbank, Jeremiah 68
Milbank Memorial Fund 65, 70, 93
Milder, Jay 290, 305
Millett, Kate 158, 164, 311,
    319–320, 326
Moody, Howard 24, 108, 117,
    130–131, 137, 139, 147,
    166, 212, 219, 240, 286, 313
Moody, Lorry 108, 117, 185–186
Moore, Carman 138, 220–221, 236,
    363, 371–376
Moorman, Charlotte 237, 311, 312,
    317, 330–331, 337,
    340–342
Mulberry Health Center 62
"Multiple Relationships" (Tungate) 36
Murphy, Betty 119, 140, 148, 215,
    216, 252
Muyskens, Joan 35, 152, 172–176
Myers, William 88

N

Nam June Paik 311, 312, 317, 331,
    340
Napoli, Maryann 171, 186, 187
Newman, Robert 125, 126, 130, 251,
    253–257

New York Baptist City Society 10–15,
    87–90, 107–108, 114,
    116–117
New York University 87, 107, 115
Nitsch, Hermann 313, 330, 337, 339
Novotny, Danny 113, 114, 116

O

Oldenburg, Claes 145, 147, 279–282,
    290, 292–302, 303, 373
One for Violin 312, 317, 331, 340
Ono, Yoko 158, 260, 270, 272, 308
Open Mic 52
Oppenheimer, Joel 162
Ordeals 327–329
Ortiz, Raphael (Ralph) 310, 311, 318,
    330, 335–338, 339
Ovitt, Jean 40–41, 343–345

P

Padilla, Sandy 259, 264–271, 273
Pant, Kala 149, 372
Pardue, Susie 157
Parker, Michael 138, 238, 350–351
Petty, A. Ray 13, 15, 59, 96
Picard, Lil 310, 311, 335, 336, 339
Pickle, Joe and Judy 139–146, 215,
    222, 224, 225
Poland, Albert 152–153
Police Athletic League 88, 108
Poole, Evelyn and Bob 119
Procter, Camay 116, 119
"Problem Parents" 100–105
P.S. 38 70, 85
Pursley, Joan Muyskens See
    Muyskens, Joan
Purvis, Lurline 159, 259, 265,
    272–273

R

Rabinoff, Sophie 75–77
Ratliff, Marc 279–280, 284,
    290–291, 292, 295,
    303–304
Rats 142, 217, 227–228

Ray Gun Specs 281, 299, 305
Reuben Gallery 290, 298, 301
Rice, John L., M.D, 79–81
Richter, Paul 137, 377
Rockefeller, John D. 11
Roderick, Tom 258–261, 273
Roosevelt, Eleanor, 84–85, 128
Rose, Steve 311
Rubinsky, Hannah 188
Rubinsky, Mark 191–194
Runaway House 22, 37–40,
        169–170, 238, 347–357
Russell, Melissa 107, 111, 114–115
Russell, Robert V. 89–90

S

Sargeant, Bob 149, 372
Saunders, Marjorie 149, 365
Schneemann, Carolee 310, 311, 327
Scott, Bernard (Bud) 22, 139, 215,
        277–285, 286, 288, 290, 371
Scott, Gisela 278
Sears, Charles H. 11, 81
Seeger, Pete 127, 228, 234
Silver, Stu 36–37
Simkhovitch, Mrs. V. G. (Mary K.) 75
Spike, Alice 107, 119–121
Spike, John 120
Spike, Paul 107, 120, 122–126, 256
Spike, Robert W. 20, 107, 117, 130,
        207, 255–256
Stein, Gertrude 172
Stern, Susan 137, 364, 372, 376
Stone, Mrs. Charles P. 84, 85–86
Student House 20–21, 112, 156, 165,
        245–273, 362
Sunday School 183–184, 202

T-U

Tailer Family 5, 6, 7
Tanner, Elizabeth Milbank 96
Tanner, John Stewart 96
Tanner, Milbank 96
Thacker, Jim 232–235
Thompson, Ruth 108

Tingley, Elbert R. 20, 111
Tinguely, Jean
Toche, Jean 45–46, 310, 335
Tungate, John 25–50, 152, 174, 185,
        344
    antiwar march 46–47
    city dump 49–50
    New York City firemen 42–32
Tyler, Richard O. 290, 299–301, 305,
        373
Underwood, Margaret 213, 220, 372

V

Van Twiller, Wouter 1
Vietnam War 46–47, 240, 309, 319,
        322, 325

W

Waite, Beverly 137–138, 150, 157,
        238, 259, 262, 264, 307, 367,
        372
Waite, Ralph 137, 150, 157, 372
Wakefield, Dan 143, 214
Wallace, Willie Mae 148, 163–164,
        216, 219–220, 259, 265,
        367
Waring, Jimmy 150, 269
    suicide 159–160
Washington Square Park 217, 343,
        371
    attempted privatization of 132
    military parade ground 2
    as potter's field 2
    redesign of 41
Wasson, Iva 248
Wesselmann, Tom 290, 292, 295,
        303–306
White, Patricia 116, 250–251
Whitman, Bob, 298, 301
Wiggins, Roland 24, 178, 181–184,
        185, 187, 189
Williams, Claude 249
Wolf, Daniel 145, 284
Wright, Dean 20, 87, 107, 113,
        114–118, 251, 254–255

Wright, Margaret 55, 107, 113, 115,
    121, 250
Wynne, Shirley W., M.D. 70

X–Z

Yalkut, Jud 311
Yampolsky, Phyllis 288–289, 290,
    294, 295

Yangas, Robert A. 214–215
Zipse, Margaret 163, 164, 361–362

Notes

Notes

Notes

Notes

Notes

Notes

Notes

Notes

Notes

Notes

Notes

Notes